SECOND EDITION

VIDEO
COMPRESSION
HANDBOOK

Comsewogue Public Library
170 Terryville Road
Port Jefferson Station, NY 11776

Andy **BEACH**
Aaron **OWEN**

Video Compression Handbook, Second Edition
Andy Beach and Aaron Owen

Peachpit Press
www.peachpit.com
Copyright © 2019 Andy Beach and Aaron Owen. All Rights Reserved.

Peachpit Press is an imprint of Pearson Education, Inc.
To report errors, please send a note to errata@peachpit.com

Notice of Rights
This publication is protected by copyright, and permission should be obtained from the publisher prior to any prohibited reproduction, storage in a retrieval system, or transmission in any form or by any means, electronic, mechanical, photocopying, recording, or otherwise. For information regarding permissions, request forms and the appropriate contacts within the Pearson Education Global Rights & Permissions department, please visit www.pearsoned.com/permissions/.

Notice of Liability
The information in this book is distributed on an "As Is" basis, without warranty. While every precaution has been taken in the preparation of the book, neither the author nor Peachpit shall have any liability to any person or entity with respect to any loss or damage caused or alleged to be caused directly or indirectly by the instructions contained in this book or by the computer software and hardware products described in it.

Trademarks
Unless otherwise indicated herein, any third party trademarks that may appear in this work are the property of their respective owners and any references to third party trademarks, logos or other trade dress are for demonstrative or descriptive purposes only. Such references are not intended to imply any sponsorship, endorsement, authorization, or promotion of Pearson Education, Inc. products by the owners of such marks, or any relationship between the owner and Pearson Education, Inc., or its affiliates, authors, licensees or distributors.

Credit: Table 3.2 Data from: White Paper: Blu-ray Disc Read-Only Format: 2.B Audio Visual Application Format Specifications for BD-ROM Version 2.5. Blu-ray Disc Association. July 2011; and "White Paper: Blu-ray Disc Read-Only Format (Ultra HD Blu-ray): Audio Visual Application Format Specifications for BD-ROM Version 3.0." Blu-ray Disc Association. July 2015.

Executive Editor: Laura Norman
Editor: Karyn Johnson
Copyeditor: Kim Wimpsett
Proofreader: Patricia Pane
Technical Editor, Chapter 9: Steve Llamb
Senior Production Editor: Tracey Croom
Compositor: David Van Ness
Indexer: Jack Lewis
Cover Design: Chuti Prasertsith
Interior Design: David Van Ness

ISBN-13: 978-0-13-486621-5
ISBN-10:   0-13-486621-5

Andy:

This book is dedicated to my wife, Lisa, and daughter, Davy.

Aaron:

For Katie, the love of my life.

Contents at a Glance

Table of Contents

Preface

Ten years ago, when the previous edition of this book was written, it was already established that video was a major part of our lives. Nothing has stopped this from being true, and in fact we are continually finding ways to make it an integral part of our daily lives. Digital video, compressed or otherwise, is all about bits. It seems like it should be easy to move those bits from one place to another, and yet it isn't. A myriad of little settings, tweaks, steps, and reasons make the process of moving video from one medium to another a frustration. If you mess it up, the results are unwatchable at best and unplayable at worst. With so many possibilities as to what can go wrong, troubleshooting becomes a prolonged guessing game, punctuated by panic-inducing deadline checks.

Sorry, we didn't mean to make you hyperventilate.

It's truly amazing how much video compression occurs now. The phones in our pockets are basically portable film studios, allowing us to capture, edit, compress, and publish video while we're on the move. Traditional broadcasters have capitulated and started making their shows available online, and IP video has become *the* infrastructure for modern studios. Oh, and did we mention Twitch and its army of broadcasters delivering game content to millions of viewers daily?

Now we're the ones hyperventilating.

What This Book Is Not

This book is decidedly not a technical tome on the nature of video compression and streaming media. We will not get into the science of encoding (well, maybe just a tiny bit), and we won't explain how committees of smart people came up with the standards we use to make this all work. Yes, we will discuss some fairly complex topics, but believe us, this is just the beginning. There is a world of math and science associated with this technology, but for the most part it doesn't mean a lick if you're in the last hour of your production, trying to figure out why your encodes are failing.

Though we'll discuss some aspects of video production, this book is not about shooting the best video possible. We have been on our fair share of shoots, but don't feel qualified to try to tell you the best way to shoot video. Plenty of other books do that. Also, we will not explain how to do visual effects, how to edit video better, or how to troubleshoot hardware and software.

What Is This Book About, Then?

This book focuses on the essential information you need to get your video online, on disc, in theaters, or onto some other device. Sometimes discussions in compression get bogged down in all the options available. What we'll try to do in this book is present you with some fundamentals and some best practices.

We'll start by covering the fundamentals of video and video compression, giving you the most essential background information you'll need to know. Next, we'll explore the current applications and web services you'll most likely run across while encoding your video. We'll discuss their merits and explain the most common workflows for each. Finally, we'll discuss the most common delivery media for your compressed video and use those same applications to create some specific content for various delivery media.

Our hope is that by combining the fundamental information, practical knowledge about the tools of the trade, and insight into the delivery platforms, we'll leave you well armed to tackle the variety of content that's thrown your way.

But we didn't want you to hear this just from us, so we asked a variety of friends and co-workers to contribute their own insight into the world of video compression. Their profiles are intermingled with the chapters, and although they all are involved in video compression, their professions are incredibly varied.

Who Should Read This Book

If you have ever suddenly had to add video compression to your regular work responsibilities, willingly or otherwise, then this book is for you. But if you have also been doing this for a few years and are suddenly learning about new topics such as HDR or DASH, then this book is also for you.

Video compression, encoding, and transcoding (they are all more or less the same) used to be the exclusive province of engineers who specialized in these tasks and were worried about meeting transmission specs or address- ing other technical issues. Today, pretty much anyone involved in the Web, traditional film and video production, and other interactive media realms will need to know at least a little bit about compression. In addition, the Web has created a new wave of individual publishers who stream their gameplay, publish video podcasts, or have created whole shows on YouTube.

So, if you were ever disappointed (or perhaps even shocked) by the results of your video compression, then read on, and we hope to provide some help.

That's not to say this book is just for newbies. Although this book lays out the fundamentals of video and video encoding, it contains a variety of workflow suggestions and deliverable-specific information that can help even the most seasoned compressionists improve their games. If there is one thing we have learned in this profession, it's that you will always be learning new things because the industry is ever evolving.

About the Authors

Andy Beach was a video geek who got into this business after starting in the postproduction world. He quickly realized that making video look good was hard and was worth spending time to learn to do better and to pass that knowledge on to others. His career took him to the startup world, where he built encoders and live streaming tools for a living, and eventually to his role at Microsoft, where he works with a large-scale commercial media infrastructure.

Aaron Owen got his start in live television and then continued his career in commercial postproduction, playing a key role in transforming Phoenix Editorial (now Bonfire Labs) from a three-suite boutique editorial company into a full-fledged facility. Leveraging his vast advertising and high-end corporate experience, he founded Cinematiq in 2012 with the goal of bringing high-end postproduction techniques to filmmakers everywhere.

Acknowledgments

We've had the privilege of meeting and working with a number of talented people in both the production and software development worlds, including each other!

In the combined 20 or so years of work in this industry, we have met and worked with a lot of very smart (often scary-smart) people.

In addition to the people profiled in the book, a variety of other real-world compressionists we know deserve heartfelt thanks. Thanks to Jem Scholfield, of Buttons Production and theC47, for mulling over new announcements and prognosticating their meaning (and for not being afraid to split a bucket of mussels and a few pints of beer). Thanks to Colleen Henry at Facebook, who is never afraid to offer an opinion or tell you why you are wrong about live streaming. Steve LLamb at Deluxe kept us honest when it comes to all things digital cinema. John Simmons of Microsoft is working to ensure there are standards for the video world so that the new technologies we create work everywhere we want them to (and best of all, he'll take our calls anytime we ask).

We also sorely need to thank the nice folks at Pearson who have patiently waited for us to complete this book. Karyn Johnson, who helped make the first edition a reality, patiently listened to all of our excuses and then held our feet to the fire to get things done. Likewise, Laura Norman helped keep us on track throughout the process. Production editor Tracey Croom worked with us on the layout and turned the text and images into a well-crafted book. Kim Wimpsett did an amazing job of copyediting and often turned around feedback to us so quickly it made our heads turn. Last, but certainly not least, Patricia Pane continually removed all the poor grammar, odd hyphens, and other elements we kept putting in.

Andy would also like to thank his work colleagues, who listened to him talk about the process and complain about changes to the industry and the late nights involved in writing this book. Every time he yawned in a meeting, they knew it was because he'd been up working on this book. For that, thank you, Greg Oliver, Jit Ghosh, LaBrina Loving, Luis Guerrero Guirado, Robert Eichenseer, Tiago Andrade e Silva, and Tobias Weisserth.

And, of course, none of this would have been possible at all without the love and support of our families. For Andy, his wife, Lisa Weisman, and Davy Beach couldn't care less about an inverse telecine error but are always happy when he can figure out why Hulu stopped working on the television. For Aaron, his soon-to-be wife, Dr. Katie Bean, and business partner, Paul Scolieri, deserve great thanks for allowing him the time to put the headphones in and the head down.

Understanding Video and Audio

Compression is one of the linchpins of the video production world. It is the quiet savior (and killer) of projects every day and is a process that, if done correctly, goes unnoticed. When was the last time you watched a TV show and marveled at how great the compression was? Bad compression, by contrast, is unmistakable and can render (pun fully intended) almost any video unwatchable.

The primary function of video compression is fairly straightforward: to conform the video to the desired delivery method, whether it's a TV, a phone, a computer, or a theater screen. The difficulty is trying to work within the technical specifications required and the limitations of the delivery medium to provide an audiovisual experience that's satisfying to the end user. If you're delivering content over the Internet, for example, you need to consider file-size issues as well as the ability to deliver content in real time. You might have the greatest film of all time, but if it's so big nobody can actually download it, then who exactly will be watching this masterpiece? Likewise, if your content will be broadcast on TV, you need to guarantee all the fields and frames of your edited, compressed program are still intact after the lengthy creation process.

But we're just getting ahead of ourselves. You see, there are some fundamentals at play within any discussion of video that are important to be aware of before delving into the intricacies of video compression. If you have worked with video for a long time, these are all familiar concepts. In fact, you most likely don't even think of them consciously in your everyday work. If you are new to video, getting a foundation in the basics of video will make solving your next compression problem considerably easier.

Thank You, Philo T. Farnsworth

The first demonstration of the technology that gave rise to modern TV and video occurred on September 27, 1927, in San Francisco through the efforts of Philo T. Farnsworth, who had dreamed up the idea as a 14-year-old boy in Rigby, Idaho.

There were, of course, many other individuals and corporations involved in creating and refining Farnsworth's electronic TV, but the essential idea of video came from this one somewhat-forgotten young inventor. Farnsworth's ideas still are at the core of video technology today, despite the radical evolutionary leaps the technology has taken in the past 80-plus years.

Philo Facts

- The first image transmitted was a dollar sign.
- The transmission was comprised of 60 horizontal lines.
- Farnsworth developed the dissector tube—the basis of all tube-based TVs.
- He won an early patent for his image dissection tube; he lost later patent battles to RCA.
- He invented more than 165 different devices, including equipment for converting an optical image into an electrical signal, an amplifier, a cathode ray, vacuum tubes, electrical scanners, electron multipliers, and photoelectric materials.

Elements of Video

Unlike film, which creates images by projecting light through transparent celluloid, video is an electronic signal. Though the term *video* originally was used to describe any signal broadcast (or *televised*) to a TV set, it has been more broadly redefined over time to encompass any images displayed electronically (such as those on video billboards, cell phones, ATMs, and so on).

Video has become a pervasive part of our lives, particularly since computers (and their video displays) came along. We use video daily for our interactions, for our entertainment, for our communication, and for tasks as simple as taking money out of the bank. The technology has shifted so much that we now regularly see video on the nightly news that was shot by citizens on their cell phones. As our uses of video have evolved, the technology that supports it has changed as well.

Frames and Fields

When a group of sequential images is displayed in rapid succession, an amazing phenomenon occurs. Instead of perceiving each individual picture, humans see smoothly moving animation. This phenomenon is known as *persistence of vision*, and it is the basis for how film and video work. The number of pictures shown per second is called the *frame rate* (seconds is the most common measurement of the frame rate but not the only one). It can take as few as about 8 frames per second (fps) for the viewer to perceive smooth motion; however, the viewer will also detect a distinct flicker or jerkiness. To avoid that flicker between frames, you generally need a frame rate greater than 16 frames per second (though this is a subjective opinion, and many believe you need 24–30 fps or more to completely remove the flicker). The faster the motion you are attempting to re-create, the more frames you need to keep that motion smooth. Modern film has a frame rate of 24 fps, and TV has a frame rate of approximately 30 fps (29.97 fps) in the United States, Japan, and other countries that use the National Television Standards Committee (NTSC) standard. Phase-Alternating Line (PAL) and Sequentiel Couleur Avec Memoire (SECAM) are the other standards, and they use 25 fps.

A frame can be presented to a viewer in two ways: *progressive* or *interlaced scanning*. You were probably more aware of this before we moved to high-definition TV (HDTV). If you have ever seen an HDTV's specs referred to as 1080i or 720p, the *i* and *p* stand for interlaced and progressive, respectively. (The 1080 and 720 represent horizontal lines of resolution; more on that later.)

Interlaced scanning was developed in the early 1930s as a way of improving the image quality on cathode-ray tube (CRT) monitors (basically every TV you owned until plasma and LCD TVs emerged). Inside the tube, an electron beam scans across the inside of the screen, which contains a light-emitting phosphor coating. These phosphors had a very short persistence, meaning the amount of time they could sustain their illumination was short

> **TIP** For a deeper dive into interlaced video, check out www.100fps.com.

(computer CRT monitors tended to have a longer persistence). In the time it took the electron beam to scan to the bottom of the screen, the phosphors at the top were already going dark. To solve this problem, the early TV engineers designed an interlaced system for scanning the electron beam. With an interlaced system, the beam scans only the odd-numbered lines the first time and then returns to the top and scans the even-numbered lines. These two alternating sets of lines (as shown in **Figure 1.1**) are known as the *upper* (or *odd*) and *lower* (or *even*) fields in the TV signal. So, a TV that displays 30 fps is actually displaying 60 fps—two interlaced images per frame.

Figure 1.1 *With interlaced video, the system scans the odd-numbered lines and then the even-numbered lines, combining fields to produce a complete frame. It takes both fields of the interlaced image to make a whole picture.*

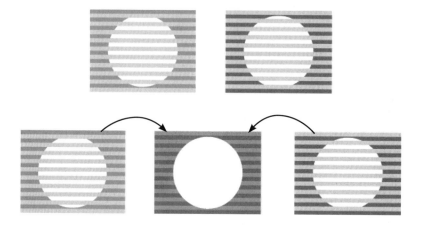

Progressive Scan Video

In progressive scan video, the entire video frame is captured and displayed in a single frame, rather than in two interlaced fields. Progressive scanning has many advantages over interlacing to deliver the same smooth motion (although when played back, the progressive image would also be a slightly higher resolution than the interlaced one). **Figure 1.2** shows the difference between interlaced and progressive frames.

Figure 1.2 *Motion in the progressive image (on the top) would appear much smoother than in the interlaced image (bottom).*

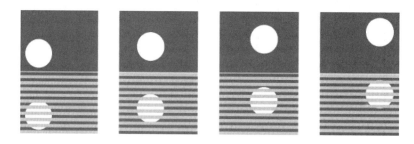

As the ball moves across the screen in Figure 1.2, the interlaced image (bottom) must display fields that are slightly out of sync (because the ball is moving constantly). This can lead to slight distortions or other poor image qualities. The progressive image (top), by contrast, shows a complete frame each time, so the image quality will be improved, and the motion will be smoother, though you are using more bandwidth to transmit the image.

Progressive video has superseded interlaced in much of the video world for a number of reasons. For one, most modern TV technologies are inherently progressive. As many manufacturers stop making traditional CRT-based monitors, newer display technologies have taken over. Most TV and monitor manufacturers have moved away from CRT technology, although some still exist as specialty items. Starting in about 2010, LCD or DLP-based screens became the dominant consumer-grade screens on the market. This technology has continued to improve, giving way to light-emitting diode (LED) or organic light-emitting diode (OLED) screens.

Resolutions

The quality of the images you see in film and video is not based just on the number of frames you see per second or the way those frames are composed (full progressive frames or interlaced fields). The amount of information in each frame, or *spatial resolution*, is also a factor. In **Table 1.1**, you can see that image resolution varies greatly for different screen types. Older standard-definition TVs max out at 720 by 486, while current high-definition TVs are 1080p (1920 by 1080). Content delivery in 4K resolution (3840 by 2160) has started to emerge, but the content library is still relatively small, and consumers have been slower to upgrade to 4K from 1080p than they were in moving from SD to 1080p.

The resolution of analog video is represented by the number of scan lines per image, which is actually the number of lines the electron beam draws across the screen or vertical resolution.

NOTE Since video was invented, resolutions have continually evolved, and they continue to scale up. The past ten years has been no different and in fact have increased dramatically. Our phones now shoot and display video resolutions higher than those of the TVs we watched a decade ago. With that in mind, be aware that over time the resolutions suggested here may seem outdated.

Table 1.1 *Today's modern video resolutions and the devices commonly associated with them*

Resolution name	Horizontal × vertical pixels	Other names	Devices
SDTV	720 × 486 (or 576)	Standard definition	Older TVs
720p	1,280 × 720	HD, high definition	TVs
1080p	1,920 × 1,080	Full HD, FHD, HD, high definition	TVs, monitors
WUXGA	1,920 × 1,200	Widescreen Ultra Extended Graphics Array	Computer monitors, projectors
2K Scope	2,048 × 858	Cinema 2K	Projectors
2K Flat	1,998 × 1,080	Cinema 2K	Projectors
2K Full	2,048 × 1,080	Cinema 2K	Projectors
UHD	3,840 × 2,160	4K, Ultra HD, Ultra-High Definition	TVs
4K Scope	4,096 × 1,716	Cinema 4K	Projectors
4K Flat	3,996 × 2,160	Cinema 4K	Projectors
4K Full	4,096 × 2,160	Cinema 4K	Projectors
8K	7,680 × 4,320	None	Concept TVs

NOTE Why are there two different aspect ratios for SD? This has to do with the pixel aspect ratio, which you'll learn about in Chapter 2 (see "Square and Nonsquare Pixels") and Chapter 4.

The resolution for digital images, on computer displays and digital TV sets, for example, is represented by a fixed number of individual picture elements (pixels) on the screen and is often expressed as a dimension: the number of horizontal pixels by the number of vertical pixels. For example, 640 × 480 and 720 × 486 are full-frame SD resolutions, and 1920 × 1080 is a full-frame HD resolution.

Vertical-Line Resolution for NTSC and PAL

The NTSC format is based on 525 vertical lines of resolution, displayed as two interlaced fields. However, some of these lines are used for synchronization and blanking, so only 486 lines are actually visible in the *active* picture area. (All video—not just NTSC—consists of more information than the visible content of the frame. Before and after the image are lines and pixels containing synchronization information or a time delay. This surrounding margin is known as a *blanking interval*.)

The PAL format is based on 625 vertical lines of resolution, displayed as two interlaced fields. As with NTSC, some of these lines are used for synchronization and blanking, so only 576 lines are actually visible in the active picture area.

Aspect Ratio

The width-to-height ratio of an image is called its *aspect ratio.* Keeping video in the correct aspect ratio is one of the more important parts of video compression. As we scale the video to different sizes to accommodate different screens and resolutions, it is easy to lose the relationship between the original height and width of the image. When this happens, the distorted image can become distracting, even impossible to watch.

The 35mm still photography film frame on which motion-picture film was originally based has a 4:3 (width:height) ratio, which is often expressed as a 1.33:1 or 1.33 aspect ratio (multiplying the height by 1.33 yields the width).

From the beginnings of the motion-picture industry until the early 1950s, the 4:3 aspect ratio was used almost exclusively to make movies and to determine the shape of theater screens. When TV was developed, existing camera lenses all used the 4:3 format, so the same aspect ratio was chosen as the standard for the new broadcast medium.

In the 1950s, the motion-picture industry began to grow concerned over the impact of TV on their audience numbers. In response, the movie studios introduced a variety of enhancements to provide a bigger, better, and more exciting experience than viewers could have in their own living rooms. The most visible of these was a wider image. Studios produced wide-screen films in a number of "scope" formats, such as Cinemascope (the original), Warnerscope, Technicscope, and Panascope.

One major problem with these wide-screen formats is they didn't translate well to TV. When wide-screen films were shown on standard TVs, the sides of the image were typically cut off to accommodate the 4:3 ratio of TV, as shown on the left in **Figure 1.3**. This process is known as *pan and scan* because the focus of the image is moved around based on the action on-screen. To solve this, studios often use *letterboxing*—black bars positioned above and below the wide-screen image—to present the entire image as originally intended, as shown on the right in Figure 1.3.

Figure 1.3 *Here's a wide-screen image cropped to 4:3 on the left, with the entire frame restored in letterbox on the right.*

The adoption of HDTV drove us to migrate from 4:3 TVs to a newer wide-screen TV format. The aspect ratio of wide-screen TV is 16:9 (1.78), which is close to the most-popular film aspect ratio of 1.85. Much of the production and postproduction equipment we use today attempts to acquire and output video to these standards. By and large, modern mobile phones and tablet devices have defaulted to screen resolutions that are close to 16:9 when held horizontally, so this has become the standard across these devices as well.

Why 16:9?

Dr. Kerns Powers of the David Sanroff Research Center in Princeton, New Jersey, a leading research lab on the advancement of TV, studied all the major aspect ratios in popular use and mapped them together. He then discovered something interesting. If he took a rectangle of a certain proportion and scaled it two different ways, he could encompass both the width and the height of all the other aspect ratios. That magic rectangle had the proportions of 16 units wide by 9 units high, or 16:9 (**Figure 1.4**). Because of this discovery, 16:9 was adopted as the new aspect ratio standard for HDTV, and most HDTV-capable TV sets have been designed with 16:9 screens.

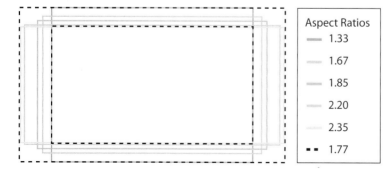

Aspect Ratios	
▬▬	1.33
▬▬	1.67
▬▬	1.85
▬▬	2.20
▬▬	2.35
▪ ▪	1.77

Figure 1.4 *Kern's approach to solving the aspect ratio problem was to take all the popular aspect resolutions of the day and lay them over each other. Upon doing so, he discovered all could be encompassed within a 16:9 rectangle.*

How Compression Works

At its most basic level, video compression works by analyzing the content of every frame and figuring out how to re-create it using less information (the technological equivalent of paraphrasing). This feat is accomplished by *codecs*—shorthand for *compression/decompression algorithm*—which reduces information in various ways. Let's say you have an entire black frame of video (say, before your content has started); all the codec has to remember is the phrase "every pixel in this frame is the same shade of black." That's a lot less data than writing "0, 0, 0" 2,073,600 times (that's 1920 × 1080 for those of you following along).

But most video isn't just one solid color, is it? So, a codec has to look at where the values begin to differ within the frame—borders between light and dark shades, for instance—and describe those values more efficiently. It does this by dividing the scene into groups of pixels, called *macroblocks*, and representing them with numbers that can re-create the patterns within them. **Figure 1.5** shows an example of a macroblock grid.

Figure 1.5 *Macroblocks represent the ability of codecs to break the image into a grid or into groups of pixels that are located near each other in order to process them more efficiently. Certain codecs have the ability to divide macroblocks into smaller groups called partitions.*

With information about preceding frames registered in these blocks, the codec needs to record only the *differences* within those blocks, rather than the entire frame, to construct the complete frame. This works extremely efficiently in video with little or no motion—such as in an interview scene or in static titles.

Despite the complexity of this process, it's an established approach and works very well. But it doesn't give a good-enough compression ratio to reduce high-definition video to manageable file sizes. This is where the notion of changes over time comes into play. You've just learned that video compression works by looking for easily describable features within a video frame. Very little information may need to be carried forward from frame to frame to render the entire image. However, in video with lots of motion, such as footage shot with handheld cameras or clips showing explosions, more pixels change from frame to frame (as shown in **Figure 1.6**), so more data must be passed along as well.

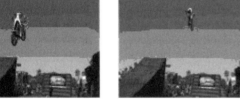

Figure 1.6 *The sequence on top, with lots of motion and little redundancy, is more challenging to compress than the sequence on the bottom, which changes relatively little from frame to frame.*

In the top set of frames, the football player is moving across the screen, and the camera is tracking his movements. This means virtually every pixel is changing from frame to frame as the sequence progresses, making it difficult to make a high-quality compression of it without using a lot of data. The bottom sequence, on the other hand, would compress more efficiently. The camera is locked down, and very little in the frame is changing except the motion path of the biker as he jumps the ramp.

That's how compression works in the most general terms, but there is of course a great deal more specific terminology used to describe how and what is occurring in the compression process. It's important to understand some of these terms described in the next sections and how they may affect your production, the actual compression and delivery, or the archival process you might use with your video content. You don't necessarily need to be able to recite chapter and verse on the topic, but you should be able to identify the words when they come up. The more compression you do, the more they will come up in the context of your work, and being able to use them correctly can only help you.

Lossless and Lossy Compression

All the codecs covered in this book (as well as all the ones not covered) are either lossless or lossy. Just like they sound, *lossless* video codecs are ones that, when decompressed, are a bit-for-bit perfect match with the original. Although lossless compression of video is possible, it is rarely used. This is because lossless compression systems will sometimes result in a file (or portions thereof) that is as large as or has the same data rate as the uncompressed original. As a result, all hardware used in a lossless system would have to be able to run fast enough to handle uncompressed video, which eliminates all the benefits of compressing the video in the first place.

With *lossy* compression, on the other hand, compressing data and then decompressing the data you retrieve postcompression may well be different from the original, but it is close enough to be useful in some way. Lossy compression is the most common method used to compress video, especially in preparing for final delivery such as on DVD, the Web, or mobile devices.

What Should You Remember About Lossy and Lossless?

Just keep in mind as you are working on your video projects that video can be stored as both lossless and lossy. Lossless may or may not come into play during your actual production. If it does, you will need some fairly powerful (and expensive) equipment to store enough of it and play it back fast enough. Even if you are using lossy compression in your production, it is still probably a higher quality (and higher data rate) than the finished product is going to be. Something that is being delivered as a finished project is probably a lossy format. Remember that this doesn't mean the quality is lower, just that the data making up the image isn't as large.

Spatial (DCT) and Wavelet Compression

Now that we've established the lossless/lossy distinction, we'll move on to explaining two other types of codecs, spatial and wavelet-based codecs. Spatial compression is the basis for what was described earlier as a general description of how video compression works—the frame-by-frame removal of redundant material over time. DCT is a form of spatial compression that is always lossy.

NOTE We discuss DCT-based codecs further in Chapter 3.

Wavelet-based video compression is a more advanced form of compression that's well suited for images and video but is less commonly used. Unlike DCT Compression, wavelet compression can be either a perfect, lossless data compression or a lossy compression. Wavelet-based codecs are fewer and further between than their DCT-based counterparts; the files created with them are often much larger, and they typically take more processor power to play back. Thus, they're less suitable for common video playback, though they are more common in acquisition systems, such as the Red camera.

One example of a wavelet video codec is JPEG 2000, considered an excellent intermediate (or *mezzanine*) format.

What makes JPEG 2000 better than DCT-based codecs? Three things:

- **Superior compression performance:** At high bit rates, where artifacts become nearly imperceptible, JPEG 2000 has little fidelity over other codecs; however, at lower bit rates, JPEG 2000 has a much greater advantage.

- **Lossless and lossy compression:** Unlike DCT-based codecs, wavelet codecs can be both lossless and lossy, allowing for a broader range of options when working with video.

- **Side channel spatial information:** Wavelet codecs fully support transparency and alpha channels.

You'll see more examples of wavelet-based codecs in Chapter 3.

What Should You Remember About Spatial and Wavelet Compression?

Spatial compression, specifically DCT compression, is much more common than wavelet compression, though wavelet will continue to increase in popularity. For the most part, you won't need to concern yourself with keeping track of whether you are using one or the other in your workflow. However, since spatial is much more pervasive now, you want to make sure you are delivering content to others in such a codec.

Quantization

The use of both DCT- and wavelet-based video compression involves quantization. *Quantization* is the process of approximating a continuous range of values by a relatively small set of discrete symbols or integer values; in other words, it's a way of mathematically finding an efficient way to describe all the pixels in an image.

Quantization plays a major part in lossy data compression and can be viewed as the fundamental element that distinguishes lossy data compression from lossless data compression.

What Should You Remember About Quantization?

Quantization is used as a measurement of quality when speaking about video. The lower the number, the better the quality of that image.

Interframe and Intraframe Compression

Earlier in this chapter, we described compression as being dependent on the ability to keep track of how the pixels evolve frame by frame over time. Interframe and intraframe are ways of describing how that compression relates the various frames of the video to one another.

With *interframe*, the most common method compares each frame in the video with the previous one. Since interframe compression copies data from one frame to another, if the original frame is simply cut or lost (either through editing or dropped during broadcast), the following frames cannot be reconstructed properly. Only video ready to distribute (and no longer edited or otherwise cut) should be compressed in an interframe format.

Some video formats such as Apple's ProRes, however, compress each frame independently using *intraframe* compression. Editing intraframe-compressed video is similar to editing uncompressed video, in that to process the video, the editing system doesn't need to look at any other frames to decode the information necessary to construct the frame at hand.

Another difference between intraframe and interframe compression is that with intraframe systems, each frame uses a similar amount of data. In most interframe systems, however, certain frames (called *I-frames*) don't copy data from other frames and so require much more data to create than other nearby frames. See Chapter 2 for more information on the types of frames that exist, including I-frames.

It is now possible for nonlinear editors such as Apple Final Cut Pro and Adobe Premiere Pro to identify problems caused when I-frames are edited out while other frames need them. This has allowed formats such as high bitrate MPEG-4 to be used for editing without requiring conversion to all I-frame intermediate codecs. However, this process demands a lot more computing power than editing intraframe-compressed video with the same picture quality because the processor is constantly looking to other frames to find the information needed to re-create the frame the user wants to edit.

What Should You Remember About Interframe and Intraframe?

Interframe compression works well for video that will simply be played back from start to finish by the viewer but can cause problems if the video sequence needs to be edited or played in reverse. Video that is still in production and therefore may need to be edited or otherwise cut should be compressed with an intraframe codec (such as ProRes or PhotoJPEG).

High Dynamic Range

High dynamic range (HDR) video is one of the newest buzzwords to enter the video lexicon. It can push video images past the previous limitations of the display contrast. Some say it offers more visual enhancement than what the move from 1080p to 4K offered in terms of picture quality. It's impressive to see on TVs that can handle it (and yes, it takes an HDR-capable display to take advantage of HDR), but it is still an emerging technology and the catalog of content available today is fairly small when compared to standard dynamic range (SDR). The amount of HDR content will continue to grow, however, and being aware of it and knowing how to handle it will be useful knowledge.

In a nutshell, SDR dates back to the days of CRT monitors, which did not support as great a range of color and brightness when compared to modern flat screens. HDR increases both the luminosity and the color depth of the image, resulting in a display image that is much closer to film quality (**Figure 1.7**).

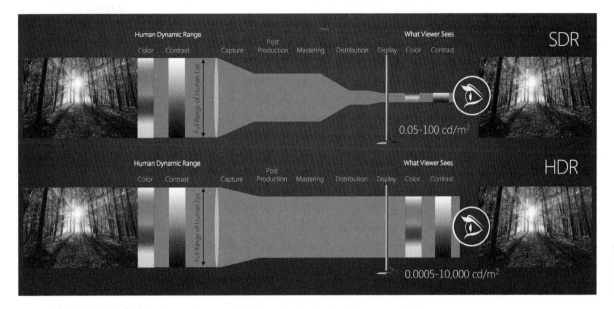

Figure 1.7 *Much more color information is sacrificed in the SDR image, and the resulting image is less rich in color.*

Audio Compression

With all this talk of video compression, it's easy to forget that video has audio with it almost all the time. In fact, many filmmakers will tell you that audio is more important than the visuals in the film-watching experience. Certainly it's no less important, though the process for capturing and compressing it is less complex, only because there is less data present to work with.

The term *compression* has several meanings in audio, so it's good to be aware of that, especially when speaking with an audio professional. There is lossy data compression (just like video), level compression, and limiting. We'll touch on compression and limiting a bit in Chapter 4 as part of the preprocessing techniques for audio.

As with video compression, both lossy and lossless compression algorithms are used in audio compression, lossy being the most common for everyday use (such as with MP3). In both lossy and lossless compression, information redundancy is reduced, using methods such as coding, pattern recognition, and linear prediction to reduce the amount of information used to describe the data.

The compression of audio can quickly go too far, however, and the results are quite noticeable, especially in music, which has a more dynamic sound than spoken words. Music is similar to high-motion video; with more action in the content, the compressors have to keep track of more information continuously. In a monologue, by contrast, where much less is happening, less data is needed to capture what is happening. When very dynamic audio is restricted to too few bits to re-create it, the results sound distorted—either tinny or degraded by pre-echo or an absence of high or low end.

As mentioned earlier, good audio compression is just as important as video compression, and with the rise in popularity of podcasting, many people have come to pay attention to it much more than they have in the past. The key to good audio, perhaps even more than video, is to acquire good source material.

There is a lot—way more—that goes into actually encoding content for delivery, but let's pause for a moment and talk about delivery. Specifically, the most prevalent distribution channel today: the Internet.

Online Video Delivery

Let's face it, in this day and age, you are likely to deliver content online in some way. Whether it's on YouTube, your own site, or somewhere else, there are some basics you'll need to understand. Or perhaps you have bigger plans and are looking to get into adaptive bitrate streaming. Not sure what that is? Let's explore all of these a bit.

Traditional Streaming vs. Download

Video and audio content can be delivered in two ways on the Internet: as a streaming file or as a progressive download file.

The same technology used to share web pages can be used for distributing media. The content can be embedded in a web page. The content is accessed through the browser, downloaded to a temporary file on your computer's hard drive, and then played by the player. This process is called *progressive download* and doesn't require a special server, other than the standard web server.

With progressive download, the browser handles the buffering and playing during the download process. If the playback rate exceeds the download rate (you run out of content that's been downloaded), playback is delayed until more data is downloaded. Generally speaking, files that are downloaded over the Web are able to be viewed only after the entire file is downloaded. With progressive download video, however, most formats allow the user to start watching before the entire video has downloaded.

Traditional What?

Please note that what's referred to as *traditional streaming* here is really just the way we streamed things prior to adaptive bitrate streaming (ABR). Unless you are in the Internet radio business, it's likely you aren't using this traditional style method very much. Still, it does show up from time to time, so it's handy to know some basics.

Traditional streaming media works differently. In this scenario, the server, like the standard web server, is connected to a high-speed Internet connection. However, in this case, the computer is running specialized streaming media server software such as Windows Media Services (Microsoft) or the Flash Media Server (Flash Video).

Streaming addresses use a different protocol than the standard Hypertext Transfer Protocol (HTTP) and appear like this:

mms://x.x.x.x/streaming_media_file_directory/media_file_name.wmv

or like this:

rtsp://x.x.x.x/directory/filename.flv

A streaming server works with the client to send audio and video over the Internet or an intranet and plays it almost immediately. Streaming servers allow real-time "broadcasting" of live events and the ability to control the playback of on-demand content. Playback begins as soon as sufficient data has been transmitted. The viewer can skip to a point partway through a clip without needing to download from the beginning.

Adaptive Bitrate Streaming

NOTE ABR will be covered in more detail in Chapter 6.

Adaptive bitrate streaming as a concept existed in 2008, but there were no practical consumer examples of it available. Today, the majority of the content viewed online is delivered this way. While not a standard to begin with, it has still become a ubiquitous method for delivery, with few competing methods. In fact, it has consolidated around one or two implementations and will likely stay that way as a few others slowly fade away. The ABR formats we focus on in this book are Apple's HTTP Live Streaming (HLS) and MPEG-DASH. Check out Chapter 6 for more details about online video delivery and MPEG-DASH in particular.

Conclusion

Understanding these basics is a good start to mastering video compression. These fundamentals are important to refer to as you progress deeper into the world of video compression. From here, we'll dive deeper into the specifics of compression and expand on delivery information for a multitude of devices.

Understanding the Language of Compression

2

All disciplines have their own specialized terminology and references for explaining various components and practices, and compression is certainly no different. It has its own specific language, and like most languages, it shares elements with other neighboring tongues, especially the video and IT network worlds.

But in some cases, the same terms have different meanings in the world of compression. Talk to a broadcaster or cable operator about video on demand, and they'll immediately assume you are referring to the video content made available on demand through cable channels. Talk to a streaming services or content provider about the same terminology, and they will assume you mean any online content. Compressionists need to know both definitions and be conscious of the context others refer to when they use these terms.

On the other hand, some words and concepts are specific to compression, and these are the ones that typically cause communication problems between compressionists and others. Perhaps the most confusing terms concern the differences between video players on computers (and embedded devices), video and audio codecs, and video and audio formats. The words that describe these different parts of compression are similar enough to puzzle anyone working in the field and confuse a client who just needs work done and has no inclination or need to learn the compressionist's lexicon.

The goal of this chapter is to clarify what exactly these three major concepts—players, codecs, and formats—mean, and then we will discuss some specific facets of compression that any compressionist should be prepared to discuss as part of the encoding process.

Compression Parameters

Before we dive into the formats, containers, and codecs you are going to come into contact with, let's drill into compression parameters. This is a term commonly used to describe the settings available with a codec. Many are global, meaning they are identical or at least similar from codec to codec. Some, however, may be specific to an individual codec family. It's important to understand all the basic settings because they are directly going to affect the quality of the finished video you are creating.

It's also a good idea to familiarize yourself with the advanced settings possible within the codecs you work with most often. This will allow you to really get in there and optimize the finished product.

Data Rates (or Bit Rates)

Data rates are the number of bits you are allowing the software to use to describe each frame of the video. If you use more bits, the detail and picture quality go up, but so does the file size. If you use fewer bits, the size goes down, but the image detail may suffer. Certain codecs are better at providing a better-quality image with less data than others.

TIP In the world of acronyms, a little b means bits, and a big B means bytes. Don't get them confused; there are eight bits in a byte, so if you get it wrong, you are off by eight times!

Data rates are typically represented in bits (whereas storage on a hard drive is typically represented in bytes). The two abbreviations you will see most often in reference to this are kilobits per second (Kbps) and megabits per second (Mbps). However, in recent years, Society of Motion Picture and Television Engineers (SMPTE) and other large standards boards have attempted to unify around Bit/s instead of bps to avoid confusing bits and bytes. So, the use of kbit/s and Mbit/s would also be appropriate in documentation or software settings.

VBR and CBR

Variable bitrate (VBR) encoding varies the amount of output bits over time, using an average target bitrate as a goal but apportioning different amounts of bits to different portions of an encoded video. VBR allows a higher bitrate (and therefore more storage space) to be allocated to the more complex segments of media files, while less space is allocated to less complex segments. The average of these rates is calculated to produce an average bitrate for the file that will represent its overall audio and video quality.

Constant bitrate (CBR), on the other hand, means that bits used per segment are constant, regardless of the complexity of the audio or image. Why would you use one versus the other? VBR is useful for web-based content that is downloaded, not streamed in real time, because the ratio of image quality to file size is high—you are being as efficient as possible with the bits being used (the most bang for your bits, as it were).

So, if that's true, why would you ever use CBR? Some playback devices expect the same amount of data constantly because it is easier for the player to maintain smooth, continuous playback of the video. Devices with lower processing power than modern DVD and Blu-ray players, as well as portable devices that have to balance processing power against power consumption, are ideal candidates for CBR video because the processor won't be overwhelmed.

> **TIP** Need a small-sized video with a decent picture quality? Try a VBR file with a low minimum data rate and a high peak. This will keep the average fairly low while allowing the codec to decide when it needs to spend more bits to get the image right.

Frame Rate

Frame rate (expressed most often as frames per second or fps) is the frequency, or rate, at which consecutive images are displayed. The term is used for film and video cameras, computer graphics, and motion capture systems. Frame rate is also called the *frame frequency* or *hertz* (Hz).

In the early days of online video, it was common to reduce the frame rate to save bandwidth (for example, delivering a clip at 15 fps instead of 30 fps). Because of the improvements in broadband speeds as well as an increase in the processing power of modern devices, most encoded video is delivered at a native frame rate, rather than a reduced one. It is, however, vital to ensure frame rates aren't accidentally adjusted during the encode process (say from 30 to 24, or vice versa). The effect of this would be to potentially add perceptual motion stutter or what is often called "judder" to the image.

Frame Types

NOTE Interframe compression encodes a frame after looking at data from many frames (between frames) near it, while intraframe compression applies encoding to each individual frame without looking at the others.

When encoding video, there are a few different types of frames that will appear within the content—intra (I) frames (also called *key frames*), predicted (P) frames, and bipredictive or bidirectional (B) frames. I-frames are frames that do not refer to other frames before or after them in the video. They contain all the information needed to display them. P-frames, however, use previous I-frames as reference points to complete them (in other words, they describe the changes made in an image since the last I-frame). Because they are describing changes only since the last I-frame, P-frames take fewer bits to create. B-frames are predictive frames that use the last two I-frames to predict motion paths that may occur. These take even less data to create than P-frames.

All My Frames

Intra frames (aka slices, I-frames, I-pictures, or key frames) have the following characteristics:

- Are pictures coded without reference to any pictures except themselves.
- May be generated by an encoder to create a random access point (to allow a decoder to start decoding properly from scratch at that picture location).
- May also be generated when differing image details prohibit the generation of effective P- or B-frames.
- Typically require more bits to encode than other frame types.
- Often, I-pictures (I-frames) are used for random access and are used as references for the decoding of other pictures. Intra-refresh periods of a half-second are common on such applications as digital TV broadcast and Blu-ray Disc storage. Longer refresh periods may be used in some environments. For example, in videoconferencing systems, it is uncommon to send I-pictures frequently.

Predicted pictures (aka slices, P-pictures, or P-frames) have the following characteristics:

- Require the prior decoding of some other picture (or pictures) to be decoded.
- Can reference previous pictures in decoding order.

(continued on next page)

All My Frames *(continued)*

- May contain both image data and motion vector displacements (that is, information that tells the encoder that an object has changed positions) and combinations of the two.
- In older standard designs (such as MPEG-2), use only one previously decoded picture as a reference during decoding and require that picture to also precede the P-picture in display order.
- In H.264, can use multiple previously decoded pictures as references during decoding and can have any arbitrary display-order relationship relative to the picture (or pictures) used for their prediction.
- Typically require fewer bits for encoding than I-pictures do.

Bipredictive pictures (aka slices, bidirectional, B-pictures, or B-frames) have the following characteristics:

- Require the prior decoding of some other picture (or pictures) to be decoded.
- May contain both image data and motion vector displacements and combinations of the two.
- Include some prediction modes that form a prediction of a motion region (for example, a macroblock or a smaller area) by averaging the predictions obtained using two different previously decoded reference regions.
- In older standard designs (such as MPEG-2), B-pictures are never used as references for the prediction of other pictures. As a result, a lower-quality encoding (resulting in the use of fewer bits than would otherwise be the case) can be used for such B-pictures because the loss of detail will not harm the prediction quality for subsequent pictures.
- In H.264, may or may not be used as references for the decoding of other pictures (at the discretion of the encoder).
- In older standard designs (such as MPEG-2), use exactly two previously decoded pictures as references during decoding and require one of those pictures to precede the B-picture in display order and the other one to follow it.
- In H.264, can use one, two, or more than two previously decoded pictures as references during decoding and can have any arbitrary display-order relationship relative to the picture (or pictures) used for its prediction.
- Typically require fewer bits for encoding than either I- or P-pictures do.

Aspect Ratios and Letterboxing

As discussed in Chapter 1, a number of aspect ratios are available; however, in the video world, 4:3 and 16:9 are the two most common. As part of the compression process, you want to be conscious of preserving the intended aspect ratio as you scale the video resolution; nothing can be as distracting as trying to watch video that has a distorted image.

But there is also one other issue to keep an eye out for: letterboxed video. Letterboxed video is 16:9 content that has black bars above and below the image to conform it to 4:3 standards. Letterboxing became popular in the 1970s to help preserve the full image of a feature film being played back on a broadcast TV. Pillar bars are another form of letterboxing, which became popular with the arrival of wide-screen TVs. Most compression applications have a built-in cropping tool that allows you to remove the black bars from the original image as well as alter the intended aspect ratio to the new dimensions needed to keep the video image from distorting.

Square and Nonsquare Pixels

Pixels in the computer world are square. A 100-pixel vertical line is the same length as a 100-pixel horizontal line on a graphics monitor (a 1:1 ratio). However, some formats (such as HDV and DVCPRO HD) use nonsquare pixels internally for image storage as a way to reduce the amount of data that must be processed, thus limiting the necessary transfer rates and maintaining compatibility with existing interfaces.

Directly mapping an image with a certain pixel aspect ratio on a device whose pixel aspect ratio is different makes the image look unnaturally stretched or squashed in either the horizontal or vertical direction. For example, a circle generated for a computer display with square pixels looks like a vertical ellipse on a standard-definition NTSC television that uses vertically rectangular pixels. This issue is even more evident on wide-screen TVs.

As you convert video meant for one delivery format to another, you may need to convert the pixel aspect ratio as part of the process. Many compression programs will already correct for this automatically; however, some may expose an option that allows the users to either select it manually or override the default options available.

Containers

A *container* (also known as a *wrapper* or *format*) is a computer file format that can contain various types of data, compressed by means of standardized audio/video codecs. The container file is used to identify and interleave the different data types and make them accessible to the player. This applies to online and broadcast content. Simpler container formats can contain different types of video or audio codecs, while more advanced container formats can support multiple audio and video streams, subtitles, chapter information, and metadata (tags), along with the synchronization information needed to play back the various streams together.

Containers for Audio

Some wrappers/containers are exclusive to audio, as listed here:

- **WAV:** This is widely used on the Windows platform.
- **WMA:** This is a common Windows audio format that supports a number of codecs.
- **AIFF:** This is widely used on the macOS platform.
- **MP3 (MPEG-1 Layer 3):** Though it has plateaued in popularity, this format is considered one of the linchpins for the rise of digital music.
- **M4A and AAC:** These are audio formats that have better audio quality over MP3 and take advantage of the MPEG-4 audio standards.

Containers for Various Media Types

Other, more flexible containers can hold many types of audio and video, as well as other media. Some of the more common containers include the following:

- **AVI:** This is the standard Microsoft Windows container.
- **WMV:** This is a compressed video file format for several proprietary codecs developed by Microsoft.
- **FLV:** This is the format specific to Flash Video. It primarily uses AVC/H.264 codec, though it also supports VP6.
- **MOV:** This is the standard QuickTime video container from Apple.

- **MPEG-2 transport stream (TS) (aka MPEG-TS):** This is the standard container for digital broadcasting; this typically contains multiple video and audio streams, an electronic program guide, and a program stream (PS).

- **MP4:** This is the standard audio and video container for the MPEG-4 multimedia portfolio.

- **OGM ("Ogg Media"):** This is the standard video container for Xiph. org codecs.

- **MXF:** This is a container format for professional digital video and audio media defined by a set of SMPTE standards.

- **Matroska/MKV:** This is not a standard for any codec or platform but instead is an open standard.

- **MOX:** This is an open source mezzanine container for use in conjunction with open source codecs such as EXR, PNG, and VC5 (CineForm).

Codecs

Ah, here we are, the core component of the compression world—the codec. Codec is an acronym that stands for compressor/decompressor or coder/ decoder, depending on whom you ask. Though codecs also exist in hardware, when you hear codecs referred to, people are typically speaking about the software codecs that actually make it possible to translate stored video and audio from their digital form into moving images and audio. Knowing when and when not to use different codecs is important throughout the postproduction, compression, and final delivery of your content.

A Time and a Place for Everything

All codecs have advantages and disadvantages. Comparisons are frequently made between which are the "best" (best being a sliding scale depending on who published the findings). Generally speaking, the trade-off between image fidelity, file size, processor usage, and popularity can be used to draw comparisons between various codecs. What do we mean by that?

- **Image quality:** Obviously, preserving image quality is of paramount concern when compressing video.

- **File size:** Quality has to be balanced by how large the file actually is.

- **Processor usage:** As the video is playing back, it is being decoded from its binary form to be displayed. Each codec requires different amounts of processor support to perform this. It can't be so intensive that it's impossible for the device or computer to actually keep up with the decoding process, so this should be considered as well.

- **Popularity:** The most popular codecs are the ones that have the widest-reaching audience, though they are not always the best-looking or the ones capable of delivering the best quality in the smallest files. A video format or codec that requires additional steps to install a custom player may not get the viewers that a lower-quality but widely supported player may get.

With these criteria in mind, you can begin organizing codecs into a few categories that make it easy to decide when—or even more importantly, when not—to use a certain codec. The following are the essential categories for video codecs.

Why Is This So Confusing?

Players, containers, and codecs often are the components of video compression most difficult to understand. This is for a number of reasons. For one thing, you can see that several of them share identical or similar names, making it hard for someone not deeply rooted in the video compression realm to differentiate between the terms. It is also hard for those who just want to watch a video clip on their computer to grasp (or even care about) the relationship between the three terms, and frankly, they don't have to understand it. If we as compressionists and content creators/distributors are doing our jobs, the content should just work (like turning on a TV). It shouldn't be hard to make it work.

Generally speaking, it is useful to remember that players are a long-term prospect—they are something that will be around for a long time (as evidenced by the longevity of such players as QuickTime Player). They will rise and fall in popularity depending on the quality and types of video they may offer.

Formats can also have a long shelf life, if they were developed with an eye to the future. Formats that limit the codecs and data they support other than audio and video (metadata) have fallen out of popularity as other more flexible formats have gained popularity. Codecs are perhaps the most expendable part of the equation. Codecs will continually be updated and created to take advantage of the newest, fastest computers and higher-resolution video monitors.

Acquisition Codecs

Acquisition codecs are the ones you capture your images in. Acquisition codecs are usually (but not always) associated with cameras. When choosing your acquisition codec, generally speaking, you should aim for the highest-quality codec that your camera (or your budget) supports. In this case, "highest quality" just means you want to capture as much information as possible: less compression, higher bit depth, and less chroma subsampling. If you start with more information at the beginning, the more flexibility you will have in post, especially in color correction and any visual effects work. In many cases, your choice of camera also dictates your choice of codec (or codec family). Choosing an acquisition codec is one of the most important decisions content producers make. But there are also a lot of pragmatic factors involved with this decision. Otherwise, we would always be shooting uncompressed 8K raw, right?

A few of the current popular acquisition codes available are the following:

- **REDCODE:** Red Digital Cinema's proprietary codec and format for camera acquisition.

- **XF-AVC:** Canon's 4K acquisition codec.

- **XAVC:** Sony Prosumer line for acquisition. XAVC is based on 4K and can support up to 4K at 60 fps.

- **XDCAM:** Sony's line of acquisition codecs based on MPEG-2. Four different product lines—XDCAM SD, XDCAM HD, XDCAM EX, and XDCAM HD422—differ in types of encoder used, frame size, container type, and recording media.

Legacy Acquisition Codecs

These acquisition codecs aren't really around anymore:

- **DV/DVCAM:** The DV codec, in terms of file-based content (as opposed to tape), has two main versions: DV-NTSC, which is the 720 × 480 default DV codec that comes installed with QuickTime for use in accordance with the North American broadcast standard, and 720 × 576 DV-PAL, which is available for European playback standards.

- **DVCPro/DVCPro HD:** This is Panasonic's answer to Sony's DVCAM format.

Mezzanine Codecs

The main purpose of these intermediary codecs is to preserve image quality (usually) regardless of file size. These codecs are mostly used during the postproduction process and are usually not suitable for delivery to the end user. These files are often huge or lack wide public support as playback formats. You would use a mezzanine codec if you wanted to export video to be used in another program during the postproduction process but didn't want to introduce compression artifacts.

A few of the current popular mezzanine codecs are as follows:

- **Apple ProRes:** This is a lossy codec developed by Apple for use in postproduction that supports up to 8K. It is the successor of the Apple Intermediate Codec and was first introduced in 2007 with Final Cut Studio 2. In 2010 it was made available as an encoder on the Windows platform as well, and in 2011 FFmpeg added support for it.

- **CineForm:** This is an open source intermediate codec first developed by CineForm in 2002 and then acquired in 2011 by GoPro. It is a wavelet-based codec that is similar to JPEG 2000, which is currently being standardized by SMPTE under the VC-5 name.

- **Avid DNX:** This is a lossy high-definition video postproduction codec developed by Avid for multigeneration compositing with reduced storage and bandwidth requirements. It is an implementation of the SMPTE VC-3 standard.

Legacy Mezzanine Codecs

These mezzanine codecs are older and not used much anymore:

- **SheerVideo:** This is an older family of fast, lossless QuickTime and AVI codecs developed by BitJazz. This hasn't been updated in quite a while, so check before using.

- **Photo JPEG:** The Photo JPEG codec implements the Joint Photographic Experts Group (JPEG ISO version 9R9) algorithm for image compression.

- **Motion JPEG (M-JPEG):** Originally developed for multimedia, the MJPEG codec compresses each frame as a JPEG.

- **Animation:** This is an early Apple codec that enabled RGB video playback in real time without special hardware requirements.

Delivery Codecs

Delivery codecs are used to distribute video and audio content to an audience. These codecs provide the tightest balance between small file sizes and image quality. They are widely adopted and supported codecs that will reach the widest audience possible.

Current delivery codecs are as follows:

- **HEVC/H.265:** High Efficiency Video Coding (HEVC), also known as H.265 and MPEG-H Part 2, is an industry standard and considered a successor to AVC (H.264 or MPEG-4 Part 10). It was codeveloped by the Motion Picture Experts Group (MPEG) and the Video Coding Experts Group (VSEG). In comparison to AVC, HEVC offers about double the data compression ratio at the same level of video quality, or substantially improved video quality at the same bitrate. It supports resolutions up to 8192 × 4320, including 8K UHD.

- **VP9:** VP9 is an open source and royalty-free format developed by Google, which acquired On2 Technologies in 2010. VP9 has a large user base through YouTube and the Android platform. This code base was also the starting point for the AV1 codec.

It's a Multiformat, Multicodec World We're Living In

While it may seem like AVC has dominated the past ten years of video delivery, it is still very much a multicodec world. True, AVC was a dominant player for delivery, but the codecs used in acquisition and postproduction have continued to expand and mature, with improved resolution, quality, decode speeds, and so on. That won't change anytime soon. In addition, as we move past 1080p delivery to the consumer, we will have a new battle between AV1 and HEVC for dominance.

- **MPEG-4 Part 10/H.264/AVC:** MPEG-4 Part 10 is a standard technically aligned with the ITU-T's H.264 and often also referred to as Advanced Video Coding (AVC). This standard is still the most popular codec currently supported on the Web. It uses different profiles and levels to identify different configurations and uses. It contains a number of significant advances in compression capability, and it has been adopted into a number of company's products, including the Xbox family, PlayStation, virtually all mobile phones, both macOS and Windows operating systems, as well as high-definition Blu-ray Disc.

- **AV1:** AOMedia Video 1 is an open, royalty-free video-coding format designed for video transmissions over the Internet. It is being developed by the Alliance for Open Media (AOMedia), a consortium of firms from the semiconductor industry, video-on-demand providers, and web browser developers, founded in 2015. It is meant to succeed its predecessor VP9 and compete with HEVC/H.265.

Business, Not Technology, Will Decide the Winner

As we look to 4K and greater delivery, it will ultimately be licensing deals, not the technology, that determines whether AV1 or HEVC becomes the dominant delivery codec. The industry is still cautious about the licensing deals that will be enforced around HEVC, and it is still not entirely clear whether AV1 will escape patent enforcement. Many believe there is underlying technology in AV1 that may infringe existing patents. Whether this is true or not, it will be something that potentially delays adoption of it. From a technology standpoint, these two codecs are on par with each other right now.

It is worth noting that while AV1 is talked about a lot right now, it is still emerging technology. The specifications for the encoder were released in the fall of 2017, and we will begin seeing companies integrating it into their compression tools soon. Remember that H.264 was commercially available for years before you saw it proliferate, so don't be surprised if AV1 takes a similar course.

Legacy Delivery Codecs

These are some legacy delivery codecs. While you might not use these in your current work, it's helpful to know about them:

- **VP8:** This is a proprietary video codec developed by On2 Technologies and used in Adobe Flash Player 8 and newer.

- **VC-1:** This is an SMPTE video compression standard (SMPTE 421M) based on Microsoft's WMV 9 video codec. It is also one of the three mandatory video codecs in Blu-ray high-definition optical disc standards (MPEG-2 and H.264 are the others). Like MPEG-4 Part 10, VC-1 uses the concept of profiles to differentiate the uses and data settings it supports through its configurations.

- **MPEG-2 Part 2:** Used on DVD, on SVCD, and in most digital video broadcasting and cable distribution systems, MPEG-2's sweet spot in the market is the quality of video it provides for standard-definition video delivery. When used on a standard DVD, it offers good picture quality and supports both the 4:3 and 16:9 aspect ratios. In terms of technical design, the most significant enhancement in MPEG-2 over its predecessor, MPEG-1 (see the next section), was the addition of support for interlaced video. We have newer codecs that do much better at the image quality-to-file-size ratio, so let's put our dear friend MPEG-2 to rest, shall we?

- **H.261:** Used primarily in older videoconferencing and video telephony products, H.261, developed by the ITU-T, was the first practical digital video compression standard. Essentially all subsequent standard video codec designs are based on it. It included such well-established concepts as YCbCr color representation, the 4:2:0 sampling format, 8-bit sample precision, 16×16 macroblocks, block-wise motion compensation, 8×8 block-wise discrete cosine transformation, zigzag coefficient scanning, scalar quantization, run+value symbol mapping, and variable-length coding. H.261 supported only progressive scan video.

- **MPEG-1 Part 2:** This was used for video CDs (VCD) and sometimes for online video. The quality is roughly comparable to that of VHS. If the source video quality is good and the bitrate is high enough, VCD can look better than VHS, but VCD requires high bitrates for this. MPEG-1 offers high compatibility, in that almost any computer can play back MPEG-1 files, and many DVD players also support the VCD format. However, it is an antiquated format that has been surpassed in terms of

(continued on next page)

Legacy Delivery Codecs *(continued)*

quality and file size by many others. MPEG-1 only supports progressive scan video.

- **MPEG-4 Part 2:** This was an older implementation of the MPEG-4 standard that was less processor intensive (but not as good at the quality-to-file-size ratio that Part 10 would later provide). As soon as devices more widely supported H.264, use of MPEG-4 Part 2 waned.

- **Sorenson Pro 3:** This was the best-looking QuickTime codec for a long time, but H.264 officially unseated it, and it is no longer used commercially.

- **Cinepak:** A precursor to Sorenson Pro 3, this should also no longer be considered a viable delivery codec.

- **Windows Media 7 and 8, Microsoft MPEG-4 version 3:** All of these have been far surpassed by WMV 9/VC-1.

Players

The term player refers to the software that makes it possible to play back video and audio. In essence, video players are the TV within the computer that plays your videos. *Player* can refer to a stand-alone application, or it can be the software used for playback that is designed for use in web pages and applications that use HTML5. These HTML5 players will vary in capabilities but are developed to be used in web pages, in purpose-built applications, on computers, on console devices, and even on mobile phones (effectively, anywhere HTML works).

Desktop Players

There are many out there; some come free from software and hardware companies, others are sold commercially, and some are open source products supported by a community of developers and enthusiasts. Sometimes these players will have compression capabilities of their own, making it possible to transcode a piece of video in addition to playing it back.

As mentioned, several players are available; there isn't one universal video player that will seamlessly play back all video and audio formats (though some try hard to do just that). As a compressionist, you want to be familiar with all these players and have them available to test and play back content you are creating to make sure it will work for your clients (and their end users) upon delivery.

If you are widely distributing your content, then you should also be checking this content in these players on multiple types of computers. Don't test just on your Mac if all your viewers are likely to be playing it back on a PC; you have to mimic the end-viewer experience as closely as possible to assure a quality viewing experience.

Built-in Players

Generally speaking, on a modern consumer PC or Mac, the default player is a fairly generic application that will play back local media but is also tied to a media catalog or store run by the platform and designed to sell you movies and TV shows. It is not expected that the average user is doing much video conversion, so the default consumer experience is merely one of playback.

Microsoft Movies and TV App

On a modern Windows 10 device, the default player is a Windows Store app called Movies & TV (**Figure 2.1**). It is a simple player but supports formats and codecs expected in general content delivery (various flavors of MPEG-4 primarily). Given it is focused on a consumer experience, it also supports closed captions or subtitles in the display and the ability to "cast" or wirelessly push playback to supported wireless devices, such as an Xbox on the same network or a Google Chromecast. It also supports the ability to add new codec support through the Microsoft store (for example, there is a free extension to add MPEG2 support to the Movies & TV app).

Figure 2.1 *Movies & TV does not support the ability to transcode video to other formats.*

macOS QuickTime and iTunes

QuickTime is still the default player for video in the Apple ecosystem (**Figure 2.2**). QuickTime X is the latest version (the previous version was QuickTime 7). The reason for the jump in numbering from 7 to 10 (X) was to indicate a similar break with the previous versions of the product that macOS indicated. QuickTime X is fundamentally different from previous versions, in that it is provided as a Cocoa (Objective-C) framework and breaks compatibility with the previous QuickTime 7 C-based APIs that were previously used. QuickTime X was completely rewritten to implement modern audio video codecs in 64-bit. QuickTime X is a combination of two technologies: QuickTime Kit Framework (QTKit) and QuickTime X Player. QTKit is used by QuickTime Player to display media. QuickTime X does not implement all of the functionality of the previous QuickTime and has focused support of codecs to primarily H.264, ProRes, and a few others.

Figure 2.2 *The QuickTime player is the default player in macOS.*

Third-Party Players

Built-in players are not the only option for playback. Several third parties have created both open source and proprietary players that will play back video and audio. The platforms and formats they support will vary for each. These players offer additional features over the default players such as expanded format support, video analysis, and some exporting features.

VLC

VLC is an open source software media player from the VideoLAN project (**Figure 2.3**). It is a highly portable multimedia player, encoder, and streamer supporting many audio and video codecs and file formats as well as DVDs, VCDs, and various streaming protocols. Versions of it exist for Microsoft Windows, macOS, BeOS, BSD, Windows CE, Linux, and Solaris.

It is well known as one of the most flexible video players on the market, able to play back virtually any format. It provides hardware decoding on supported devices and has advanced controls for adding subtitles and resyncing audio and video.

Figure 2.3 *VLC is widely used for its ability to play back virtually any format.*

Telestream Switch

Telestream, a company known for both its professional and enterprise video tools, has a player marketed directly to compressionists. Its application, Switch, lets the user play a variety of web and professional media formats and, more importantly, inspect and adjust the properties of those files and then export a new file if needed. Switch enables visual file inspection and single-file transcoding, and it is an affordable software solution for professional media quality control.

Its functionality is broken down into three levels (and price points). The most basic Switch player is $9.99 and plays and inspects movies (providing metadata, and so on). The $199 Switch Plus adds the capability of editing the metadata of the video and gives extended support for HEVC, DNxHD, and many other professional codecs. The most expensive level, Switch Pro ($499), adds many more inspection tools, panels designed for monitoring audio loudness and playback on external monitors, and a timeline that highlights GOP structure and data rate details. The Pro version also includes the ability to compare alternate media (for example, comparing encoded video to source) and allows for exporting video as an iTunes-friendly package for those submitting content to the Apple Store for sale.

Switch is available for both Windows and macOS, which makes it an ideal cross-platform tool for testing and finding issues with your encodes.

HTML5 Players

HTML5 video is intended by its creators to become the new standard way to show video on the Web. The video tag is meant to replace the previous de facto standard, which was the proprietary Adobe Flash plug-in. Early adoption of the tag was hampered by lack of agreement as to which video-coding and audio-coding formats should be supported in web browsers. The <video> element was proposed by Opera Software in February 2007. Opera also released a preview build that was showcased the same day, and its manifesto called for video to become a first-class citizen of the Web.

Other elements closely associated with video playback in HTML5 are Media Source Extensions (MSE) and Encrypted Media Extensions (EME). Both are World Wide Web Consortium (W3C) specifications. MSE allows browsers to directly decode content supported by HTML5. EME provides a secured communication channel between web browsers and digital rights management (DRM) software. This allows the use of HTML5 video to play back DRM-wrapped content without the need of a plug-in like Adobe Flash.

The HTML5 specification does not specify which video and audio formats browsers should support. Browsers are free to support any video formats they feel are appropriate, but content authors cannot assume that any video will be accessible by all complying browsers. Next we want to go through a few of the common HTML5 players you may see referred to. It is worth noting that unlike desktop players, HTML5 players are more what framework developers will use either in an application or online to play back the media. Each will have its own supported features and quirks.

How to Choose an HTML5 Player

The compressionist is not the one who typically has to choose the HTML5 player as part of a larger media project. This role will most likely fall to the developer building the site or application. However, multiple factors will go into the decision, so the compressionist and developer should make sure that the player that is chosen matches the following short list of criteria:

Format and codec dependencies: Ensure that the player supports the choices made for video delivery.

Performance and quality: How quickly does the video start up and play back? How efficient is the player in regard to memory usage?

Custom features: Does the player need to support closed captions or subtitles? Is there DRM support required? Is there an advertising model that needs to be supported?

Video.js

Video.js is one of the most popular open source HTML players available (**Figure 2.4**). It is sponsored by Brightcove and is now used in more than 400,000 web sites. Video.js plays both HTML5 and Flash Video and works on mobile devices and desktops.

Figure 2.4 *Video.js is widely used as an open source HTML player.*

Projekktor

This is an open source video player project. Projekktor was released under GPLv3 for the Web, and it was written using JavaScript. This platform is capable enough to manage all compatibility issues and cross-browser problems while providing a huge set of powerful features such as preroll and postroll advertising, playlist and channel support, and Flash playback.

Bitdash

The HTML5 and Flash-based web player Bitdash can be used in web browsers on desktop computers and smartphones (**Figure 2.5**). This player enables the streaming and playback of MPEG-DASH or Apple's HTTP Live Streaming, using either MSE or Flash, depending on the platform. DRM is enabled through the usage of EME as well as Flash. Bitdash is a product from Bitmovin, a multimedia technology company that provides services that transcode digital video and audio to streaming formats using cloud computing and streaming media players.

Figure 2.5 *Bitdash, from Bitmovin, streams and plays back video using either MSE or Flash.*

JW Player

JW Player was developed in 2005 as an open source project. The software is named after the founder and initial developer Jeroen Wijering and was initially distributed via his blog. JW Player has several different versions, including a free basic version under Creative Commons and a commercial software as a service (SaaS) version.

JW Player supports MPEG-DASH (in the paid version), digital rights management (DRM), interactive advertisement, and customization of the interface through Cascading Style Sheets (CSS).

The Rise and Fall of Flash

Adobe Flash Player is a multimedia and application player developed and distributed by Adobe Systems. Already a major tool in interactive web design, it became a major player in online video starting in 2005 when Adobe introduced support for On2's VP6 codec. Flash continued to mature, adding AVC support and even supporting its own ABR streaming protocol. Until around 2013, Flash was the gold standard for delivering a rich video experience online.

But while Flash dominated on the desktop, mobile support was always a struggle. Steve Jobs famously drew a line in the sand in 2010 announcing iOS would never add support for Flash. Even in Android devices that had support, the experience was poor, with battery life suffering and the experience being subpar.

At this same time, the industry was pushing forward with advances to make video a first-class citizen using HTML5, with the video tag and support for SME and EME. As mobile continued to gain popularity, the lack of Flash made these HTML5 technologies all the more important. By 2015, Flash usages in video had definitely plateaued. Major websites were providing alternatives to Flash for video playback, and browsers began limiting its ability to run or removing it outright. By the summer of 2017, Adobe announced that support for Flash would be phased out by the end of 2020. In technology terms, 15 years is a pretty good run (remember, Flash was already ten or so years old by 2007; we're just focused on its years of video support). But at this stage there is little Flash could provide for video playback that can't be done on more platforms via HTML.

Conclusion

These are the basic tenets of the compression part of video compression. To use them effectively, you need to consider how they apply to your daily workflow. Now that you are better informed about the fundamentals of video compression, in Chapter 3 you'll learn what type of equipment and process you need in place to use that knowledge.

Planning and Preparation

3

The Boy Scouts have it right: Always be prepared. Many first-time compressionists assume that preparing to compress video means choosing your equipment and firing it up or shooting and editing the video you intend to compress.

These are important topics, but the most important step you need to take before you start compressing video is to identify what type of compressionist you are. Taking a moment to ask yourself a few questions and understanding the various requirements of the tasks you'll need to accomplish will allow you to make better choices along the way. Once you've established your position in the production pipeline and what kind of compression you need to do, you'll be able to come up with a few workflows for how best to get your compression work done. Even though all compressionists ultimately use similar setups, different jobs have different needs, so in this chapter you'll take a look at some of those needs. Once these preliminaries are out of the way, you can then turn a critical eye on your equipment and make some decisions about what gear you'll need to compress your video effectively.

Once you do all that, you'll be well prepared for video compression. In this chapter, we'll also offer some suggestions for optimizing both your equipment and your workflow.

What Are Your Compression Needs?

Different types of content have different requirements in terms of how the content is handled and the type of equipment you'll need to use. So, let's figure out what type of compressionist you are and what kind of compression you'll be doing by answering some questions.

Final Delivery or Work in Progress?

The first question to ask is *where* in the production process the majority of your work will be done. Will you be compressing video for the final delivery of finished titles? Are you facilitating viewing of works in progress? Both? Understanding a bit of the big picture will help you optimize your work for the task at hand. It's useful to start your work by thinking about the end result and working backward. If your role includes delivering final outputs, you may tune your process toward delivering high quality at low data rates or efficiently encoding for multiformat delivery. If most of your work is distributing screening copies of work in progress, your process may be optimized for speed and security.

Are You the Master of Your Destiny?

How much control do you have of your decision-making process? If you are working as a one-man band, you'll have freedom and flexibility that compressionists working in a more collaborative environment may not have. Are you generating your own content, or will someone else be handing it to you? Are you part of an established workflow, or are you creating a new pipeline from scratch? Knowing what external requirements that you don't have control over will help inform the decisions for things you can control.

Long-Form or Short-Form Content?

Once you've established where your work exists in the production process and how much flexibility you have, determining the length and type of content will help you make some basic decisions, especially once you also know the target delivery medium. Different lengths of video lend themselves better to different delivery platforms. Generally speaking, video meant to be viewed in a web browser is shorter than video meant to be viewed on a TV. This is not a hard-and-fast rule, and every year the lines between online and offline delivery systems get a little fuzzier.

Let's say you are planning on delivering long-form content that is meant for a progressive download player on the Web. You will have to factor in length and encode the video at a much lower data rate than you would for short-form content. This will help keep the file size down to a manageable download. After some experimentation, you might find that your long-form show is better suited to an adaptive bitrate streaming platform that requires specialized encoding tools. All of these considerations are length-dependent and may change dramatically if the total run time changes too.

What Is Your Final Delivery Target?

Knowing your target delivery medium will help you determine the video quality limitations of the final product. You may be asked to deliver for broadcast, theatrical, web, mobile, optical discs like Blu-ray and DVD, or some combination of those. Most likely, you are not just compressing your video for one particular targeted delivery. Identify all the places to which you'll ultimately deliver your content and then determine what specific needs each destination has.

How Is Your Content Delivered to You?

If you're working in a collaborative environment where content is not origi-nating with you, you'll likely receive content you haven't seen before.

There are a lot of ways to deliver content to a compressionist. In some pro-duction environments (broadcast, for example), the most common delivery mechanism may be old-fashioned videotapes like Digibeta for standard definition, or HDCAM-SR for 1080i. In other realms, you may be asked to work with a digital source file, which might be delivered on a drive or over the Web. The medium used to deliver content to you matters for several reasons.

First, you must be prepared to accept the delivery format your clients or colleagues commonly use, and then you also have to know the practical limitations of it.

Do you have the right equipment to accept your content source's format of choice? If not, you need to ask for something else or budget time into the process for troubleshooting issues that may come up when you try to access the delivered source material. For example, your client may prefer using Mac-formatted drives, but you only have a Windows PC that cannot read the Mac drive. You may need to buy special software to read the Mac-formatted disk or ask for the delivery drive to be formatted using a cross-platform file system before it gets to you.

Is the source material of high-enough quality for the output destination? Video compression is the art (and science, but mostly art) of eliminating information. If you don't start with enough information in the source, it doesn't matter what sort of golden touch you have; your output results will always be poor. This is a game of garbage in, garbage out. Make sure the client is delivering a file or tape format that is high-enough quality that you can encode a decent finished deliverable from it.

How Much Content Are You Compressing?

How many minutes or hours of content are you working with actively in a given week? What about at one time? Do you have enough equipment to do the workload?

Overcommitting your time and equipment will lead to delayed or rushed results. Determine how much work you have to accomplish and then make sure you have the appropriate amount of hardware and software available to accomplish it.

Some video clips take longer to compress than others, so budget your time based on the length of video, ingest format, export format, and complexity of compression to decide whether you can keep up with your workload. Unfortunately, there isn't a fast or easy way to determine this—you have to learn the capabilities of your setup over time.

Thoughts on Quality

Video quality is a difficult thing to determine because it is simultaneously completely subjective as well as objectively measured. How can that be? For compression purposes, you can measure the quality of a source input by a qualitative measure (i.e., how pleasing the image looks to the eye) or by a quantitative measure (i.e., how many bits there are in the image data and what those bits describe).

Video compression is the art and science (though mostly art) of getting rid of redundant data that humans can't perceive. To get rid of data, it has to exist in the first place. If you start with an image that is highly compressed, most encoders will produce an inferior end result compared with an encode that originated from an uncompressed source, even using the same settings.

The best way to know if you have the highest-quality source possible is to know about the history of the file in question. What camera was it shot with? What sort of edit process did it go through? How many conversions did it go through before landing on your desk? Knowing (or being able to infer via some detective work or experience) what sort of process your source material has gone through will oftentimes play a role in what tools you might choose or what sort of preprocessing you may need to do.

Even if you can't know or deduce the history of the file, you still have quite a bit of information at your fingertips about the file itself. How large is the file? What sort of attributes does it have in terms of frame size, frame rate, and codec? In most but not all cases, files that are larger will have been subjected to less compression and will be more suitable for compression.

Is Compression All You're Doing?

Where does compression fit into your job description? Is it your only responsibility in the project at hand? Are you also playing some other role? If you are going to be doing things other than encoding video, where does video compression rank in your job priorities?

Quality or Timeliness?

Which is more important to you and to the client: quality or on-time delivery?

There's much more to video compression than subtracting or reassigning bits, and oftentimes the better the compression, the more difficult it is for the computer to encode. The tougher the encode, the longer it will take. When it comes to crunch time (and you will find that almost every project has hard deadlines), do you or your client simply need all the work done in a specified time frame, or is it better to take an extra few hours or days to get the right results? Rushing to complete a project when it will only be rejected because the results are suboptimal could mean you'll be doing the work twice (and maybe getting paid only once).

How Knowledgeable Are Those with Whom You Work?

A little knowledge is super dangerous in any field, and compression is no exception. Some clients know a little of what they want, or their knowledge may be out of date.

This kind of knowledge usually does more damage than good. There are lots of examples, but a favorite is when a client asks for an "uncompressed H.264" file. Both of those are actual video compression terms, but they are contradictory. You might have to read between the lines or ask additional questions to figure out what a client or colleague is asking for. Help educate them so they can work with you to get what they need, instead of making arbitrary demands based on poor, outdated, or incomplete information. This, of course, means *you* need to be up to date and knowledgeable, too—which is as good a reason as any for you to be reading this book and asking these questions well before your actual compression work begins.

You may find that people have an idea of the results they ultimately want but not the specifics of how to get them. You as the compressionist—and, consequently, the person most knowledgeable about the compression pro-cess—should be in a position to make suggestions to the client or colleague who needs a particular end result. If you see something that doesn't make sense, say something. You may be surprised to discover you have informa-tion that others in the chain may not have that will make the process easier or the results better.

Equipment and Workflows for Different Scenarios

Now that you've taken the time to establish answers to a lot of questions about the work you'll be doing, let's look at how to equip yourself for the job to be done. Though the equipment may not vary much from one compressionist to another, it's good to identify the type of setup that will best suit your work needs. The following sections highlight some real-world scenarios to illustrate how to match encoding equipment to the demands of the job at hand.

Encoding as an Editor

Let's say you're an editor and you need to encode video. You might be sharing rough cuts with a client or delivering dozens of finalized short clips meant for the Web. Perhaps you're a blogger packaging your own content for YouTube. Regardless of the reason, you're working with video in a nonlinear editing (NLE) system, and your ultimate goal is to prepare content to go somewhere outside your edit suite. If this is the case, then video compression is almost always a second- or third-tier priority in your workflow. If you're busy trying to carefully edit a video, get all the titles finished, and ensure the audio levels are good, chances are by the time you're ready to encode, you will be running low on mental energy. Compression is an afterthought—something you do while you get up and stretch after a long editing session.

In this situation, you probably aren't encoding heaps of content at once. Most likely you will edit a sequence together, encode it, send it off for review or to the next postproduction stage (whether that's the graphic artist, the colorist, or the sound editor), and then carry on editing. The good news is that if you are using an NLE system, you don't really need much more specialized equipment. Your NLE system will feature encode/export presets for all kinds of contingencies (**Figure 3.1**) and usually will have the ability to tweak them to your specifications if needed. One word of caution: Make sure you have enough disk space. Editors tend to use a lot of storage for source material, media caches, and renders. Confirming you have enough space on your drive before you export your compressed version will save you a lot of head- and heartache.

Figure 3.1 *Here's where you choose encoding options in Apple Compressor, the compression tool available from Apple's App Store.*

If you are a hobbyist just editing together home movies, you may not want to invest in an overly expensive setup. In fact, you may not have to invest any money at all. Most Macs and Windows machines ship with video-editing software that allows you to export compressed video suitable for many different purposes. These tools come with some video-compression capability—usually the ability to encode video for Windows Media Player or QuickTime Player, plus Blu-ray and DVD authoring. Your encoding options might be limited to good/better/best or similar categories, but this is enough to get you started compressing video that's reasonably suited to your output choices.

Maybe you're getting paid to edit and need a bit more than the free tools provide. Or perhaps you're just the type of avid hobbyist who wants the best equipment possible. Then you'll want gear categorized somewhere between the inexpensive consumer equipment and the high-end professional stuff. This in-between tier is called *prosumer*. Equipment manufacturers and software creators love prosumers because they tend to spend more on equipment than the average hobbyist-type consumer. Prosumer equipment tends to have a better set of features but not quite as many as a full-time professional might need (**Figure 3.2**).

Figure 3.2 *Transcode settings in Adobe Media Encoder CC, the encoding tool in Adobe Creative Cloud.*

Maybe you're a professional editor and your equipment reflects it. You might have somewhere between $25,000 and $200,000 parked in a climate-controlled edit suite (or you just rent other people's gear). You might even have multiple systems in your studio—the high-end setup for high-paying clients and maybe a smaller setup on a laptop that you use to bang out jobs on the go (**Figure 3.3**).

Figure 3.3 *Professional editors may simply choose to use the default export settings within their NLE system of choice to expedite the compression process.*

No matter the situation, in all these cases, you're an editor first and a compressionist second (or third or fourth). Even though it might not be the top priority, you'll still need to output video in a compressed format at some point. Generally speaking, the more expensive the tool, the more options you'll have, and the more you'll need to know to use it effectively. Sometimes this means that expensive toolsets can be difficult to use, but they can be powerful. You'll want to know as much as possible to use your encoder to its full potential and achieve high-quality results.

Encoding as a Compressionist

Maybe you don't bother with editing and content creation. Maybe your part of the pipeline is to take the stuff already made and turn it into something else. Well, you, my friend, are a compressionist—*mazel tov*. You probably don't need quite the same equipment your friend the editor needs, but the setups will still look shockingly similar (although you will have a wider variety of tools on hand). Because editors typically are their own encoding customers, they usually only need to accept content from one primary source—their NLE system. However, you'll need to be equipped to decipher lots of video formats and content from many sources.

What are the basics you need to consider? These are the fundamental requirements:

- You need to be able to successfully open and play back content that comes your way.

- You need to get that content into a format from which it's easy to encode.

- You need to encode it (duh).

- You need to organize and archive it.

- You need to deliver it.

In short, if you're encoding as a compressionist, you'll need to know more about encoding than your editor counterparts and be prepared for many different scenarios.

In the ever-changing world of digital video, there's at least one constant: the need for compression to make video manageable and deliverable to the end user. Entire content platforms rely on the work of compressionists who understand the ins and outs of video-encoding workflows.

Automating the Encoding Process

As a compressionist, you'll likely be working with much higher volumes of content to encode. This means you'll want to be as efficient as you can be and let the computer do as much of the work as possible.

Many encoding applications have various automation tools built into them that allow for higher efficiencies. In actuality, you're not so much removing yourself from the process as allowing the computer to handle the simpler mundane tasks and jobs, which leaves you free to focus on the more difficult segments or to manage a larger volume of work.

The most common automation feature is the watch folder. The compressionist designates a folder on the computer through the encoding application as an incoming compression source and assigns a template or groups of templates to the folder. When the watch folder is activated, the encoding application monitors the folder looking for new files. When files are copied to this folder, the application automatically begins encoding the content based on the templates that were assigned.

Some systems further support automation by allowing finished files to be copied across the local network or remotely to FTP servers for delivery. Chaining together actions in an automated way can be crucial in time-sensitive environments. One example of how a watch folder might be useful is the creation of dailies by a postproduction house for overnight delivery to a director on set.

If the content is always in the same format (frame size, frame rate codec, etc.), a watch folder system can be relied on to deliver consistent results. But if you receive a variety of types of content, this type of automation may be less useful.

Enterprise Systems: The Big Leagues

Automation on a single encoding system may help you speed up a production environment, but in many cases it may not be enough. Some broadcast facilities and outfits dedicated to the business of encoding have to deal with upwards of 200 or more hours of content a week. When you hit that scale of work, it's time to invest in an enterprise encoding solution that enlists multiple computers in the encoding process. Telestream's Vantage and AWS Elemental Server are two popular on-premise enterprise solutions, but many others are also available in the cloud.

An enterprise solution means more than just being able to split compression jobs over several computers (known as *grid encoding*). It also means giving the compressionists running this system some options that might not be present in lower-end systems such as segment re-encoding or support for adaptive bitrate packaging. Such tools aren't cheap—expect to spend at least $40,000 to $60,000 just to get into the entry-level models. But if you are encoding that much content at a time, you probably have a business case to spend the money.

Encoding in the Cloud vs. On-Premise

Traditionally, video encoding has been done by computer systems physically installed on-site, at the office or facility in which the compressionist works. This is known as *on-premise* encoding. But in recent years, companies such as Amazon, Google, Microsoft, and IBM have all started renting out infrastructure as a service (IaaS). This infrastructure that is accessed over the Internet has been deemed the *cloud*. Cloud platforms can give compressionists access to large amounts of processing power at a relatively low price point. Using these cloud services has become much more popular in recent years as the amount of content to encode has grown exponentially because of technologies such as adaptive bitrate streaming (ABR). See Chapter 6 for more details on ABR.

Essential Encoding Equipment

Unless you're working in a studio that specializes in high-end theatrical delivery, you're probably not working with a hardware encoder. More likely, you're doing your encoding with software, perhaps using a supporting application that shipped with your NLE system (such as Apple Compressor or Adobe Media Encoder). You might even be using a stand-alone encoding application such as Sorenson Squeeze, FFMPEG, or Apple QuickTime. But that doesn't mean you aren't using hardware to support your encoding work or that your hardware setup isn't critical to the process. Make no mistake, video encoding is nothing if not a processor-intensive application, so making sure you have enough power in your system to support the process is a key step in your preplanning efforts.

Hardware

If you're about to build (or buy) your encoding system, it's a good time to be doing so. Most computers on the market today ship with two or more processors; these multicore systems deliver a noticeable improvement over older single-core and even hyperthreaded systems, which do a decent job of acting like multiprocessor systems but aren't the real deal. Video encoding demands lots of encoding horsepower and, more to the point, needs the full attention of your processor, or as close to it as possible. Whenever possible, your encoding system—even a multiprocessor one—should be a dedicated one since asking your computer to perform other tasks while encoding just slows down the process. Multicore systems are great for focusing the full resources of one or more encoders on the encoding tasks at hand while relegating routine operations to other system resources that don't interfere. Keep in mind that not all encoding software is optimized for multicore systems, but you can expect to see that change as new iterations of the tools emerge.

Encoding on the Road

Thanks to the increased storage and processor speeds of modern high-end laptops, compressing video is not something confined to large desktop computers any longer. A fairly recent laptop with a good amount of random access memory (RAM), fast storage, and capable central processing units (CPUs) paired with a decent graphics processing unit (GPU) will serve as a great encoding tool on the go for compressionists who need to balance portability with power.

Another advantage of multicore systems is that the processors themselves don't need to be as honkin' fast; in other words, clock speed is less important than the number of processors you have. If you have multiple older, single-processor systems you want to use for encoding applications, you can network them into a cluster, but keep in mind that this process—which actually breaks up an encoding job into multiple segments, sends the pieces to the other systems on the network for encoding, and then retrieves the encoded segments and pieces them back together—might not increase your efficiency as much as you'd imagine. In many distributed encoding systems, the longer the clip to be encoded, the more time that is spent shipping it back and forth across the network, which cuts into your encoding time savings. In addition, breaking up the clip will reduce your encoder's ability to identify redundancies in the data that make efficient compression possible.

The Ideal Setup

An ideal setup doesn't exist. Each type of workflow may lend itself to a different type of hardware configuration. So, while it may not be possible to pin down one "ideal" setup, the following is a good guide to getting off the ground.

A good setup for video encoding is one high-horsepower machine and a few lower-powered workhorses. You can save space and lose the keyboard, mouse, and monitor, and access the low-powered grinders over a remote access program such as a VNC viewer or something like TeamViewer or Anydesk. Your initial setup also has a dedicated, multiterabyte Redundant Array of Independent Devices (RAID) and some active encoding storage (either internal or high-speed external) of 1 TB per CPU.

If you feel like setting up and maintaining it, go with a shared storage solution like a storage area network (SAN) or network-attached storage (NAS)—that way, the encoders have access to the same file system. All of this should have a backup storage in place: either big external drives that you manually back up to or a network-attached storage solution with backup management software.

Figure 3.4 *Storage may be the most important feature to the compressionist. All the encoding horsepower in the world doesn't mean a thing if you do not have enough space to properly store the source material as well as all the files you plan to create in the encoding process.*

Monitors aren't as important as processor power, although you'll want to make sure that you have enough resolution to view your encoded output at full resolution. If you're encoding 4k material, you'll want to be able to view the output without scaling it down. If you're using multiple machines in a cluster, you can also use a keyboard-video-mouse (KVM) switch and let multiple machines use one on-screen keyboard if you can.

Storage

As for storage, there's no way around it: You need a lot, and it needs to be fast (**Figure 3.4**). Fortunately, high-performance storage has gotten cheaper and faster over the years. In addition to capacity, you must consider the performance of the drive's connection because you will be moving around very large files. The slower the drive, the longer your encodes will take. **Table 3.1** shows the different transfer speeds for various common hard drive interfaces.

Table 3.1 *Transfer speeds for common interfaces (100 GB)*

Interface	Max speed (M/bits)	Time in minutes (approximate)
Thunderbolt 3	40,000	1
Thunderbolt 2	20,000	2
USB 3.1/10 GB Ethernet/Thunderbolt	10,000	3.5
USB 3.0	5,000	6.5
eSATA	3,000	11
Gigabit Ethernet	1,000	33
FireWire 800	800	42
USB 2	480	67
100 Base Ethernet	100	328

NOTE Transfer times vary from drive to drive. Even if your device uses one of these connections, it is possible the drive inside the enclosure is slower than the maximum speed of the connection interface. The transfer times listed in Table 3.1 are for reference only.

High-Performance Storage

Depending on how high-quality the source is, you may need a RAID if your work requires playing back the video in real time. At the least, you'll want a NAS solution for offloading work. A SAN can be annoying (well-specialized knowledge is needed to set up and manage one) but handy. All these systems share the same basic concept: using multiple hard drives combined to act as one large storage device (**Figure 3.5**).

Figure 3.5 *If compression is your main job, consider investing in a high-capacity storage system such as a SAN.*

The higher the volume of work you are performing at any given time, the larger-capacity storage your encoding system needs to be, and potentially the more encoding machines you need. The number of jobs and length of content will dictate how much active space you need, but 1 TB per CPU is a good start.

Note how we said *active* storage space. After you have been encoding video for a while, you'll discover that doing so means creating a lot of files. Some files are tests, and others are intermediate or mezzanine files. It is quite easy to run out of space, lose files, or generally become confused about where everything is. As part of staying organized with your files, you should also create and follow a storage policy. A storage policy is a guideline for how files get treated as part of your workflow. Depending on how long your project cycles are, try storing files based on what is active and keeping those files close at hand. Then, in descending order, create a storage hierarchy for files older than 30, 90, and 120 days. Active files are regularly needed for work and are on the main system, as are files that are less than 30 days old. You can back up older files to external hard drives such as a NAS solution once you no longer need to access them regularly. Every six months or so, it is worth reviewing this *cold storage* to decide whether the files still need to be retained on a local drive or can be uploaded to a cloud backup service, LTO tape, or other form of even colder storage.

In addition to backing up the video and audio files you are working with, don't forget to back up your settings and applications. If you can afford to do so, keep an external hard drive available as part of your backup system that is an exact copy or clone of your entire encoding system, and plan on recloning it once every 30 or 60 days. This way, if anything happens, you have a perfect image of your entire system that can be used to quickly get you back online. Apple's operating system comes with a built-in backup system known as Time Machine, but many other backup systems are available for both the Mac and Windows machines. The best backup system is the one that gets used!

Input and Output

We've talked a little bit about storage connections (refer to Table 3.1), but it's worth taking a moment to dive a little deeper. If you think about each step of the encode process as parts of a pipeline, the goal is to remove as many bottlenecks in the pipeline as possible. This will allow the system to reach its maximum encode speed.

Generally speaking, the steps of the encode process go something like this:

1. Read source data from disk.

2. Decode source data and store in RAM.

3. Encode decoded source data to destination format.

4. Write encoded data back to disk.

When you break it down like this, you can see that there are at least three factors that can affect overall encode speed: CPU clock speed, amount and speed of memory, and disk throughput. If you've purchased or built a new machine in the last couple of years, then it's likely that your CPU and memory are up to speed. However, your disk speed (or lack thereof) might be slowing you down.

In many situations, your CPU is able to process data faster than you are able to feed it. This means the CPU might be wasting clock cycles waiting for the hard drive to give it more data to work on. Even the fastest and most expensive systems are only as strong as the weakest link, which could be your storage system. Note that we say storage *system*. This is because there can be many parts of a storage system depending on your exact hardware. Solid-state disks are typically faster than spinning hard drives, and drives that use a faster connection usually transfer data faster than those that use slower connections, but these aren't hard-and-fast rules. A striped (RAID 0) set of ten spinning hard drives connected over Thunderbolt 2 could be faster than a single SSD connected over Thunderbolt 3.

When it comes to disk throughput, you can't just look at the max speed of the connection used because the speed of the drive inside the enclosure could be the limiting factor. Real-world speeds of devices also tend to vary from the stated theoretical maximum speed. One rule that does tend to hold true is that the faster the performance of the drive, the more expensive it tends to be, especially at larger capacities. An economical storage strategy is to have a lower amount of high-performance active storage used for encoding, and a lower-cost, higher-capacity storage system for bulk storage of encoded files.

Although you may not specifically have to purchase storage separately, be conscious of your system's hardware input/output (I/O) ports because each protocol typically has different supported read/write speeds, which will greatly affect your performance for copying files back and forth and compressing files on external drives.

Software

Hardware, of course, is only one piece of the compressionist's toolkit. You're also going to need a variety of software to help you get the job done.

Operating System Agnosticism

Although choosing an operating system is a religious issue for many people in this industry, no operating system is inherently superior for video encoding. The most important thing is to choose the one that best matches your existing workflow. There are lots of transcoding software options on the Mac side, and the software is typically a little cheaper; however, the hardware will cost more. Like many things, it's a trade-off.

Players

The first part of being able to encode video is being able to play it back. With the range of file formats and codecs in use (see Chapter 2 for more details), you may often find yourself presented with a file that doesn't conform to your production standards. Keeping a variety of video players handy is a useful way to verify that the video file you need to encode works and is in a format that will work in your particular workflow. Another thing to keep in mind is that many players interpret color differently (even on the same monitor!), so the ability to view material via multiple players can be crucial to the quality control (QC) process.

Disc Rippers

The term *ripper* sounds like the evil tools of pirates and misguided college kids, but the fact is they are a perfectly legal and necessary tool that should be part of any compressionist's toolkit. A ripper is a specialized encoder that allows you to convert DVD or Blu-ray discs into a format readily understood and usable by your encoding workflow. Though not the best source material for encoding video, authored optical discs are a popular way of moving files around because they are small and lightweight (easy to ship) and nearly universally playable. The problem with using a DVD or Blu-ray Disc as source material for re-editing and re-encoding is not playability but access.

Although a DVD or Blu-ray Disc has the ability to act as just another data storage medium, like hard drives or flash media, these discs are most often written in a playable format. This means that the video is formatted specifically for set-top and software players. For DVDs, the video data is stored as MPEG-2 files in video objects (VOBs), which include metadata that makes the discs readable in consumer players. These VOBs need to be disassembled—a process often described as *unpacking* or *ripping*—to extract MPEG-2 video files that can be edited and re-encoded on your computer. Blu-ray Discs store the video data in .m2ts files, which stands for MPEG-2 Transport Stream. Transport streams are optimized for playback and also need to be converted for any other use.

A popular (and useful) DVD ripper on the Mac is DVDxDV (*www.dvdxdv.com*), which allows you to extract whole sections or just small clips by marking in and out points from a video DVD. Another option is the open source and cross-platform application Handbrake (*https://handbrake.fr*). With both of these tools, you can export the files as a number of high-resolution file types, making it easy to then transcode them to whatever formats are needed. Several PC ripping tools are also available; however, many automatically transcode the video to another editing or delivery format on the fly, which means they're optimized for speed rather than quality. Although this seems appealing and can save time, we haven't been impressed with the results of such direct-from-disc encoding and, as such, prefer to keep the extraction to a high-quality format and do the transcoding later. Something to keep in mind is that DVD is inherently a standard definition format, so the largest frame size you'll be able to extract is 720 × 480, while Blu-ray supports the two popular HD frame sizes—1280 × 720 and 1920 × 1080—as well as 4k UHD (**Table 3.2**).

Table 3.2 *Blu-ray frame sizes (interlaced formats are listed in fields per second)*

Format	Resolution	Aspect ratio
4K UHD	3840 × 2160 60p	16:9
	3840 × 2160 59.94p	16:9
	3840 × 2160 50p	16:9
	3840 × 2160 25p	16:9
	3840 × 2160 24p	16:9
	3840 × 2160 23.976p	16:9
HD	1920 × 1080 59.94i	16:9
	1920 × 1080 50i [a]	16:9
	1920 × 1080 24p	16:9
	1920 × 1080 23.976p	16:9
	1440 × 1080 59.94i [a]	16:9
	1440 × 1080 50i [a]	16:9
	1440 × 1080 24p [b]	16:9
	1440 × 1080 23.976p	16:9
	1280 × 720 59.94p	16:9
	1280 × 720 50p	16:9
	1280 × 720 24p	16:9
	1280 × 720 23.976p	16:9
SD	720 × 480 59.94i [a]	4:3 or 16:9
	720 × 576 50i [a]	4:3 or 16:9

a. Interlaced formats are listed in fields per second.
b. MPEG-2 at 1440×1080 was previously not included in a draft version of the specification from March 2005.

Compression Tools

Chapter 5 discusses compression applications in specific detail, but we'll lay the groundwork for that chapter now by discussing the categories of compression tools in use today. Some applications—usually the free or lower-cost tools—are meant to encode only one video clip at a time. Some applications that are meant for other purposes, such as editing, creating motion-graphics, or authoring DVDs, can also encode video clips. These single-encode tools are useful for one-off projects and jobs that use simple settings but are typically used as part of some other workflow, not just video compression.

If you are reading this book, you probably have more than just one clip at a time that you need to deal with, so you'll likely need a batch-encoding tool to get your compression jobs done. Using a batch encoder will allow you to save specific settings as a template that is stored separately from the videos, then apply them to lots of files at the same time, and finally send them off to encode. The application still encodes each video one format at a time but will keep the rest queued and begin encoding them one after the other until all files have been completed. Batch encoding is incredibly handy because hours of content can be queued at night or on dedicated machines while you accomplish more important or creative tasks.

Although you will most likely pick one compression tool as your primary workhorse, it's a good idea to have a few of these tools installed so that you can switch between them as needed. Certain applications perform better than others for certain types of files and certain types of source material. For example, Andy used to regularly receive uncompressed music-video files from record labels in New York for encoding to various sizes meant for delivery on the Web. One band regularly sent videos that were shot and edited in such a way that the standard deinterlacing options available in his normal compression application produced poor results. He knew that when that band's content came in, he'd want to use a different application that had a wider range of deinterlacing options available.

Another reason to be familiar with several different compression tools is that, over time, support and features may change enough to merit switching from one to another for your day-to-day work. The flexibility to switch between different applications to get the best performance and results will help set you apart as a top-notch compressionist.

Aspect Ratio Calculators

In the course of normal compression work, at some point you'll be asked to change the frame size. In scaling and cropping all that video, you end up doing a lot of math to determine the new dimensions. Several handy tools have cropped up to make this easier on those of us trying to crunch the numbers quickly. Although it might not be the kind of tool you use daily in your workflow, this type of product can come in handy from time to time. Several aspect ratio calculation tools can be used online, and others are available as small downloadable applets. Some of the better ones we've tried include the following:

- The Aspect Ratio Calculator (cross-platform), *www.wideopendoors.net/design/aspect_ratio_calculator.html*

- The Screen Aspect Ratio & Dimension Calculator (online tool), *www.silisoftware.com/tools/screen.php*

- Andrew Hedges Aspect Ratio Converter, *https://andrew.hedges.name/experiments/aspect_ratio/*

Video Storage and Data Rate Calculators

NOTE You can find the video storage calculator widget at *www.digital-heaven. co.uk/videospace.*

Because storage is one of the most important parts of the compression process, tools to help calculate storage requirements are also super handy.

VideoSpace is a useful macOS dashboard widget that can help calculate the amount of disk space required given a duration, frame size, frame rate, number of audio channels, and codec.

If you're more inclined to use a mobile app, AJA's DataCalc for iOS or Android can be found in Apple's App Store or on Google Play, respectively.

Both apps also work in both directions, so you can calculate time to space, or space to time. Having a data rate calculator in your toolbox can prevent you from creating files that are too large for your destination and are a must have for any compressionist.

Analysis and Quality Control

It's not enough just to encode the video. You need to make sure it actually works as it should and that it doesn't contain unacceptable artifacts. This is the fundamental premise of quality control. QC isn't just about making sure the video file opens and plays back either. True QC means replicating the environment in which the video will be consumed and testing its performance there. As a compressionist, this means having access to a variety of DVD or Blu-ray players, computers, mobile devices—or whatever gives you the broadest representation of your target platforms—to assure that the content you are creating will play back on them. Ideally, the files should be tested in their entirety; it's tempting to test just the first few seconds of any clip, but until you've reviewed the entire video to verify full playback without losing audio/video sync, dropping frames, and so on, your compressed video has not passed QC. After all, nothing can be more embarrassing than delivering files that do not work.

As you can imagine, this process can be quite time-consuming. It may be impossible to check every single frame of every video you encode, so you have to decide what level of spot-checking you are comfortable with in order to catch any serious problems. Some encoding tools, such as ProMedia's Carbon Coder, have some analysis tools built into them, allowing the QC process to be done as part of the encoding process. Stand-alone products such as Tektronix's Aurora or Telestream's VidChecker analyze video after the encode process to verify specific settings. Several companies have also developed software and hardware designed to perform the same QC in a matter of seconds that would take a human all day to do. However, these industrial-strength products can be quite expensive, so again it's a matter of how important QC is to your work when deciding how much time and money to invest in performing it.

But QC in the lab or studio environment isn't enough on its own. It's important that the encoded video be tested under the real-world conditions that the end user will encounter. For example, video meant for progressive download via the Internet should not only be checked for visual and audio quality but also for the appropriate file size that allows the user to watch the video without buffering during the download. Regardless of how great the video looks, if the file is too big to download and watch simultaneously, then the video ultimately fails to deliver the desired experience. It may be better to reduce the quality slightly to get the file down to a manageable size and thus make the viewing experience more enjoyable.

Pick Your Poison

Now that you are fully armed with information about the tools of the trade, it's time for you to build out or at least enhance your encoding workflow. What is important to note here is that every encoding solution can be as specific as you need it to be. There is no need to pick a specific platform or operating system that *you have* to support to make your encoding solution work. If you are more comfortable on PCs, stay on PCs. If you're a Mac fan, then geek out and let your Mac flag fly.

Supporting the compression of lots of video on a regular basis is hard enough, so there is no need to make the process harder on yourself by adding some specific solution that is marketed as *the* encoding solution. No single encoding solution is superior to all others in every situation. The solution that's right for you is the one you develop to answer the needs you have. So, get out there and check out all the options available, and start testing them until you find the one that works for you.

Productivity Tips

Now that you have your compression setup and workflow in place, let's review some best practices to follow while encoding.

Minimizing Quality Loss Without Overdoing It

Typically, though not always, the goal of video compression is to get the best-possible quality out of the smallest amount of data (the most bang for your bits, as it were). So, what exactly does that mean in terms of encoding?

To begin with, you want the best-quality source material you can get your hands on. We can use a painting metaphor to describe the bits that make up a video clip. The more paint (or bits) making up the source, the better the end result will be, regardless of the file sizes involved.

Until the moment you are creating your delivery format (the clip the end user will actually view), you want to stay in what is referred to as *production* or *authoring* formats and codecs that will retain as much data as possible. Production formats typically take a fairly powerful machine to open and play back, but that's OK—you aren't sharing this version outside your post-production workflow, so leave it big and buy more storage if you need it. You want all the data possible available right up until the moment you create the final version. At that point, you are going to subject this super-high-quality, super-high-data-rate file to all the magic, trickery, and science you can to maintain superior video and audio quality while removing as much of the data (bits, paint, whatever) from the process as possible.

That said, don't be silly and take low-resolution source files and convert them to some high-quality format in the hopes that you will get a superior end result. You can't invent bits that weren't there to begin with. You will waste your time and end up with just-as-ugly video as the end result—just in a lot larger file. The quality of the source you get to work with, whether it is uncompressed or something else, is the highest priority you should concern yourself with for the duration of the job.

Stay Organized

As mentioned earlier in the "Storage" section of this chapter, if you are doing any kind of serious encoding, regardless of the volume of work, you are going to make a lot of new files. If you're not organized, it becomes easy to lose track of files or, worse, erase something you didn't mean to erase. How do you need to stay organized when it comes to encoding?

- **Don't work on your desktop.** It is tempting to keep all the files you are working with on your desktop. Do not do this! Your desktop should be a temporary space, and it can get cluttered quickly. Instead, set up a working folder, preferably on a dedicated media storage drive. If you are working on a laptop or do not have a dedicated media drive, create this folder in your local user account.

- **Use source and export folders.** Within your work folder, set up both an incoming work area and an outgoing work area (just like the little baskets people used to have on their desks). This way, all your source material has an assigned spot in which to live for the time you need it, which can be regularly erased to make more space. Your newly created files have a special location to go until you have time to back them up, upload them, or do whatever needs to happen after encoding. This is an area that will also be regularly deleted to make room, but since you know all the files that live here were newly created, make sure they have been archived somehow before deleting.

- **Create client or project folders.** If you have a lot of different unrelated projects, maybe across multiple clients, it's also a good idea to give each project or client its own unique folder within the incoming and outgoing sections. Nothing is more embarrassing than delivering the wrong content to the wrong person.

- **Develop a storage policy.** As described in the "Storage" section, make keeping your storage organized part of your daily or weekly schedule. Regularly move files you no longer need on your active system to some sort of backup and then review the backup from time to time to make sure it is also organized.

Filenaming Conventions

Choose a method for naming your files, and stick to it as best you can. It's easy to get lazy about naming files and give them generic names like Finished Movie.mov, but will you remember what that was in a month when you need to use the file again? Probably not—especially if you've used similar names for other video files. Even just a few years ago, we were limited to only a few characters for filenames. Both OS X and Windows XP made it possible to have much longer filenames, but often only the first dozen characters or so will be visible in the operating system, making it hard to differentiate between similarly named files.

Filenames should be long enough to help you describe what the file is without opening it but short enough to work in the computer environment. Spaces in filenames were also once taboo but have become acceptable to use on local machines. However, files on remote servers such as a web or FTP server typically cannot read across a space in a filename, so substituting a dash or underscore is a good policy.

Also, remember that at minimum when encoding, you are going to have two similar files: the source and the export. And these days you will typically have more than just one export; you may have half a dozen exports from one source clip, formatted for a variety of destinations with various data rates, formats, and resolutions.

File extensions will help you easily differentiate many of these different formats, but in some cases, the file type isn't enough. For example, all the movies exported for the Web may be in the same format but at different data rates meant to target different qualities of the same source. In this scenario, it's common to denote the different qualities with a numeric value of the target data rate. So, if you have three encodes of the same movie—one meant for low-bandwidth or mobile connections, one for middle-of-the-road broadband, and one super-high-quality movie meant for high bandwidth—you can easily differentiate between them. By adding the target data rate to the filename (which, in this example, would mean adding something like _56, _200, and _800 to the end of the filenames), you can tell which file is meant for which delivery without opening each one. It's also a good idea to keep the numeric value in the same base, so convert the earlier data rates in megabits per second to their equivalents in kilobits per second (for example, 1.5 Mbps would become 1500 Kbps for naming purposes).

Last but not least, try not to use superlatives like the word *final* in your file-names. Many professionals disdain the use of this word—for good reason! Almost every project will come back for a revision of some sort after you create your deliverables. Files named *final* will almost always be out of date at some point in the future, and thus the word *final* loses its meaning. A better practice is to stamp files with a version number or a date (**Table 3.3**).

Table 3.3 *A few examples of some do's and don'ts when naming your files*

Bad	Why it's bad	Better
Cicada princess Final.mov	Nothing is ever final. Use a date, version number, or both.	CicadaPrincess_02-23-2018_v4.mov
Revised cicada Final2 copy.mov	Nothing is ever revised just once. Use a date, version number, or both.	CicadaPrincess_02-28-2018_v5.mov
CP low quality new.mov	Title abbreviations are hard to understand. "Low quality" and "new" are both relative examples. Without any context, both descriptors are meaningless.	CicadaPrincess_h264_800kbps_480.mov
cicadaP ProRes master.mov	This isn't terrible, but it could be more descriptive as to what "master" means.	CicadaPrincess_ProRes422HQ_1080_stereoMix.mov
cicada_princess_final_final_v3_client_approved_20180228_AWO	This name is overly underscored, making it really long and difficult to read. The version number is hidden in the middle, and it uses not one but two *finals*. Using year, month, day, date formatting means that the dates should sort chronologically if the date is always in the same spot, but it can be hard to read as a date sometimes. Putting the version number at the end will help sort the files correctly if all the versions are in the same folder. Oftentimes the date in the filename isn't necessary because the end user can look at the date created/modified metadata in the Finder/Explorer for more accurate data.	CicadaPrincess_approved_AWO_v5.mov

Experimenting Can Be a Good Thing

Even the most proficient compressionist has to do some trial-and-error encoding from time to time to optimize the settings for a specific video. The less experience you have with encoding, the more trial-and-error work you may need to perform to get the exact results you want from a clip. Save yourself a lot of time and effort by performing these dry runs on short clips rather than on your entire video. Many encoding tools allow you to mark in and out points around a specific part of a video, but if yours doesn't, find a way (through an editing tool) to create a short, self-contained clip you can use to tweak and perfect your settings. Take care to alter only the length of the source clip so that the short clip you've created represents the full-length source in every other way.

If the image of your video content changes dramatically from beginning to end (for example, cutting between fast-moving outdoor scenery and indoor headshot interviews), then you may want to perform experiments on one or two sections of the video to make sure you aren't optimizing it for one specific type of scene at the detriment of the others. Using these short clips allows you to quickly adjust and re-encode your content several times quickly until you get the results you want. Then set the entire video (or multiple videos) to encode using the final setting.

Keep a few clips around as test encodes for new applications as they come out (or even upgrades of the same application). These clips should run the gamut of the same types of video you are likely to receive for encoding (for some, this may mean from super-high-quality, gorgeous 4k content all the way down to video shot on a mobile device). When new products or upgrades release, it's useful to run this baseline test video through once at some fairly standardized settings so you can see what type of results you may expect from the application during your regular work. This basic diagnostic experiment can quickly help identify pitfalls in your workflow before they cost you time and money in the middle of a big project.

Make Your Own Recipe Book

Many of us in the encoding business refer to our compression settings as *recipes*. And if you are going to have recipes for video compression, you might as well organize them into a cookbook. You may not have to refer to it every time you work with content, but it's comforting to know that you have a reference somewhere when you need it.

A compressionist's cookbook can be as simple as a handwritten book or an electronic document full of the settings that work specifically for certain clients, including specs sent as the deliverable they wanted (though often these get tweaked slightly over time). A program like Evernote is a great place to keep all of this organized. Check out Chapters 6 through 10 for some starter recipes for your cookbook.

Mezzanine, or In-Between, Files

It isn't practical for most people to try to keep uncompressed versions of every video they create; it is possible to "lightly" compress the same video to some format in between the finished deliverable and the source. These files are known as *mezzanine* versions. Mezzanine is an architectural term for an intermediate floor found between two main floors of a building. In the encoding world, it describes a file that is high-enough quality to act as an archive and encoding master but sufficiently smaller than the original source to be stored and handled practically.

Some people refer to this as an *intermediate* format, but this can get confusing because the term digital intermediate (DI) is used in the postproduction world to describe a digital color-correction session. To avoid confusion, compressionists have adopted the term *mezzanine*, and though it hasn't been accepted as a standard, it's used widely enough that others should generally know what you're talking about if you use it.

I-frame-only MPEG-2 video is a popular mezzanine format for many encoding facilities because it is still edit friendly but relatively small in file size when compared to 10-bit uncompressed video. Apple's ProRes 422 and GoPro's Cineform are also high-quality codecs that are popular both in postproduction and in compression as mezzanine formats.

Archiving and Transcoding

Video clips that get used as part of marketing such as movie trailers or commercials may be first released in one format or size but, over the life of the marketing initiative, may need to be sent out in as many as 20 or more different resolutions and formats. Rather than repeatedly ingesting the same source again and again, you can save a step by storing a mezzanine version of the content somewhere safe and then transcoding from it repeatedly whenever needed. This can potentially save a great deal of time as part of your workflow.

Conclusion

By now you should have some idea of what type of compressionist you are and the gear you need to get the job done. But there is still one area of knowledge compressionists need if they are to be considered world-class professionals. This area is the difference between just being able to convert video simply and efficiently from one format to another and being able to take any video and draw out the best quality and the most detail from each frame when compressing or transcoding it to a deliverable format. Skill in this area is invariably referred to as the "magic of video compression" because the results are sometimes nothing short of a miracle. While some might call it a "dark art," we in video compression just call it *preprocessing*, and although it can be a little specialized (and sometimes a hit-or-miss process), it can be taught to mere mortals. How do you think we learned it?

Interview with a Compressionist

Name: Derrick Freeman

Location: Columbus, Ohio

Title/role: Instructor, Video Streaming and Compression Consultant, Webcast Producer

Company: Freeman Compression

URL: *www.freemancompression.com*

How did you get started in video compression or video streaming?

Around 1999, I got started with video compression at the City of Dayton when I needed to encode videos for our SCALA system, which was being used to display graphics, text, and other information for our government TV station's channels. I came across a program called Media Cleaner Pro 4.0, and it helped me get the compression done and taught me a great deal about compression by reading the product manual.

What role does compression/streaming play in your daily work?

In addition to the work with my company, I work full-time at the Ohio State University Wexner Medical Center as a webcast producer for our Continuing Medical Education webcast. Streaming and compression are big parts of what I do weekly. We produce a weekly webcast, and I periodically need to encode videos of medical procedures and surgeries as video segments in our webcasts. In addition, I compress a three- to five-minute video of the beginning our webcast to upload to our YouTube channel. I then embed the YouTube video in our blog. We also have an audio podcast created from our webcast recordings for listeners.

For trainings, with my training company, most of my time is spent researching and testing encoding with the latest codecs and formats for teaching training classes and providing consulting to clients. In addition, I write articles and tutorials on streaming and compression for our readers as well as other websites. During classes, I'll teach students hands-on about video encoding for computers, tablets, and mobile devices. I'll also guide them through encoding workflows for adaptive streaming. Students are also being taught about live streaming.

For consulting projects, I create video compression presets for clients encoding for on-demand streaming or live streaming. I also install and set up their Wowza Streaming Engine streaming server and will make recommendations and configure the desired type of media delivery with Wowza for the client.

What surprises you most about video compression today?

There appears to be so much more science involved with compression today, and many cloud encoding tools are available. In addition, many CDNs have taken the need for the hands-on compression experts out of the workflow. Many encoding tools and products allow content producers to perform video compression without an expert. Although video compression experts are still needed, their roles have changed, and they may be more involved in creating educational resources, creating manuals, or providing consulting to encoding and streaming companies.

I'm really surprised at the influence of YouTube and Facebook and the interest of many to deliver live streaming on their social media networks. I'm also surprised that we live in a day where everyone knows what streaming is and that it's so prevalent around the world. In 2002, I remember having to do a search for streaming video, and you could barely find it on most websites. At that time, NASA and the White House were two of the early adopters of delivering streaming media. Today, it seems that almost every website has streaming media available.

How has video compression changed in the time you've been working with it?

Video compression has changed and become much more advanced. There's also a greater need for compressionists in many companies and organizations. From my view, there are more individuals involved in the video compression and streaming space, and money dedicated to encoding and streaming appears to be more extremely plentiful.

What's the one thing you wished you had known about video compression when you were starting out?

I wish I would have known that video compression and streaming media would become more mainstream. I also wish I would have known that everyday people (nontechnical folks) would be viewing streaming using computers, tablets, mobile devices, and OTT devices, and that large social media companies would be driving the growth of the streaming media marketplace.

What's the next big thing we should be watching in the world of video compression?

I think AV1 is the next big thing in the world of video compression. I'm excited to see what will occur when this new codec is available in encoding tools, in streaming servers, and on devices.

Preprocessing Video and Audio

4

You have shot and edited your video, and now it's time to compress, encode, and deliver it. But one more step is left before final encoding can begin. This step is called *preprocessing*, and it consists of a variety of optimizations you need to perform on the video and audio before you can hand them off to the encoder. These optimizations can include deinterlacing, inverse telecining, cropping, scaling, aspect ratio adjustments, noise reduction, brightness and color corrections, and audio adjustments.

Preprocessing of some sort is almost always necessary to get your video to look its best. The goals of preprocessing are to clean up any noise in the video and to optimize its basic elements for playback on the devices you are targeting (TVs, mobile phones, computers, and so on). Preprocessing is sometimes referred to as the "magic" part of compression because it takes a lot of practice to achieve the desired results. This is the most artistic and frequently misused part of the compression process. It's easy to go overboard with the changes until you get a feel for how much you really need to do to your video and audio to optimize it for encoding.

Fortunately, preprocessing is a craft that can be learned, and practice will only make you better at it. Understanding why you preprocess video and audio and how the various types of optimization that occur at this stage affect your final product will help you make your preprocessing choices.

When and What to Preprocess

To some degree, every piece of video will need some preprocessing, but the amount is wholly dependent on both the source video and the format you are creating. There are basic things such as scaling and changing the frame rate that will often be required, but color and luma changes should be used judiciously to avoid taking away from the intent of the content. Often, new compressionists will want to pull out all the bells and whistles when preprocessing, and the results may be negligible at best. Add to that the fact that any additional processing you are asking the machine to do to the content will lengthen the overall encoding process.

Remember, the goal of preprocessing is to improve the quality of the video and audio and to maintain the original creative intent. So, it's best to use a light hand most of the time.

Spatial/Geometric Preprocessing

Whether it's simply changing the frame size and aspect ratio to match the destination or reframing the video entirely, spatial preprocessing is one of the most common types of preprocessing you'll encounter as a compressionist.

Cropping: Title and Action Safe Zones

Cropping is a way of identifying a specific region of the video to use in the compression, excluding the other areas of the source frame. Cropping can be used to change the aspect ratio of a wide-screen 16 × 9 video to the older 4 × 3 format, or it can be used to crop out unwanted picture areas at the edge of the frame.

Most TVs do not display the entire image that is transmitted. Instead, they are *overscanned*, meaning slightly larger than the viewable area of a consumer-grade television. This is done for several reasons, most of which culminate in needing to hide irregularities that exist in the edges of the video frames. Production people are aware of this and have created three regions of a video image that affect how they frame shots and incorporate graphic overlays: overscan, action safe, and title safe. **Figure 4.1** will be familiar to anyone who has looked through a video camera viewfinder. It depicts the action- and title-safe areas that a camera operator needs to be conscious of when framing a shot.

Title Safe

Action Safe

Figure 4.1 *Compressionists need to be aware of the action- and title-safe regions of the frame and use them as a general guideline for cropping nonbroadcast content.*

The outermost region of the video is known as the *overscan* region. This area may not appear on standard consumer TV screens, and it often contains the edge of the set or cables and other equipment. Professional-grade monitors have a mode that allows this overscan area to be viewed, known as *underscan* mode. These monitors may also include action-safe and title-safe indicators.

The *action-safe* area is the larger rectangle within the image area. This area displays approximately 90 percent of the video image and is where camera operators will make sure to keep the primary action framed to keep it viewable on TVs.

The smaller rectangle in the image is the *title-safe* area (comprising about 80 percent of the visible image). It is far enough in from the four edges of a standard TV that text or graphics should show neatly without being cut off or distorted. The title-safe area started out as a guide for keeping text from being distorted by the rounded corners on old cathode ray tube (CRT) TVs. Most modern TVs display a lot more of the area outside of the title-safe zone than their CRT counterparts. However, as a rule of thumb, text and titles should still be contained within the title-safe area.

Cropping can be a useful tool to ensure that the video displays the same regardless of delivery and playback format. While TVs routinely overscan, mobile devices and online video players do not. If you want the video to appear to display the same on all devices, it may be necessary to crop the overscan area on the formats that do not overscan.

Scaling

Scaling is another key part of the preprocessing process, and it simply means either enlarging or shrinking the frame size. A *proportionate scale* means that the same scaling factor is applied to both the horizontal and vertical axes. Many times you'll crop an image and then scale it up so that the frame size stays the same as it did when you started. Other times, it may mean shrinking a video from the original size to a size more appropriate for delivery (**Figure 4.2**).

Figure 4.2 *These images demonstrate how a 720 × 480 source clip (left) can be scaled down to 320 × 240 (right) for web delivery with no loss in quality.*

Scaling video up is called an *upconvert*. Going from a small frame size to a higher frame size (as shown in **Figure 4.3**) is not recommended but can be necessary in certain situations. In these situations, the different scaling algorithms in different tools can produce dramatically different results. Some tools will simply scale pixels, while others will *interpolate*, or create new pixels. There are lots of options for tools in this area ranging from lower-cost plug-ins for After Effects all the way up to dedicated hardware for real-time SDI conversions. As always, your mileage may vary, and it's always best to test your content against multiple tools to determine the best tool for the job.

Figure 4.3 *Upscaling, unlike downscaling, is a bad idea—you can't add pixels that weren't in the image to begin with without compromising quality.*

A key question when scaling is what size should you scale to? The answer will be determined by your destination and the frame sizes supported. As bandwidth has increased and technologies such as adaptive bitrate streaming are invented, the answers to these questions have gotten both simpler and more complex.

While there are all sorts of possibilities, there are two general facts: the larger the frame size, the bigger the output file will need to be to maintain good quality, and the slower it will play on some machines. Of course, small frame sizes could also be low quality, so you need to find a good balance that works for your projects. One thing to keep in mind, however, is that it is always best to scale down rather than scale up. That means if you have a video finished at 1920 × 1080, creating an upconverted 4k/UHD version won't mean higher quality.

Here are some general guidelines, regardless of aspect ratio:

- **Height of 2160 pixels:** At double the size of HD video, this is a great high-quality encode if you don't need to worry about file size or playback speed (some older computers will have difficulty playing back files this large without dropping frames).

- **Height of 1080 pixels:** This is probably the most common delivery size today. Most platforms and players support some version of 1080p.

- **Height of 720 pixels:** This is a good choice if you need to prioritize file size over spatial resolution. It can also be appropriate if your target machine is older and slower.

- **Height of 480 pixels and smaller:** What used to be called *standard def*, these frame sizes are pretty small. These are more suited to mobile video, given the screen resolution and bandwidth.

For more details on general guidelines for frame sizes, see **Table 4.1**. These ratios assume that the pixel aspect ratio is 1:1 (square).

Table 4.1 *Common frame sizes*

Output	Full-Screen (4:3)	Wide-Screen (16:9)
Ultra-high definition	2880 × 2160	3840 × 2160
Extra-large broadband	1920 × 1440	2560 × 1440
Large broadband/high definition	1440 × 1080	1920 × 1080
Small broadband and large mobile	960 × 720	1280 × 720
Large mobile	640 × 480	854 × 480
Medium mobile	480 × 360	640 × 360
Small mobile	320 × 240	426 × 240

Temporal Preprocessing

Whatever the reason, sometimes you'll need to adjust the frame rate of your video. Most of the time this is done to better match the source to the destination. Whatever the reason, temporal processing can be one of the most difficult steps to get right.

Easy Frame Rate Conversions

Certain frame rate conversions aren't too hard and usually yield good-quality results. For example, when the source frame rate is a fractional frame rate, say 29.97 fps or 23.976 fps, converting to its corresponding integer frame rate—30 fps or 24 fps in this case—isn't too hard. You'll just change the amount of time each frame appears on the screen slightly. Audio will need to be adjusted to stay in sync, but most modern tools can do this compensation for you. Another simple conversion is when you want to go from a higher frame rate to one that is half as fast (or the other way around), such as 59.94 fps to 29.97 fps. In this conversion, you'll simply drop (or duplicate) every other frame to get from the source rate to destination rate. Most modern nonlinear editing (NLE) systems can do these conversions in the timeline.

Telecine and Inverse Telecine

Telecine is the process of transferring motion-picture film into electronic form. The term is also used to describe the machine used in this process. Traditional motion-picture film runs at exactly 24 fps progressive scan, which doesn't easily convert to 29.97 fps for NTSC.

Converting from film to PAL is easy. The video is sped up 4 percent to 25 fps and converted into progressive PAL.

The telecine process for NTSC is more complex: the film is first slowed down 0.1 percent to 23.976 fps and is then converted to 29.97 fps by using a process called *3:2 pulldown* (**Figure 4.4**). In this process, the first frame of film becomes three fields of video, the next frame becomes two fields of video, the next becomes three fields, and so on, resulting in two out of five frames having fields that come from different source frames.

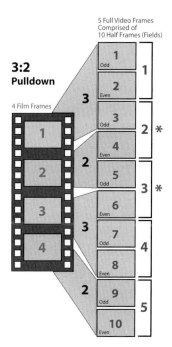

Figure 4.4 *In the 3:2 pulldown process inherent to NTSC telecine, four frames of film become ten fields/ five frames of video by using a three-then-two field pattern to maintain the smooth motion of the film in the newly created video.*

To correctly compress video that has been telecined, it is crucial to be able to identify these duplicate frames and then remove them. *Inverse telecine* basically reconstructs the four frames from every five to turn the source back into progressive video.

The Difficult Conversion

There's one particularly tricky conversion to be aware of. It occurs when your source is 30 fps (or 29.97) and your destination is 24 fps (or 23.976). Now when we say "tricky" or "difficult," we mean that it's difficult to get it to look good. Let's dive in to see why.

When you want to get from 24 fps to 30 fps, you can add interlaced 3:2 pulldown to a clip to achieve the desired result with minimal unwanted motion artifacts. This is because you're using fields created from a progressive image to create additional frames in a pattern that gives six additional frames per second that are distributed in an even cadence. You can reverse this process to get from 29.97i to 23.976p.

The problem arises when you start with a progressive source sequence and need to remove frames from it to lower the frame rate. To keep the dropped frames in an even cadence, you need to drop every fourth frame. The problem is that if you have smooth motion in your shot, like a car driving through the frame from left to right. The change in the car's position between each frame is consistent, which means when you remove one of those frames, the car appears to move further between the third and fifth frames, which makes it look like it jumps. When this is repeated six times per second, the result is a really jumpy-looking video that is unpleasant to watch.

Just like with the upconversion process, the way to try to deal with this motion artifact is through interpolation. While there are a lot of standards converters on the market, there are a couple to take a look at for this specific conversion: Cinnafilm's Tachyon and BlackMagic Design's Teranex. But be warned, these tools can be fairly expensive and sometimes often yield subpar or unacceptable results depending on the content. Many times, the best way to deal with this situation is to manage expectations or try to find a solution that doesn't involve this conversion.

Color and Image Preprocessing

When working with finished content that has already been color corrected, most of the time you won't need to make further adjustments. However, certain situations where adjustments are necessary do arise from time to time. For example, if you have a show that's being encoded for broadcast and mobile, you might need to adjust the mobile version to match the look of the broadcast version since the two formats use different color spaces. Understanding what adjustments are available will allow you to evaluate your outputs and determine whether any adjustments are necessary.

Luma Adjustments

Image adjustment is the process of using controls, similar to those in image-editing applications, to change aspects such as brightness and contrast. Digital video is described in either RGB or in Y'CbCr (aka YUV) color space. A *color space* (or *model*) is a way of describing and specifying a color. RGB and the Y'CbCr color space formulas contain three variables, also known as *components* or *channels*. RGB's variables are red, green, and blue, while Y'CbCr breaks down as follows: Y is luma (or black and white or lightness), and CbCr is chroma or color (Cb is blue minus luma, and Cr is red minus luma).

This representation addresses the human eye's predisposition to green-light sensitivity, which is why most of the information about the proportion of green is in the luma (Y), and only the deviations for the red and blue portions need to be represented. The Y values have twice the resolution of the other two values, Cb and Cr, in most practical applications, such as on DVDs.

Because different color spaces are used by different codecs and video playback devices, image adjustment may be required as part of preprocessing.

Luma Range Expansion

The RGB color space breaks the steps from black to white into 256 even steps (0 to 255, with 0 being black and 255 being white). Standard TV has only 220 steps from black to white, using black as 16 and white as 235 within the same scale (**Figure 4.5** on the next page). Generally, modern postproduction applications automatically keep black and white consistent. However, if blacks and whites appear either crushed (too black) or faded (too white), the luma range may need to be remapped.

Figure 4.5 *Television and computer-based video use different luma ranges to depict the range between black and white. When this is not compensated for in preprocessing, the distortion of the luma range can leave video either washed out or too dark.*

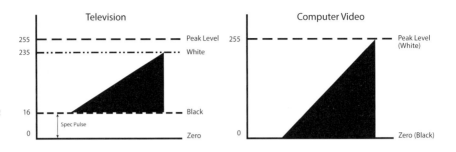

The Digital Color Meter

Apple users have some built-in help when figuring out luma and chroma values. In the Utilities folder (Application > Utilities) is the Digital Color Meter (**Figure 4.6**). This little application launches a small magnifier and a table that shows the specific RGB value of the samples part of the screen. This application is a handy way of checking values, rather than just trusting that your display is calibrated correctly. You can learn more about it here: https://support.apple.com/guide/digital-color-meter/welcome/mac.

Figure 4.6 *Apple's Digital Color Meter makes it easy to check luma and chroma values.*

> ⚠ **TIP** Using noise reduction in addition to adjusting the luma may make achieving proper levels easier.

Gamma Adjustments

Gamma is a measurement of how the luma range turns into brightness when it is displayed. Although black and white will look the same under different gamma values, the middle of the range will look different. Gamma correction is a complex mathematical concept that works to best encode images according to how human image perception works. Different computer platforms and TVs all have different default gammas, with the majority of gamma values falling between 2.2 and 2.4. Before OS X 10.6 Snow Leopard, Apple used a default gamma value of 1.8. CRT television sets used a gamma of 2.2, and Windows systems used gamma values ranging from 2.2 to 2.5. Modern LCD televisions use a gamma value of 2.4. If the value used to encode the video is not the same as the display/output gamma value, the image will appear either slightly darker, which will lose detail in the shadows, or slightly brighter, which will make colors appear washed out and "milky."

If you are encoding for a mixed environment or are unsure of what playback device the end user has, it's best to target an encode value of 2.2.

Brightness and Contrast

Brightness filters adjust the overall intensity of each pixel in a frame by a fixed amount. *Contrast* settings, on the other hand, increase or decrease each pixel's value by an amount proportional to how far away from the middle value it is (the farther away, the bigger the change). These values are often used together, rather than separately, because just brightening an image without adjusting the contrast can leave the black levels too muddy gray, rather than the desired black.

Chroma Adjustments

Chroma adjustments affect the color (*chrominance*) of a video image, similar to the way luma affects the brightness. Changes to the color of the video aren't commonly required. In fact, some compression tools do not even include these filters.

Saturation

NOTE Digital video has a narrower saturation range than RGB, so slightly increasing the saturation will make video look more vibrant on computer screens.

Saturation controls the intensity of a color. Increasing saturation will brighten a color artificially, while decreasing it (or desaturating) will remove the color, all without affecting the luminosity of the image (turning it to black and white).

Hue

Hue is the way of describing a color (for example, red or blue). The hue adjustment in compression tools shifts the color spectrum of the image. It is used to do simple color correction, most often when white levels or flesh tones do not appear correctly. This is a pretty coarse adjustment and should be used with care or not at all.

Noise Reduction

Noisy video is a big headache for video compressionists. Random noise causes pixels to change rapidly and constantly, making it difficult for the codec to encode the clip correctly.

Figure 4.7 *Here are two versions of a DV-NTSC clip. On the right it has had a median filter applied. Note the increased softness in the image on the left but the smoother quality of the image also.*

Noise reduction encompasses a variety of techniques to remove that noise from an image, making it easier to compress. Simple noise reduction algorithms are just blurs that hide grain but make the image softer, such as when a median filter is applied (**Figure 4.7**). More advanced algorithms try to blur only the parts of the image that have grain and may take advantage of differences among frames.

Noise Reduction Before Compression

If the damage from video noise is significant enough, such as dust or scratches in film, no amount of blurring will help remove this damage completely from the image during compression. In this case, you may want to use a stand-alone application, such as Adobe After Effects or Photoshop, to digitally remove the scratches either manually (with a clone tool) or with an automatic scratch removal filter. Once you've treated the source footage to remove the damage, you can then compress the footage as you normally would.

Noise reduction is not always required. If you have a clean video source to work with, simply skip the noise reduction step when preprocessing your work. If you do have damaged footage, it may take several experiments to find the right balance of cleaning up the source without degrading the finished video image.

Legacy Video Issues

There has been a lot of change in the realm of digital video. We've moved from interlaced to progressive formats. The number of standard aspect ratios has exploded. So-called high-definition resolutions have gone from being in the minority to the majority. Even higher resolutions like ultra-high definition, 4k, and even 8k are now coming into play. But as a compressionist, you'll be asked to work with all sorts of video from various periods in time. That means there's a whole host of issues that come with older video that you'll need to understand and be comfortable with fixing.

Deinterlacing Video

In the past, most digital video was interlaced because it was assumed that at some point it was meant for playback on a standard CRT television, which had an interlaced display. We've now moved to a world where most displays are progressive scan, and they are not always televisions. Because interlaced video is unacceptable for web and mobile delivery, deinterlacing video for playback on the Web or other progressive displays is a fundamental and necessary step.

If the source video is left with interlacing lines intact, the output will appear as jagged lines sometimes referred to as *combing*. The lines do not make for a good viewing experience and are also difficult to encode for a couple of reasons. Moving objects will keep merging and reassembling (with the two fields moving out of step), and motion estimation will become difficult, thus making the encode inefficient. The interlaced image will also have more detail than is necessary to display the image, so additional bits are wasted when relaying this redundant detail.

You can perform a deinterlace in several ways. Each is designed to optimize different types of images and different types of motion within the video. All in all, there are approximately eight ways to perform a deinterlace, though those eight have several different names by which they are recognized, depending on the tools you are working with.

> **TIP** It is rare for a compression application to offer all the deinterlacing options listed here, and each tool may have its own naming scheme for them. Experiment with the options to find the ones that work for your content.

Blend

The first common deinterlace method is referred to as *blending*, also known as *averaging* and *combining* fields. This method involves both fields being overlaid. This method gives you good results when there's no movement, but it results in unnatural, low-quality movements. The advantage of this approach is that it's a fast way to deinterlace and is good for low-motion scenes, such as interviews, but you will get ghosting every time an image moves.

Weave

Another commonly used method is *weaving*, which shows both fields in each frame. This method basically doesn't do anything to the frame, leaving you with jagged edges but with the full resolution, which can be good.

Area-Based Deinterlacing

Area-based deinterlacing blends nothing but the jagged edges. You do this by comparing frames over time or by space/position. It gives you good results in quiet scenes with little movement because in those circumstances there is nothing to blur.

Motion Blur

The *motion blur* method blurs the jagged edges where needed, instead of mixing (that is, blending) them with the other field. This way, you get a more filmlike look. You may have to apply motion blur with a program such as Apple Final Cut Pro or Adobe After Effects before using a compression application.

Discard

With the *discarding* method, you throw away every second line (leaving the movie at half the original height) and then resize the picture during play-back. Because this is the same as skipping Field 2, Field 4, Field 6, and so on, you could also call this *even fields only* or *odd fields only*. Although you won't get artifacts from trying to blend or merge the images, you'll lose half the resolution, and motion will become less smooth.

Bob

The *bob* approach displays every field (so you don't lose any information) one after the other (that is, without interlacing) but with double the frames per second. Thus, each interlaced frame is split into two frames (that is, the two former fields) at half the height. Sometimes bobbing is also called *progressive scanning*. However, since the bob approach doesn't analyze areas or the differences between fields, the two approaches are not really the same (see the next section).

Progressive Scan

Progressive scanning analyzes the two fields and deinterlaces only the parts that need to be deinterlaced. The main difference between progressive scanning and area-based deinterlacing is that progressive scanning gives you a movie with twice the frames per second instead of the standard 25 fps or 30 fps movie, thus leaving you with perfect fluidity of motion. To say it more academically, it has high temporal and vertical resolution.

This method is also variously called *motion adaptive*, *bob and weave*, and *intelligent motion adaptive*.

Motion Compensation

NOTE If you control the video production process for your content and know you don't plan to distribute via a traditional broadcast, then try to keep your whole project in progressive mode to avoid issues with deinterlacing.

The *motion compensation* method analyzes the movement of objects in a scene when the scene consists of a lot of frames. In other words, it involves tracking each object that moves around in the scene, thus effectively analyzing a group of consecutive frames instead of just single frames.

Although effective for horizontal motion, some software for this technique does not handle vertical motion at all and may fall back on selective blending or other techniques when it is unable to resolve the motion vectors.

Image Aspect Ratio Correction

The film world has dealt with the difficulty of matching the source aspect ratio to the screen ever since movies were invented. For the video world, this is somewhat of a new challenge. Much like Henry Ford's Model T that came in any color as long as it was black, if you worked with video, the aspect ratio was 4:3. This was a much simpler time because most of the video displays were also 4:3. We're now living in a multiscreen/multiformat world, and it's become a lot more complicated. Most of the time, it's advisable to keep the aspect ratio the same as the source and allow the playback system to account for any difference in aspect ratio. An example would be if your source file is a movie trailer that was delivered to you at 2048 × 858. If you divide the width by the height, you get the result of 2.3869, which is generally rounded up and written as a ratio to one like so: 2.39:1. This is one of the standard aspect ratios for cinema. Let's say you want to upload this to YouTube and have it look correct. You could reformat the source video to 16 × 9 by adding a letterbox, which is simply black bars that take up the remaining space between the original 2.39:1 aspect ratio and the destination 1.78:1 player aspect ratio. The problem with this approach is that if the end user plays the YouTube video full-screen on a computer or tablet that doesn't have a 16 × 9 display, the black bars are "burned in," and the player may not format the video optimally for that display.

The better choice is to resize the video to a standard/optimal width and keep the original aspect ratio. In the previous example, this would mean keeping the 2.39:1 aspect while resizing to 1920 wide. The end result would be a file that is 1920 × 804. The YouTube player will automatically letterbox the video with the appropriate amount of black for the final output display.

Some facilities will also ship finished content in the *anamorphic* format—that is, wide-screen content that is horizontally squished to fit in 4:3. During playback, specialized hardware is used to restore the wide-screen aspect ratio. When working with content that is either letterboxed or anamorphic, it's important to correct the image appropriately. In the case of letterboxing, this probably means cropping out the black bars, and in the case of anamorphic, it means changing the aspect ratio from 4:3 to 16:9 to correct the image.

Take care when dealing with aspect ratio conversions to ensure that you aren't losing content by accident or distorting the picture in a way not intended by the creator.

Pixel Aspect Ratio Correction

An important element of scaling is pixel aspect ratio correction. What is pixel aspect ratio? You already know that *aspect ratio* just means the relationship between the height and width of the image. *Pixel aspect ratio* is the same concept, but instead of being applied to the image as a whole, it describes the actual shape of the pixels.

Three common pixel aspect ratios are in use today. The first is taller than wide; the second is the same height and width, which makes a perfect square; and the last is wider than tall. Let's take a closer look at where you'll most likely run into each of these now.

You'll find pixels that are taller than they are wide when working with legacy standard-definition content. These pixels are referred to as *nonsquare* pixels or 0.9 pixels. Pixels on the old CRT televisions had this shape.

Computer displays and modern HD televisions use pixels that are square. Square pixels are the most common pixel aspect ratio today and by far the easiest to work with.

A few codecs store the image in an anamorphic (squeezed) way but use a special pixel aspect ratio to stretch that squeezed image back out upon display. These codecs use pixels that are wider than tall to do this. Depending on if you're in a standard-definition environment or an HD environment, the codec will stretch by slightly different amounts: 1.21 for SD and 1.33 for HD.

Make sure you get the aspect ratio correction right when you convert to square-pixel sources from nonsquare-pixel sources by verifying that the output frame size matches the source aspect ratio. So, if you use a 4:3 source, a 4:3 frame size such as 1440 × 1080, 960 × 720, 640 × 480, and 320 × 240 are all acceptable choices, even if the source frame size is 720 × 480, 720 × 486, 640 × 480, or 352 × 480 (all nonsquare pixels).

Audio Preprocessing

Audio is a huge part of any production and can make or break the viewing experience. There isn't typically a lot of preprocessing that needs to be done with well-produced audio, however. Raw captured audio may need some preprocessing (sometimes referred to as *sweetening*) to clean it up, but this is typically done during the edit process, rather than during preprocessing for compression. When it comes to audio, the job of the compressionist is to make sure that the program's audio is appropriate for the distribution channel.

Adjusting Volume

Volume is one of the elements easily adjusted in preprocessing, and you can do this in a few different ways. The quickest way is to raise or lower the volume, either by an absolute decibel (dB) amount or by a relative percentage amount. This is another fairly coarse adjustment, akin to turning up or down the volume on your radio. For those needing a little more finesse, there are other possibilities, such as normalization and compression.

Normalization

Normalization is the act of adjusting the audio levels in the content and then raising or lowering the volume of the entire clip so that the loudest sound matches the level you have specified. This is a global adjustment, affecting the volume of the entire track the same way, rather than affecting the relative levels.

Audio Compression

This is a totally different type of compression than what we have discussed so far in this book; with regard to audio, *compression* refers to a specific type of audio filter known as a *compressor*. Loud noises in a digital audio track can cause distortion, and likewise, quiet sounds, such as whispering, can be lost. An audio compressor can smooth out these issues in an audio track by removing dynamic range. By pulling down large spikes and lifting up those quiet parts, compression will ensure that the average loudness is fairly constant.

Noise Reduction

Just as with video, there are also noise reduction filters for audio, although these are more often found in professional audio-editing tools, not in compression tools. Unwanted noise in audio tracks is just as bad for compression because noisy video (meaning bits) will be wasted, and the end result will be lower quality than desired. Some compression tools have simple hum-removal filters that will help clean up the audio during encoding, but truly bad audio may need to be preprocessed separately in a professional application such as Avid Pro Tools or Adobe Audition.

Stereo Mixdowns of 5.1 Surround Mixes

Depending on the type of content you normally work with, you may be given source material that has a 5.1 surround sound track and asked to encode it for a destination that supports only stereo audio. Nine times out of ten, if you ask for a stereo mix, you'll be able to get it because a typical surround mix session produces both the 5.1 and stereo mixdown. It's almost always preferred to have an audio professional produce mixdowns, but in the rare case where you have only the 5.1 source and you're the only resource available, you'll need to know how to properly convert the six channels into two.

The most straightforward stereo mixdown is referred to as Lo/Ro, which stands for "left only and right only." Sometimes referred to as an *ITU downmix*, the formula to create this two-channel mix from a 5.1 source is as follows:

1. Discard the LFE (subwoofer) channel. This channel is of little use to small speakers that will most likely be the destination and will overdrive them.

2. Leave the left and right channels alone, each continuing to be mapped to Ch1/Left and Ch2/Right, respectively.

3. Map/pan the center channel to both Ch1 and Ch2 equally while lowering its volume –3 dB.

4. Map the left surround channel to Ch1 while lowering its volume –3 dB.

5. Map the right surround channel to Ch2 while lowering its volume –3 dB.

If you are asked to deliver an Lt/Rt (which stands for "left total/right total"), this is a different type of downmix, often referred to as *matrix encoding*. It is much more complicated to create and is best left to an audio professional.

Conclusion

Being aware of the preprocessing techniques covered in this chapter will no doubt make you a better compressionist. However, the application you use determines how well you will succeed with your content almost as much as the skill set you're developing. Each application, through supporting multiple formats, typically has one or two specific workflows or techniques it does better than most, so knowing how to use several applications can be crucial to successful compression.

Interview with a Compressionist

Name: Bryce Castillo

Location: Austin, Texas

Title/role: Video/Livestream Producer

Company: Bizarre Magic

URL: *http://neshcom.com*

How did you get started in video compression or video streaming?

While studying fine-art production in college (2008–2012), I started my first podcast, so the video, audio, and live pieces started to blossom around then. This was around the time when AVCHD camcorders and video DSLRs were making HD production much more viable but still a beast to handle. Concurrently, video streaming was still in its infancy, and it was a Wild West of services, software, and viewers. Working through both of those periods early on really frames the current ease of video production and streaming as a miracle in simplicity.

What role does compression/streaming play in your daily work?

I manage the streaming of about 12 hours of live video a week, plus another 3 hours of on-demand/edited video material, so compression is key. We record our livestreams to WMV—not the most elegant, but it's saved our butts in the past—and edit those down in Premiere for content and export to various H.264 and MP3 bitrates depending on if it's a podcast download or a YouTube HD stream. It's not fancy, but it works and is accessible on consumer consumption devices.

What does your encoding workflow look like?

Our live production is cordoned across three computers (a content computer feeds into a switching computer, which feeds into a streaming computer), so it means our streaming/compression PC can be relatively low end for today's standards. My computer for postproduction is a quad-core, 4 GHz i7 with 16 GB of RAM. Because accessibility is key, almost all of my non-live work comes in H.264 and MP3 flavors from Adobe Media Encoder. For any graphic elements, I tend to stick to QuickTime Animation for clean transparencies and compatibility with vMix.

What surprises you most about video compression today?

How efficient they're able to deliver solid video feeds for sure. The fact that I can download an HD offline stream from Netflix in seconds is a testament to how far compression has come—and it's still got a lot of room to grow as mobile processing keeps climbing.

How has video compression changed in the time you've been working with it?

Access to simple compression, which has been a huge boon to the advancement of consumer video streaming. General access to powerful computing means the barrier to entry is lowered, and the understanding of compression is wide-reaching (shallow though it may be). Every young kid who wants to be a vlogger and streamer will start to experiment with compression, not out of necessity but because it feeds directly into their goals.

What's the one thing you wished you had known about video compression when you were starting out?

To do it at all! My very first video experiments in high school were unimportant labors of love and were certainly not worth the dozens of gigabytes and hours of rendering. Given that they'd never be seen on an HD display— hell, most were burned to video DVDs—the act was doubly futile.

What's the next big thing we should be watching in the world of video compression?

I think we've got another big peak or two we can climb in terms of efficiency as hardware gets more powerful. There'll be a new format everyone can decide to work with that compresses tight, unpacks easily, livestreams with lower lag, and becomes ubiquitous. There's too much demand on the creation and consumption sides to accept anything other than "easy."

Compression Tools 5

Up to this point we've discussed various concepts associated with video compression. We've briefly covered the hardware and software that support a compressionist's work, but we have not addressed the compression tools in depth. There are more video compression software applications on the market than ever before. Because no single product can be all things to all people, each tool has its own strengths and weaknesses that suit it to different situations. The tools available today run the gamut in terms of cost and complexity. On the lower end, there are free and easy-to-use tools meant for people who want to convert small amounts of content quickly without knowing much about how the technology works. At the other end of the market, there are enterprise-level applications designed for business-class customers who have hundreds of hours of content daily or weekly to convert, manage, and maintain. Unfortunately, many users do not understand what differentiates the free applications from the more costly ones. Therefore, it is important to explore the wide range of tools available, examine their capabilities, and understand what sets them apart from each other.

This chapter will identify several of the major compression tools you are likely to run into in your regular work and point out their strengths and weaknesses. Then we'll show how to set up a different type of compression job with each application, keeping in mind that the next few chapters will go into further detail on compressing video for delivery to specific platforms such as the Web, mobile, optical discs, and digital cinema. In those chapters, we'll outline specific compression "recipes" to help get you started with your compression project.

As we're evaluating compression tools, we won't focus on the quality of one over another. Generally speaking, each of these products does a good job at what it's designed to do. Instead, we'll focus on the nature of how each tool operates and call out formats and features that may make it a better choice than competitors in specific situations. We'll be covering everything from the least expensive tools to the most expensive enterprise-grade tools available so that when you finish this chapter, you'll have a better understanding of the vast spectrum of encoders.

It's important to remember that no one tool may be the answer to all your needs when it comes to video compression—in fact, it can be a detriment to how you operate over the long run if you use a single tool for all your compression tasks. If you become too reliant on one application, you then become reliant on its manufacturer and developers to ensure they stay up-to-date with the most modern codecs and features that allow you to do your job most efficiently. Spreading your workflows out over a few applications breaks that reliance and allows you to choose the most appropriate tool for each job. It's only natural that one application may dominate your workflow, serving the majority of your encoding needs, but it's important to be aware of competitive tools and how they operate.

Free and Low-Cost Tools

As video has become a ubiquitous communications medium, the number of free and low-cost tools for compression has exploded. A quick online search yields a plethora tools available for free or less than $50. Here are a couple of our favorites.

HandBrake

NOTE You can download HandBrake from *https://handbrake.fr.*

This open source tool is a staple of the video-encoding industry. Originally developed as a pirate tool to rip DVDs and Blu-ray Discs to digital files, it's evolved into a powerful general-purpose encoding tool that supports many common source video formats and outputs them to MP4, M4V, or MKV files. It bundles the high-quality open source versions of the popular H264 and H265 codecs called x264 and x265, the VP8 and VP9 codecs, and the traditional MPEG-4 and MPEG-2 encoders. This full-featured tool includes features not normally found in free tools, such as encoding batches of files, cropping and scaling videos, and handling surround sound. Given the price point, it's quite the encoder for the money!

What Does It Look Like?

The user interface (UI) of HandBrake is quite simple yet is filled with lots of options not normally found in free tools. The following sections give a full breakdown of the features of HandBrake (**Figure 5.1**).

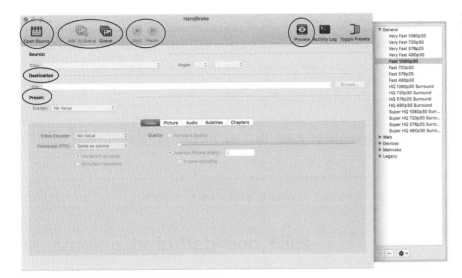

Figure 5.1 *The HandBrake interface at startup*

- **Open Source button:** At the top left of the main window is the Open Source button. You select the source file or disc you'd like to work with in HandBrake here. Once the window opens, the title and other information such as angle, chapters, and duration will appear in the Source section just below the button bar.

- **Destination field:** Specify where you'd like to save the encoded output file here. Simply hit the Browse button, navigate to the folder you'd like to save your file to, and give the file a name.

- **Preset option:** Under the Destination field in the main interface is the Output Settings section (labeled Preset in the Mac interface). You can select the format you'd like to output, as well as configure options for the format selected. In the middle of the window are the Video, Picture, Audio, Subtitles, and Chapters tabs. Clicking the Toggle Presets button at the top right of the main window shows/hides a list of presets configured for specific uses. Clicking one of the presets loads that preset into the Output Settings section.

- **Queue buttons:** One of the more advanced features of HandBrake is the batch encoding tool, also known as a *queue*. Clicking the Add To Queue button adds the current opened source to the queue with the current settings. You can view the queue by clicking the Queue button.

- **Start and Pause buttons:** These buttons control the encoder and allow you to start encoding or to pause encodes currently underway. It's important to understand that HandBrake is a batch encoder and works on what's loaded into the queue in the order listed in the queue window. If you haven't added anything to the queue, the currently loaded source is added to the queue, and HandBrake begins encoding when you click the Start button.

- **Preview:** This button pops open a secondary window where you can view a picture preview. This allows you to adjust the cropping and scaling visually and gives you the option to do a preview encode of a segment according to the current output settings.

How Does It Work?

Although it can be used for a wide variety of encoding jobs, HandBrake is really good at certain tasks. In this example, we'll show how to convert video from a non-copy-protected Blu-ray Disc into an MP4 that can be either uploaded to the Web or ingested into a nonlinear editing (NLE) system such as Adobe Premiere Pro for editing.

To export an MP4 file from a Blu-ray Disc using HandBrake for upload to a site such as YouTube, follow these steps:

1. Open a BDMV folder from a Blu-ray Disc in HandBrake by clicking the Open Source button.

2. Specify the output destination and filename.

3. Check the source's properties, such as frame rate, number of audio channels, and so on.

4. Select Preset/Configure Output Settings. For this example, you want to encode a 1080p file from the Blu-ray Disc, so start with the Fast 1080p30 preset and make the following changes:

   Video: The source for this particular video is 23.98, so change the frame rate (FPS) to 23.976 (NTSC Film).

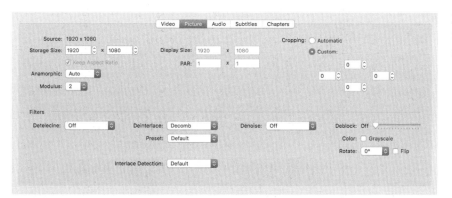

Figure 5.2 *Configuring the picture settings in HandBrake*

Picture: You want to make sure that the output frame size is 1920 × 1080. Since the Blu-ray source for this particular disc is already 1920 × 1080, select Custom Cropping and set the value to zero on each side. This source is already progressive, so leave the Deinterlace and Detelecine filters off (**Figure 5.2**).

Audio: The source is stereo, so choose the AAC codec using the Stereo settings. Leave the Bitrate setting at the preset of 160 (kbps), with a Gain setting of 0.

Subtitles: This source doesn't have subtitles, so skip this section.

Chapters: This particular disc doesn't have chapters, but if it did, those chapters could be automatically encoded into the output file, which is pretty nifty.

5. Click Start.

What Makes It Special?

As mentioned earlier, HandBrake gives you a ton of options that are normally not found in a free tool. Batch encoding, subtitles, chapter markers, and granular control over video and audio bitrates are all useful in controlling the output. But the thing that makes HandBrake special is the ease with which you can convert video that's been authored onto optical discs. If your client gives you a Blu-ray or DVD as the source material and asks you to do something with it, odds are you'll be turning to HandBrake to make that conversion. Another interesting thing about HandBrake is that there's a command-line version that allows advanced users and developers to automate encoding by using a scripting language such as Bash or Python or by using a Windows batch script. This is really handy for working with lots of content or for automating workflows that need to follow the same procedure each time. It's also one of the only tools available for all three major OS platforms (Windows, Mac, and Linux).

HandBrake on the Command Line

If you're a developer or know a little bit about coding, you might be interested in playing around with HandBrake's command-line interface (CLI). With the HandBrake CLI, you'll be able to programmatically encode videos according to logic that you determine in your program. Whether you're running a web server that receives video uploads from users and need to convert them into a standard format or you want to automate a standard encode and upload workflow, using the CLI version of HandBrake offers more power and flexibility. You can install the HandBrake CLI using Homebrew on the Mac or using apt-get on Linux. You can launch it from the HandBrake program folder on Windows by running HandBrakeCLI.exe.

For more information about HandBrake's CLI options, visit *https://handbrake. fr/docs/en/latest/cli/cli-options.html*.

What Should You Watch Out For?

TIP HandBrake's community has created a robust online manual to help you get the most from the application. Access the quick-start guide at *https:// handbrake.fr/docs/en/1.0.0/ introduction/quick-start.html*.

Because HandBrake is an open source tool, it may not receive updates in the future, and there's nobody to turn to for support if the tool isn't working like it is supposed to. Also, there are a few options that aren't labeled with units that are immediately recognizable, or in a way that communicates exactly what the option gives you control over. Like any encoding software, you'll have to do some trial-and-error work to see exactly how each option affects the output.

What Should You Remember?

If your output file is going to be an MP4 file that uses the H264 or H265 codec, HandBrake is a good option that doesn't cost anything. The availability of advanced features such as batch encoding and good presets to use as a starting point make this an easy-to-use yet powerful encoding tool.

MPEG Streamclip

MPEG Streamclip rose to prominence between 2008 and 2010 because it was a free tool that could open and export almost anything. Supported source formats include a veritable alphabet soup: MPEG, VOB, PS, M2P, MOD, VRO, DAT, MOV, DV, AVI, MP4, TS, M2T, MMV, REC, VID, AUD, AVR, VDR, PVR, TP0, TOD, M2V, M1V, MPV, AIFF, M1A, MP2, MPA, AC3.

If you're given a random file that's giving you problems in other tools, there's a good chance that MPEG Streamclip might be able to decode it and allow you to convert it into something a little easier to work with. This handy little app is great for converting source files from nonstandard video sources that save video in "strange" formats (e.g., surveillance cameras) and are going to be edited in an NLE.

NOTE Download MPEG Streamclip from Squared5's website at *http://www.squared5.com.*

What Does It Look Like?

Don't let the simplicity of the initial interface fool you. There's plenty of power packed into this little app. Almost all of the options are driven from menus or keyboard shortcuts (**Figure 5.3**).

Figure 5.3 *The MPEG Streamclip interface after loading a video file*

- **File menu:** Load your source files, web streams, or DVD image here. Display metadata about the open file and select the type of file you'd like to export. Most of the "actions" in MPEG Streamclip take place in the File menu (**Figure 5.4**).

Figure 5.4 *MPEG Streamclip's File menu contains a lot of the program's functionality.*

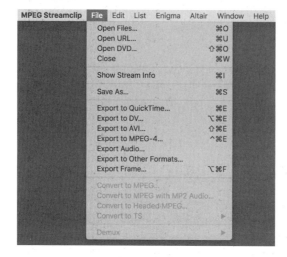

- **Edit menu:** If you need to trim the video to export just a portion of the clip, you'll find those options here along with a few other tools for navigation and fixing timecode (**Figure 5.5**).

Figure 5.5 *The MPEG Streamclip Edit menu*

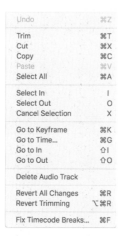

- **List menu:** Despite its simple appearance, MPEG Streamclip has the ability to do rudimentary edits that can be displayed in an edit list. It has a batch list window where you can operate on multiple files at once.

How Does It Work?

For this example, we'll demonstrate how an M4V file that was ripped from a Blu-ray disc using HandBrake is converted to a ProRes QuickTime file for editing.

Follow these steps:

1. Load the clip by choosing File > Open Files and select the M4V file.

2. Choose File > Export To QuickTime.

3. Select the appropriate options from the QuickTime Exporter (**Figure 5.6**).

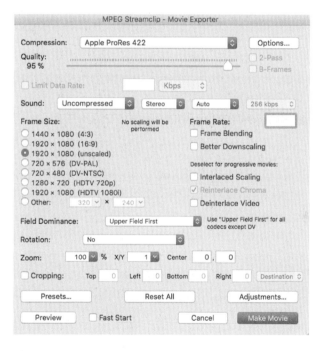

Figure 5.6 *The QuickTime Exporter contains a lot of options, not all of which may apply to the task at hand.*

What Makes It Special?

MPEG Streamclip can open a wide variety of multiplexed (muxed) video formats that can prove too esoteric for some of the more mainstream applications. It allows you to work with transport streams that are normally meant for playback only and can be difficult to transcode.

What Should You Watch Out For?

While this tool can be quite powerful, there are no built-in presets to get you started. However, it does allow you to build and save your own presets. The user interface is quite simple, but the QuickTime Exporter isn't very organized and can be a little intimidating for compressionists who may be just starting out. MPEG Streamclip assumes you know what you're doing and gives you just enough rope to hang yourself. As always, be sure to test the settings on short test clips first (or use the built-in preview function) to avoid wasting lots of time encoding files with the wrong settings.

Also, it's a free tool that seems to be built by a single developer, which means that it may not get updated when new video formats come along.

What Should You Remember?

MPEG Streamclip is a solid free tool that gives you a lot of options for dealing with MPEG-related files. If a file floats across your desktop that has a file extension you've never seen before, this tool just might be the right one for the job.

NOTE Many of the low cost/no cost tools are built on FFMPEG, a command line encoding tool. Users can directly install and use FFMPEG, but if they are unfamiliar with command line or need more features, using it via one of the low cost tools is a good option.

Other Low-Cost Tools

While we've highlighted only two of the more popular free/low-cost tools available today, there are many others. Here are a few other low-cost tools worth mentioning:

- VirtualDub, *www.virtualdub.org/*
- Cyberlink PowerDirector, *https://www.cyberlink.com/products/power director-ultra/features_en_US.html*
- Adobe Premiere Elements, *https://www.adobe.com/products/premiere -elements.html*
- Apple Final Cut Pro X, *https://www.apple.com/final-cut-pro/*
- Nero Video 2018, *https://www.nero.com*
- Pinnacle Studio Ultimate, *https://www.pinnaclesys.com/en/products/studio /ultimate/*

Middle-of-the-Road Tools

For professional compressionists, it's worth stepping up and paying a little bit more for features you probably won't find in the lower end. While they won't break the bank, these next two applications are probably two of the most popular encoding tools on the market today when measured by the active user base.

Adobe Media Encoder CC

Adobe Media Encoder CC (or AME) is part of a suite of products called Adobe Creative Cloud, available through a monthly subscription license ($50/month). The good news about the subscription model is that feature updates and bug fixes are constantly being released. The downside is that you will be paying the monthly fee for as long as you want to use the toolset.

At the time of this writing, AME requires Mac OS X 10.11 or newer, or Windows 7 SP1 or newer (64-bit). For hardware, the requirements include a multicore processor with 64-bit support, 8 GB of RAM, and an Adobe-recommended graphics processing unit (GPU) for GPU-accelerated performance.

AME is highly integrated with Adobe's other video and audio applications such as After Effects, Premiere Pro, Audition, and Character Animator. This makes it an ideal choice for projects originating in the Adobe ecosystem. You can even launch the application directly from within Premiere Pro.

> **NOTE** Learn more about Adobe Media Encoder at *https://www.adobe.com/products/media-encoder.html*.

What Does It Look Like?

When you first look at the interface, you'll find it divided into four panels (**Figure 5.7** on the next page).

- **Media Browser:** Just like it sounds, this is where you browse the file system for media to import. Features such as search functionality/file filtering and the ability to scrub and play video clips directly in the browser without opening them make finding the correct version of your media a bit easier.

- **Preset Browser:** You'll find loads of built-in encoding presets geared toward specific workflows and use cases here. Whether you're encoding H264 for Blu-ray or the Web or outputting for broadcast, odds are you'll find a good starting point with one of the built-in presets. You can also

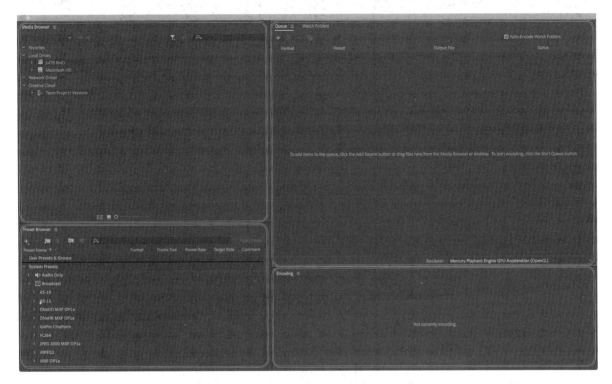

Figure 5.7 *The Adobe Media Encoder CC 2018 interface*

customize, save, and export your own presets, which makes sharing settings across multiple computers really simple.

- **Queue:** This panel displays a list of items to encode, along with the associated setting and output directory. The list is shown in a hierarchical outline view where you can have one source exported to multiple outputs. Each item can be collapsed or expanded, which makes dealing with files in bulk a more manageable task.

- **Encoding:** When an encode is running, the progress of the current item is shown in this panel along with an output preview thumbnail and a quick look at the basic encode settings. This window also displays the time elapsed, as well as the estimated time remaining for the current encode.

How Does It Work?

As mentioned earlier, one of the main benefits of using Adobe Media Encoder is the integration with Adobe Premiere Pro. To better understand the AME workflow, let's use it to export a handful of sequences from Premiere Pro for upload to YouTube.

To export a file for web delivery, do the following:

1. In Premiere Pro, select the sequences for export in the Project window and choose File > Export > Export Media (**Figure 5.8**).

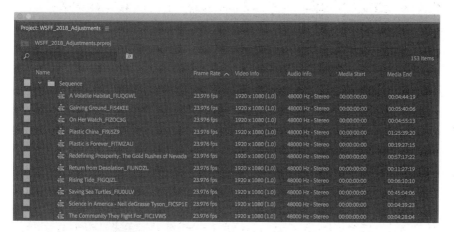

Figure 5.8 *By selecting multiple sequences in Premiere Pro, you can use Adobe Media Encoder to export sequences in the background while still using Premiere.*

2. In the Export Media dialog, choose the YouTube preset and click the Queue button (**Figure 5.9**).

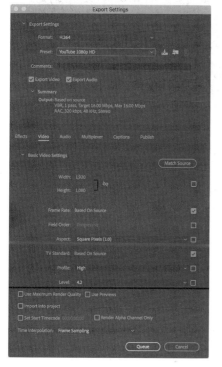

Figure 5.9 *Clicking the Queue button in the Export Media dialog in Premiere sends the selected sequences to Adobe Media Encoder for final encoding and allows you to continue editing in Premiere while AME encodes in the background.*

Figure 5.10 *Adobe Media Encoder's batch interface with lots of sequences loaded and ready for encoding*

NOTE When you click on the Output File path, a system Save dialog box pops up (not pictured) where you can specify the filename and folder where the file will be output.

3. In Adobe Media Encoder, select all items and click the output path to bring up the Save As dialog. Navigate to the folder where you want the encoded files to be saved and click the Save button (**Figure 5.10**).

4. Click the green play button at the top-right corner of the AME window; each sequence will encode one after the other, so feel free to leave it running and come back later.

What Makes It Special?

For those working in After Effects and Premiere Pro, Adobe Media Encoder is an excellent choice for quickly rendering your current sequences and edits to a specific file format and setting. This workhorse of an application has come a long way over the years and is responsible for encoding a staggering amount of content.

What Should You Watch Out For?

As it has gained popularity, most of AME's serious pitfalls have been addressed to the point where there's not a lot you'll have to watch out for. If you're working within Adobe's ecosystem, it's a no-brainer tool to choose. However, you may run into cases where the encoder doesn't support an option or format you'll need, so we caution you to remember that there are other tools out there and that while AME might work for 90 percent of your encoding workflows, there are times when it won't be the right tool for the job.

What Should You Remember?

The built-in presets are a great starting point, but don't feel constrained to using only what's available out of the box. Experiment with different settings and tweak the options to get the best results for the task at hand. Save your custom presets and give them descriptive names that accurately describe the changes you've made and why you might want to use that preset a year from now.

Apple Compressor

Initially developed primarily as a batch compression tool for creating DVD-ready MPEG-2 files, Compressor has expanded over the years to include new formats such as 360 VR, H265/HEVC, HLS, and HDR to offer delivery to various platforms.

Like many of the encoders covered in this chapter, Compressor comes installed with hundreds of ready-to-use templates, as well as the ability to create new ones easily for custom parameters. There are a variety of advanced preprocessing controls as well as some special controls for passing through, editing, and creating chapter markers for DVDs and QuickTime movies (a popular feature with podcasters).

> **NOTE** You can find Apple Compressor in the Apple store for $50, and it is compatible with macOS 10.12.4 or newer. Learn more about Apple Compressor at *https://www.apple.com/final-cut-pro/compressor/*.

Another feature unique to Compressor among desktop encoding applications is the concept of grid encoding (submitting jobs to multiple computers from one interface). Normally, only high-end enterprise solutions have this distributed processing feature, but by adding multiple Compressor instances, an operator at one station can submit encoding jobs to the cluster of systems on the same network.

What Does It Look Like?

Out of the box, Compressor 4's panel-based interface is simple, with most of the options hidden. Click the show/hide buttons located at the top-left and top-right corners to expand the interface and display two additional columns. In the expanded interface, starting from left to right, are the following components (**Figure 5.11**):

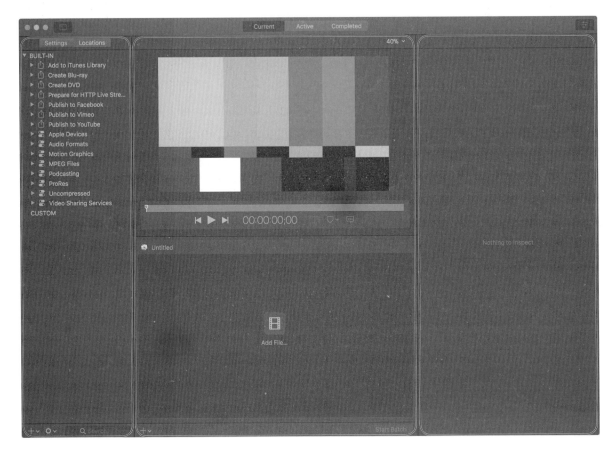

Figure 5.11 *Clicking the expand buttons at the top-left and top-right corners expands the interface to show the settings & locations and inspector panels.*

- **Settings and Locations tabs:** When the Settings tab is selected, this column shows you a list of all the built-in presets as well as any custom presets you've created. They are organized into tasks such as Create DVD, Publish To YouTube, or Podcasting. When the Locations tab is selected, this column shows a list of favorite locations, both built-in and custom. You can bookmark output folders here that you'll use often.

- **Preview window and batch queue:** The preview window shows a thumbnail preview of what your output file will look like. There's a split screen to show the before and after effects of any preprocessing actions you may have selected such as crop and scale or color effects. There are buttons to add chapter and compression markers and display captions. This is also where you can set in and out points to encode only a portion of the source clip.

  Directly below the preview window is the queue or batch list. This is where you add source items to be encoded. Each item can have multiple settings applied that will create multiple outputs. Each setting has a location associated with it, which is where the file will be saved.

- **Inspector window:** The Inspector is both a summary of your settings and a place to change advanced parameters such as preprocessing filters, image resolutions, and cropping. If you are changing settings for a template applied to a piece of video already, the changes you make will automatically appear in the preview window.

- **Active and Completed tabs:** When selected, the Active tab allows you to view a full log of all batches submitted from your computer, including progress bars of those still being transcoded. In this window, you can monitor active encoding jobs, as well as pause and cancel them.

How Does It Work?

Let's walk through a sample Compressor workflow to understand it better. Starting with a 1080p ProRes file, we'll show how to use Compressor to output for HTTP Live Streaming (HLS). You can learn more about HLS and adaptive bitrate streaming in Chapter 6.

1. Start either by dragging the file into the batch area or by clicking the plus button at the bottom left of the batch list and navigating to where the movie is stored on your hard drive (**Figure 5.12**).

Figure 5.12 *You can either drag video and audio files into the batch list or click the plus button at the bottom left to add files to a batch.*

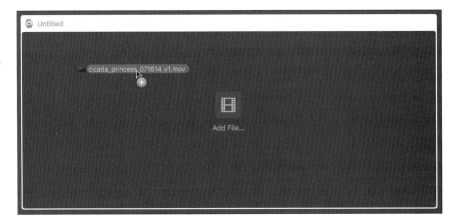

2. On the Settings tab, locate the Prepare For HTTP Live Streaming settings bundle. Drag this entire bundle onto the item in the batch list or click the Add Outputs button in the batch list and select the entire settings group (**Figure 5.13**).

Figure 5.13 *Drag the settings group onto your source movie in the batch list.*

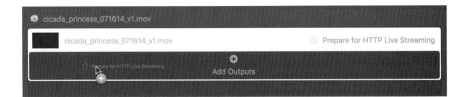

3. By default, Compressor chose the source location as the destination. In an effort to stay more organized, let's change that to a new specific location. Right-click (or Control-click) your setting. Choose Location > Movies Folder from the contextual menu (**Figure 5.14**).

Figure 5.14 *Change the default location to a new location.*

4. There should be seven outputs associated with your source file. These outputs represent the various levels of bandwidth available to the user's video player (**Figure 5.15**).

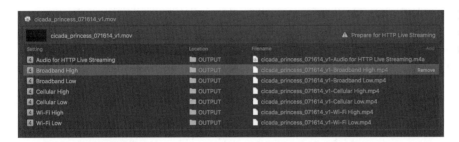

Figure 5.15 *All seven outputs associated with the source file*

5. You need to tell Compressor where the HLS package assets will be saved (the index, readme, and playlist files). To do this, click the top-level source item in the batch list, and in the Inspector panel locate the Action section. Make sure that the When Done action is set to Prepare For HTTP Live Stream, and click the Choose button to name and save these package files to the same location your encoding outputs are set to (**Figure 5.16**).

Figure 5.16 *Save the HTTP Live Stream assets to the same folder as in step 3.*

6. Scrub through the clip in the preview window to confirm the quality of the settings applied (**Figure 5.17**). For this particular file, no custom settings are needed (to see customized settings in Compressor, check out Chapter 8.

Figure 5.17 *The preview window showing a split view of the video (before and after encoding)*

7. At the bottom of the batch list, click the Start Batch button. If you had added multiple source files and settings to the batch list, all of them would be submitted into this one batch.

8. The job now appears on the Active tab as a collapsed name showing the batch name and the percentage of file (or files) encoded. Click the down arrow next to the batch name to view a list of all the movies associated with that batch (**Figure 5.18**). If you had used multiple source movies, each would appear with its applied settings organized beneath its name.

Figure 5.18 *The Active tab, showing the encode progress of the current batch*

9. Once the batch job has finished encoding, click the magnifying glass next to the movie name, and a Finder window for the destination folder opens. Double-click one of the MP4 video files to launch it with Quick-Time and determine the correct playback (**Figure 5.19**).

Figure 5.19 *The finished encode playing back in QuickTime Player*

The files are now ready for upload to your web server. Use your favorite FTP program to upload. There are additional instructions in the readme HTML file for how to embed this HLS package in an HTML page.

What Makes It Special?

Compressor is tightly integrated with Final Cut Pro X, which makes it an obvious choice for Final Cut Pro X editors needing to export video in a variety of QuickTime-friendly codecs and formats. The existing templates are an excellent jump-start for anyone needing to use them, and creating custom settings is just as easy.

There are also many production formats supported within the Compressor interface. For example, it is quite easy to downconvert 1080i HD clips to anamorphic SD formats. Compressor is also a fairly fast encoding tool when used on modern Macs. If you're in a studio environment with lots of Macs, you can take advantage of Compressor's ability to use shared computers for processing in a cluster. Basically, this allows a single user to take advantage of all the encoding resources on a network by submitting jobs to all the active encoding nodes.

Compressor's ability to add chapter markers to video is also a unique and valuable feature. In the world of DVD authoring, chapter markers are used to determine points within the video to start playing based on user interaction. Likewise, chapter markers can be used in movies designed to be video or audio podcasts to create a series of shortcuts to quickly jump to specific parts of the timeline. Although you can also apply DVD chapter markers in your DVD authoring tool, podcasters don't have any other option for enhancing their content with chapter markers.

The last thing of note is that Compressor is capable of creating 5.1 surround sound AC3 files for DVD and BluRay out of the box. Adobe Media Encoder has the same capability, but you must purchase a separate Dolby Digital license to access the feature, while it is built into Compressor.

NOTE Compressor also has command-line control, allowing developers to script encoding events and control the encode process without ever accessing the UI.

What Should You Watch Out For?

Though its image and preprocessing controls have been improved over past versions, Compressor still lags behind other stand-alone applications, making it less suited for specialized work where a great deal of noise filtering or other preprocessing is required. Scaling in either direction also yields mixed results based on the source image.

What Should You Remember?

If you're already using Final Cut Pro X for other work, it would be silly not to use Compressor. For many straightforward projects it will perform exactly as you want it to. When things start to get tricky, it might be best to find a more robust encoding solution, or you can rely heavily on external preprocessing tools before using Compressor to encode. The user base for Compressor is large, which means Apple is fairly active in its development and adds new features regularly.

Other Mid-Level Tools

The encoding toolsets from Adobe and Apple represent a huge user base with a staggering amount of the market covered. But they're not the only tools in this mid-level category. These are two other tools to consider:

- Sorenson Squeeze, *https://www.sorensonmedia.com/*
- MainConcept TotalCode Studio, *https://www.mainconcept.com*

Enterprise-Grade Tools

The tools you've looked at up to this point have all been aimed at single users with desktop workstations who are encoding content ranging in length from a few seconds to several hours. But if you're a media company needing to process hundreds or thousands of hours of content for multiple distribution channels in a handful of formats, it's likely that you'll need to step up to an enterprise-grade solution. This section looks at the two types of encoding platforms meant for serious encoding business: on-premise and cloud-based. There are advantages and disadvantages to both approaches. *On-premise* (sometimes referred to as *on-prem* for short) means that you have the equipment installed in your studio or facility, while *cloud-based* solutions are web-based and run on someone else's hardware off-site.

One thing to be aware of with enterprise-level solutions is that when you step up to these expensive solutions, they are far more difficult to use, and their graphical user interfaces (GUIs) tend to be less straightforward. Oftentimes what you're buying is raw power, flexibility, and customizability, or a combination of these. The trade-off with the increased power is sometimes a drop in the ease of use. Since enterprise-grade tools serve a smaller, more specialized market, their interfaces and niceties often take a back seat to pure performance numbers and interconnectivity to existing production infrastructures. This isn't true of all enterprise encoding solutions but is something to be aware of if you're evaluating solutions for purchase.

On-Premise: Telestream Vantage

Telestream is a video technology company with a long history of creating tools for television broadcasters. Many of the company's high-end tools are developed with this type of broadcast customer in mind. Vantage is its on-premise enterprise media-processing platform. It's a *modular* system, which means instead of purchasing a license for software that includes features you may not use, you purchase various licenses for different pieces of functionality, which allows you to build a system with only the capabilities that apply to your workflow.

What's the Big Deal?

Here's a look at the Vantage Workflow Designer (**Figure 5.20** on the next page). The first thing you'll notice is that it operates on a different paradigm than the middle-of-the-road tools. Instead of using a batch list, the Vantage workflow module is node-based, which allows you to design a fully automated workflow with preprocessing operations flowing into the processing and encoding operations, which can be followed by postprocessing delivery automation.

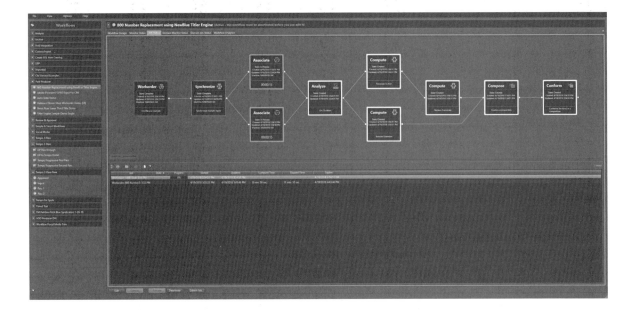

Figure 5.20 *The node based Workflow Designer in Telestream's Vantage allows users to string together actions to create complex automated encoding workflows.*

The ability to design elaborate and "intelligent" encoding workflows is one of the features that separates Vantage from the pack. When combined with special computing hardware, Vantage is also very fast. Other features, such as GPU acceleration, really high-quality deinterlacing, and scalability via distributed processing, make Vantage the go-to encoding system for many large media companies.

On-Premise: AWS Elemental Server

AWS Elemental is another video transcoding company owned by Amazon Web Services, which makes a variety of products for both on-premise and in the cloud. AWS Elemental Server started as an on-premise product aimed squarely at file-based video conversions, also known as transcoding. It is now available as an appliance, software-only, or in-the-cloud product, and is known as AWS Elemental MediaConvert.

What's the Big Deal?

AWS Elemental Server is best known for being a GPU-based encoding system, which means it's blazing fast. A single server is able to encode as much content as between four and seven comparable CPU-only encoding systems. Instead of launching an application on the server, the user accesses the UI via any web browser that is on the same network (**Figure 5.21**).

This allows many users to submit jobs concurrently from all over the facility and use a shared queue that is managed via a job priority system. The platform can also be automated over a web-based application programming interface (API). By using the API, compressionists and developers can integrate AWS Elemental Server into an existing video infrastructure. This integration allows other software applications to trigger actions or, in some cases, allows AWS Elemental Server to trigger actions in other systems. Automation via API is a really powerful feature but one that requires knowledge

Figure 5.21 *Creating a new job in AWS Elemental Server*

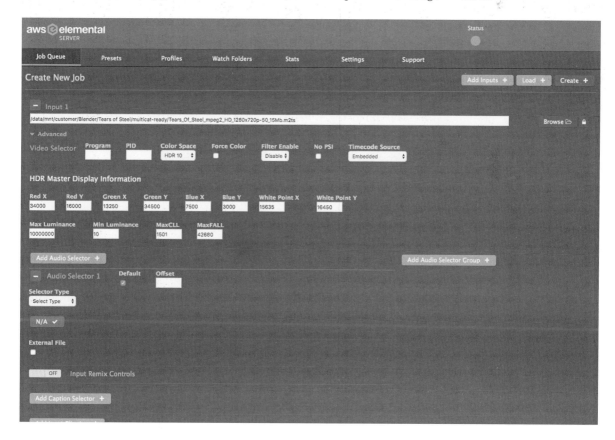

of web development technologies such as Extensible Markup Language (XML) and JavaScript Object Notation (JSON). AWS Elemental Server is ideal for large-scale uses where speed and ease of integration with other systems is a must.

Cloud-Based Systems

So far you've only looked at enterprise systems that you buy, install, and use "on the ground" inside your studio. While these larger, more expensive, and fancier systems have different and more powerful features, they act just like any other piece of computer equipment in your environment: They are physically located in your building, consume your electricity, and are able to access the local resources available in your facility such as networking and disk storage.

Cloud-based encoding platforms are a very different beast altogether. These are systems that run on hardware that is owned and maintained by someone else and operated off-site. These platforms are essentially "rented" in one way or another. Cloud-based platforms have sprung up as broadband speeds have made it more feasible to transfer large video files to remote servers and as public cloud platforms like AWS and Google Cloud have gained popularity.

What's the Big Deal?

The two main advantages of using a cloud-based system are that you can throw a lot of compute resources at an encoding problem and you can do it in a cost-effective manner. You're not buying each server you're using for your encoding tasks; you're renting time on someone else's machines and paying only for what you use. When combined with low unit prices, it suddenly becomes cost effective to assign 100 or 1,000 computers to get your heavy-duty encoding done in a fraction of the time it would take dedicated, on-prem solutions. The rental model can also lower the barrier of entry to the enterprise-grade tools. Instead of an up-front cost of $50,000 to $75,000 for an on-prem platform, you may be able to access similar tools in the cloud, often by the same manufacturers, for a fraction of the price.

While there are distinct economic advantages of cloud-based systems, the disadvantages of using cloud-based systems can also be economic. Sometimes cloud platform providers will make compute and storage resources quite cheap but charge you a lot to transfer the data out of their platform. Also, if you're processing a lot of content, eventually you may end up spending more over time for the rental model than if you simply bought a system to use in-house.

There are far more cloud encoding services than we have time to mention here. Amazon, Microsoft, and Google all have their own encoding systems included as part of their respective platforms; besides them, here's a list of a few we think are notable:

- Hybrik, *https://www.hybrik.com/*

- Encoding.com, *https://www.encoding.com/*

- Brightcove Zencoder, *https://zencoder.com/*

- Bitmovin, *https://bitmovin.com/*

It's worth noting that both Telestream Vantage and AWS Elemental Server can seamlessly integrate with the cloud offerings of their respective companies. This brings us to the concept of trying to get the best of both the on-prem and cloud-based approaches by using a hybrid approach.

Hybrid Cloud Systems

Delivery approaches like adaptive bitrate streaming have caused an exponential increase in the amount of hours of video encoded. As these file-based video-delivery technologies burst onto the scene, large media companies have needed to keep up with the demand.

What's the Big Deal?

Many of these facilities may have originally invested in on-prem systems but have now found that they cannot keep up with the workload. The manufacturers of these on-prem solutions started to build the software in such a way that it could be run on virtual machines in the cloud just as easily as dedicated hardware on the ground. They also began creating their own cloud-based services that allows their on-prem systems to integrate directly with the cloud and provide facilities with a way to add encoding capacity when needed without installing additional equipment in the studio. Each hybrid cloud system is unique in its own way, but all consist of both hardware and software on the ground and software running as a service in the cloud.

So, while the average user may not run out and buy these enterprise-grade tools, or even be aware of them, these tools offer important features and capabilities required by industries that deal with high-quality and high-volume video content. It's not uncommon for such companies to need the capacity to encode upward of thousands of hours of video content, and that takes specialized enterprise tools.

Conclusion

Encoding tools run the gamut from free to hundreds of thousands of dollars, and they service diverse industries that all want to use video and audio to communicate or simply entertain. Even hobbyists have become savvy and are starting to use compression tools to manage their video consumption.

The information in this chapter is an excellent jumping-off point to get anyone started using a specific application for their compression needs, but you still need a little more knowledge to encode video efficiently. The remaining chapters of this book will inspect the various delivery platforms you are likely to encounter in your work.

Interview with a Compressionist

Name: Alex Zambelli

Location: Seattle, Washington

Title/role: Senior Product Manager, Playback Experience

Company: Hulu

URL: *http://alexzambelli.com/blog*

How did you get started in video compression or video streaming?

I was a sophomore in college the same year the first DVD ripping tools and a codec named DivX were released online. I had a DVD-ROM drive, an overclocked Intel processor, a Blockbuster membership, and all the nighttime in the world that an insomniac college kid needs to learn how to expertly compress a DVD movie down to CD size. A year or two later I bought a DV camcorder and learned how to edit digital video in Adobe Premiere, manipulate it in AviSynth, and author my own DVDs. By the time I graduated college, I was too far down the rabbit hole of video compression to even consider climbing back out.

After graduating, I was fortunate enough to get a job at Microsoft as a software tester on the Windows Media Player team during the heyday of Windows Media 9. That exposed me to a whole bunch of new (to me) technologies such as live encoding, streaming, DRM, and so on. I never would've suspected at the time, though, that 15 years later so many of them would still be relevant to my job.

What role does compression/streaming play in your daily work?

In my current job as a product manager at Hulu, I deal with compression and streaming on a daily basis. My job is to continually improve the playback experience for Hulu users, which ultimately boils down to making sure the content looks and sounds great and making sure it gets delivered to the user at the highest quality possible. Rarely a day of work goes by that acronyms such as HEVC, DASH, or HDR do not come up somehow.

What does your encoding workflow look like?

On the rare occasion that I still get to encode video at home, my workflow is largely the same as it's been for the past decade. I start by preprocessing the video in AviSynth. From denoising to deinterlacing to converting the frame rate to resizing—you name it, AviSynth and its plug-ins can do it. Then I encode it with FFmpeg, typically using either x264 or x265 (with standard presets) for video compression. Sometimes I encode the audio separately and then mux everything together with MP4Box, while other times I just let FFmpeg handle everything.

What surprises you most about video compression today?

I'm surprised that Internet streaming has been around for two decades and we still haven't yet agreed on a single video codec for streaming that's both free and universally supported.

How has video compression changed in the time you've been working with it?

Besides the obvious fact that it keeps getting better, the biggest change I've seen in the past 20 years is the general acceptance of software-based video tools and open source software in particular. There was a time not so long ago when suggesting to a customer that a free open source encoder could produce better video quality than a $25,000 rackmount hardware encoder would've been greeted with utmost incredulity. Now it's almost standard practice for Fortune 500 software companies to build their encoding platforms on top of FFmpeg or x264, open source tools that were once used almost exclusively by digital video hobbyists like myself. So, I find it somewhat amusing that FFmpeg went from being a dirty word to being a job requirement.

What's the one thing you wished you had known about video compression when you were starting out?

I wish somebody had told me in school to pay better attention in linear algebra class or maybe take a signal processing class or two. It would've saved me from a lot of late-night wiki comas.

What's the next big thing we should be watching in the world of video compression?

360-degree virtual reality video. It seems most likely to drive the need for more efficient compression and streaming solutions.

Compression for Video-on-Demand Delivery

6

At this stage, we don't think we need to sell you on the idea that video is a major part of the online experience. Once video moved from a plug-in experience, with technologies such as QuickTime and Flash, to a more native interactive experience with HTML5, things began changing rapidly. Add to this the rise of mobile video usage and the birth of video-game broadcasting, and we now have a plethora of types of video online for anyone to consume on virtually any device.

The State of Online Video

The general populace made a mental shift to online video being a viable replacement for traditional broadcast solutions around 2017. Now, that is not to say many early adopters weren't already using over-the-top (OTT) solutions for entertainment prior to this. And traditional entertainment isn't the only place video is used online. Social media sites are moving toward video across the board. Facebook has already publicly announced that it favors live video and gives these videos greater reach. The algorithmic favoring of video content is perhaps one of the reasons why two-thirds of all Internet users between the ages of 18 and 34 have watched live video online.

Video is a regular part of most online users' experience (**Figure 6.1**). When analyzed by country, in 2017 India had the highest average online viewing times per week at 7.12 hours, followed by Singapore at 6.62, the United States at 6.58, and the Philippines at 6.35 hours. Germany had the lowest online viewing time per week at 4.23 hours, with 47.8 percent reporting they watch 1–2 hours per week.

Figure 6.1 *This chart from Limelight Networks, "State of Online Video 2017," shows that online media consumption is not a U.S. phenomenon. India and Singapore lead the way in hours viewed per week, with the United States a close third.*

Country	1-2 hours per week	2-4 hours per week	4-7 hours per week	7-10 hours per week	More than 10 hours per week	Weighted Average Viewing Time (Hours/Week)
France	37.8%	21.0%	17.8%	9.4%	13.9%	5.07
Germany	47.8%	22.4%	11.0%	8.9%	9.8%	4.23
India	15.3%	22.3%	20.7%	17.9%	23.7%	7.12
Philippines	18.7%	24.5%	22.3%	16.4%	18.2%	6.35
Singapore	22.8%	19.8%	21.0%	14.5%	22.0%	6.62
South Korea	28.1%	32.7%	20.0%	8.2%	11.0%	4.84
U.K.	36.3%	22.5%	16.4%	10.2%	14.7%	5.18
U.S.	25.9%	19.5%	16.3%	16.0%	22.4%	6.58
Global	29.1%	23.1%	18.2%	12.7%	17.0%	5.75

The distinction between traditional broadcast video and online video is also breaking down. By 2021, it is predicted that 202.1 million people will be watching video delivered over the Internet through connected TVs and that 80 percent of all Internet traffic will be video (**Figure 6.2**).

Figure 6.2 *Cisco's annual white paper, the "Visual Networking Index," is an often-cited source of both future-looking bandwidths and video usages online. As you can see from the projected numbers, video becomes increasingly important online as bandwidth expands to users globally.*

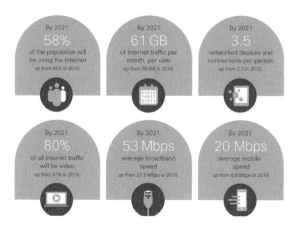

Because video is such a pervasive option, quality and delivery have become even more important. Expectations around the quality of online video content continues to grow, and users become impatient for video that buffers or takes a long time to play back. With so many options for content available at the tap of a finger, if yours doesn't play right from the start and look great, it will be quickly abandoned for something else that does.

Video-Hosting Websites

Video-hosting services are websites or applications that allow users to distribute their video content. Other types of websites such as file-hosting services, image-hosting services, and social network services might support video sharing as an additional feature of their primary business. Sites such as Vimeo and YouTube are among the most well-known versions of these hosting sites. As part of the hosting service, they usually transcode your source content into multiple resolutions to target specific devices and bandwidths.

Publishing for Yourself

If you are publishing content for yourself—content to share with friends and family or some sort of online video blog—these free sites may be a good option because you will be able to deliver content anywhere in the world through their tool sets. There may even be options for monetizing the content through advertising or other means, if the service supports it.

Publishing as a Business

Many businesses use these same channels to deliver or promote their content. However, if their business is in selling content or creating an overall branded experience around the content, then they may look to more specialized (and more expensive) solutions for delivery. These options are often referred to as *online video platforms*.

Online Video Platforms

An *online video platform* (OVP) enables users to upload, convert, store, and play back video content on the Internet, often via a structured, large-scale system that can generate revenue.

Users generally will upload video content via the hosting service's website, mobile app, or desktop application, or programmatically through an application programming interface (API). The type of uploaded content can be anything from short video clips to full-length TV shows and movies. The OVP stores the video on its server and offers users the ability to enable different types of playback, through traditional web pages or video applications on devices (such as mobile phones, game consoles, and so on). It also typically offers various monetization options, including advertising and subscription options. Because monetization is involved, there is also a great deal of analytics data around how the video was used—who watched it, how long they watched, and so on. This information helps content publishers better monetize content over the long run by providing feedback on what viewers were most interested in.

Examples of OVPs

A quick search will bring up lots of different OVPs, but here are a few popular options:

- **Brightcove:** *https://www.brightcove.com/*
- **Ooyala:** *www.ooyala.com*
- **Dacast:** *https://www.dacast.com*
- **Kaltura:** *https://corp.kaltura.com*

Web Application Video Ecosystem

NOTE While it's not mission critical today for a compressionist to worry about projects such as the WAVE Project, it's better to be aware of such standards groups like it so you can track the work they do long term. The work they support will likely impact the work you are doing for years to come.

Despite all the video being delivered, there are still lots of gaps that exist in standardizing how that video is delivered. This is bad because it leaves open the possibility that a certain display manufacturer may not ensure a specific resolution works with its screens. Or, a specific web browser or computer manufacturer might choose not to support a specific codec or container. The Web Application Video Ecosystem (WAVE) Project, hosted by the Consumer Technology Association (CTA), seeks to improve Internet-delivered video on consumer electronics devices. Its goal is to make it easier for content creators to distribute video to all devices without having to think about compatibility.

Generally, the WAVE Project does not create new protocols or other standards and instead references accepted industry standards where possible, such as HTML5, MSE/EME, DASH, and HLS.

Recipes for Encoding Video for the Web

Now that we've talked through some of the delivery mechanisms for online video, it's likely you're ready to encode some content! Whether you're using a service to deliver your material or just hosting it yourself, we'll offer you some guidance on how to best encode your content.

Encoding for YouTube

YouTube is one of the most popular sites for videos belonging both to individuals and to businesses. It has launched a whole new genre of entertainment personality (aka the "YouTube star") and has led to many new genres of content to view.

As soon as you upload your video, YouTube's servers start transcoding your file into a set of optimized video streams. This allows your video to play back smoothly on everything from mobile phones to your living-room television. The individual video streams range in resolution and video quality from tiny postage stamp–sized videos all the way up to 1080p and 4K.

But your video will be only as good as the source you give it to work with. You don't want to start with a highly compressed, low-bitrate video. After all, it's just going to get compressed again.

It used to be the case that you could try to match the top-end settings for what you planned to deliver and then allow YouTube to transcode and deliver a lower version of your content but have your source available as well. This isn't practical anymore. For one thing, YouTube delivers in multiple codecs, each of which will drive multiple qualities and resolutions. Plus, let's be honest, as a platform, it has gotten really good at transcoding content. H.264 is still one of the most popular codecs used to deliver YouTube content today; however, VP8 is still used for older devices, and VP9 is used to deliver 4K content.

YouTube Facts

You may know that YouTube has been around since 2005, but here are some other fun facts:

- The first YouTube video was uploaded in April 2005.
- The total number of people who use YouTube is 1,300,000,000.
- 300 hours of video are uploaded to YouTube every minute!
- Almost 5 billion videos are watched on YouTube every single day.
- YouTube gets more than 30 million visitors per day.
- In an average month, eight out of ten 18- to 49-year-olds watch YouTube.
- The total number of hours of video watched on YouTube each month is 3.25 billion.
- 10,113 YouTube videos have generated more than 1 billion views.
- 80 percent of YouTube's views are from outside the United States.
- The average number of mobile YouTube video views per day is 1,000,000,000.
- The average mobile viewing session lasts more than 40 minutes. This is up more than 50 percent year over year.
- Female users comprise 38 percent of the overall YouTube audience, while male users make up the other 62 percent.
- YouTube overall reaches more 18- to 34-year-olds and 18- to 49-year-olds than any cable network in the United States.
- You can navigate YouTube in a total of 76 languages (covering 95 percent of the Internet population).
- YouTube has launched local versions in more than 88 countries.
- 9 percent of U.S small businesses have content on YouTube.

Sources:

youtube.com/yt/press/statistics.html

statisticbrain.com/youtube-statistics

https://www.thinkwithgoogle.com

Video Formats Accepted by YouTube

YouTube's ingest pipeline has matured to the point that you can upload virtually any kind of video to the site and it will figure out what to do. YouTube's supported codec list includes all the normal formats and codecs you'd expect, but it also includes professional formats such as ProRes, DNxHD, and uncompressed 10-bit HD video. But just because you can do something doesn't mean you should. Depending on your bandwidth, uploading uncompressed files could take a long time. Likewise, you may have interlaced HD files, which will need to be deinterlaced before you upload for ingest since YouTube expects progressive files to be delivered. So, ultimately, it will pay to spend some time preprocessing—scaling, deinterlacing, and encoding to a format that works well with YouTube and doesn't waste time on the upload.

File Size and Duration

YouTube has limits on how long your videos can be. With a standard account, your video can't be more than 15 minutes in duration. If your video is longer than that, you'll have to either get your account verified or split your video into shorter pieces. Verified accounts can upload videos that are up to 12 hours long or 128 GB in size. Verifying your account status is fairly straightforward. You'll need to enter your mobile phone number, and as long as your account is in good standing (not in violation of the terms of service), you'll be sent an activation code that will allow you to upload longer videos. Once you've verified your account, you'll be good to go.

Resolution and Pixel Aspect Ratio

You want all of your videos to have a square-pixel aspect ratio when you're uploading them to YouTube (**Table 6.1**).

Table 6.1 *Recommended SD and HD resolutions for YouTube*

Format	Resolution
SD 4:3	640 × 480
SD 16:9	854 × 458
HD	1280 × 720, 1920 × 1080
UHD	3840 × 2160

If your video is already progressive and uses one of the recommended square-pixel resolutions, then you can just export your timeline and start uploading your file immediately. For example, if you're exporting a progressive ProRes 1080p timeline, then you're ready to upload.

However, if your editing format doesn't match—for example, if your timeline is interlaced or it's using a nonsquare-pixel aspect ratio such as 0.9 or 1.33—then you'll need to correct these issues prior to uploading.

Frame Rates

NOTE The easiest way to create content with a correct frame rate is to have your project settings match the footage you ingest, and when you encode, choose a preset that matches your project settings.

The general rule of thumb is to encode and upload your content in the same frame rate it was recorded in. In most cases, this will be 24 or 30 frames per second in North America and will be 25 or 50 in Europe. However, YouTube supports most frame rates you can dream of. The most common rates are 24, 25, 30, 48, 50, and 60 frames per second, but you're not limited to those. It is worth also noting that YouTube can manage fractional frame rates without any issue.

Progressive Only

As we mentioned earlier, the video you upload to YouTube should be progressive. While interlaced footage is becoming scarcer by the minute, it does still exist, and many modern cameras offer an option to shoot interlaced footage. If your timeline is interlaced, be sure to deinterlace the video when exporting.

Bitrate

YouTube provides some recommendations for bitrates (listed in the following tables), and they vary pretty substantially depending on the resolution of the video you're looking to upload.

For 4K video (2160p) at standard frame rates (24, 25, or 30 frames per second), the recommendation for standard dynamic range (SDR) uploads is 35–45 Mbit/s and for higher frame rates (48, 50, or 60 frames per second) is 53–68 Mbit/s. For high dynamic range (HDR) video of the same frame size, the recommendations are 44–56 Mbit/s at standard frame rates and 66–85 Mbit/s at higher frame rates.

There are recommended settings for a handful of other resolutions, from 360p through 2K and 4K, both for SDR uploads (**Table 6.2**) and for HDR (**Table 6.3**) uploads.

For audio, the recommended bitrates are 128 Kbit/s for mono, 384 Kbit/s for stereo, and 512 Kbit/s for 5.1 surround sound.

NOTE To view new 4K uploads in 4K, use a browser or device that supports VP9.

Table 6.2 *Recommended video bitrates for SDR uploads*

Type	Video Bitrate, Standard Frame Rate (24, 25, 30)	Video Bitrate, High Frame Rate (48, 50, 60)
2160p (4K)	35–45 Mbit/s	53–68 Mbit/s
1440p (2K)	16 Mbit/s	24 Mbit/s
1080p	8 Mbit/s	12 Mbit/s
720p	5 Mbit/s	7.5 Mbit/s
480p	2.5 Mbit/s	4 Mbit/s
360p	1 M Mbit/s	1.5 Mbit/s

Table 6.3 *Recommended video bitrates for HDR uploads*

Type	Video Bitrate, Standard Frame Rate (24, 25, 30)	Video Bitrate, High Frame Rate (48, 50, 60)
2160p (4K)	44–56 Mbit/s	15 Mbit/s
1440p (2K)	20 Mbit/s	30 Mbit/s
1080p	10 Mbit/s	15 Mbit/s
720p	6.5 Mbit/s	9.5 Mbit/s
480p	Not supported	Not supported
360p	Not supported	Not supported

Codec

To reiterate, you want to use the highest-quality codec you can. If your timeline is ProRes but it's interlaced, you don't have to export an H.264 file. Instead, you can deinterlace and export a ProRes file to maintain your image quality. The only reason to export an H.264 file is to make the upload and processing speeds faster. But remember, once your file is uploaded, it's locked in, and you can't change it. It may be worth a few additional hours spent on uploading if your video is going to remain online for years to come.

TIP The official YouTube upload settings page can be found at *https://support.google.com /youtube/answer/1722171?hl=en.*

YouTube's Recommendations at a Glance

YouTube's core upload recommendations are as follows:

- Choose the MP4 container for your upload file.
- Don't use edit lists (or the video might not get processed correctly).
- The movie should be saved as "fast start."
- Use an audio codec of AAC-LC.
- For the audio channels, use Stereo or Stereo + 5.1.
- For the audio sample rate, use 96 kHz or 48 kHz.
- For the video codec, use H.264.
- The video should be progressive scan (no interlacing).
- It should use a high profile.
- It should have two consecutive B-frames.
- It should have a closed GOP. The GOP size should be half the frame rate.
- The video should have a variable bitrate. No bitrate limit is required (keep in mind the higher the bitrate, the larger the file and the longer to upload).
- For chroma subsampling, use 4:2:0.
- For the frame rate, the content should be encoded and uploaded in the same frame rate it was recorded in.
- Common frame rates include 24, 25, 30, 48, 50, and 60 frames per second (other frame rates are also acceptable).
- Interlaced content should be deinterlaced before uploading. For example, 1080i60 content should be deinterlaced to 1080p30, going from 60 interlaced fields per second to 30 progressive frames per second.
- See Tables 6.2 and 6.3 for bitrates.
- Use a 16:9 aspect ratio at your preferred resolution.

One final note on encoding for YouTube. It is such a large player in the online space that many editing applications have output presets that will match YouTube's recommendations. So, don't get nervous if there's a term or two you don't understand. In most cases, if your footage was shot and edited properly, you'll be able to select a YouTube preset output and be ready to upload. However, always double-check that YouTube (or any site for that matter) hasn't updated its recommendations.

Encoding for YouTube with Adobe Premiere Pro CC 2018

Adobe has made it incredibly easy to upload content to YouTube and many other websites directly from the Export Settings dialog. The video in this example was shot on a GoPro Hero 5 and is a 2K progressive video. It was edited in a sequence that matched the native video's settings (so no additional render or transforming should be required to export the footage).

1. With the timeline selected, you can either press Ctrl+M on the keyboard or choose File > Export > Media in the main menu (**Figure 6.3**).

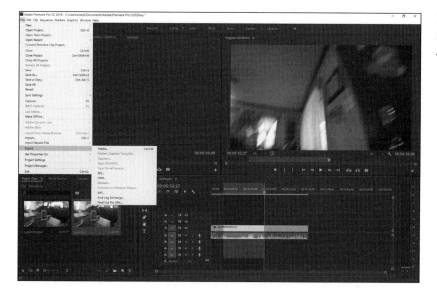

Figure 6.3 *The File > Export > Media menu item in Adobe Premiere Pro*

2. You've now opened the Export Settings dialog, and there are many settings to choose from. Since the example content already falls within YouTube's acceptable range, we'll select the Match Sequence Settings checkbox, which immediately updates all settings to match the sequence. If you are not sure if your content is in the acceptable range or if the video contained a mix of different video qualities, you can also scroll down and choose the YouTube 1080p HD preset (**Figure 6.4** on the next page).

Figure 6.4 *Depending on your content, choose the YouTube setting or match the source setting in the Export Settings dialog.*

3. Click the Publish tab below your export settings and scroll down until you reach YouTube (**Figure 6.5**). If you haven't done so already, log in to your YouTube account directly in the panel. A pop-up dialog opens to complete the task.

Figure 6.5 *Premiere Pro's YouTube export settings*

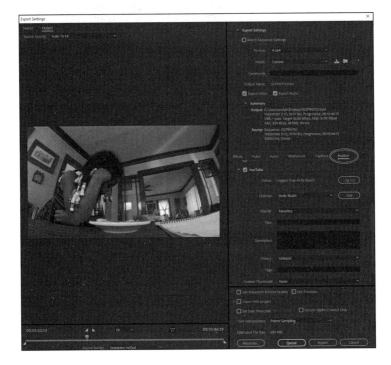

4. Now choose the channel, the playlist, and a title for the video
   (**Figure 6.6**).

Figure 6.6 *Choose your settings for exporting to YouTube.*

5. Set the privacy (for example, public or private) as well as any tags you want the video to have as soon as it is uploaded.

6. Choose a custom thumbnail if you want. The first frame of the video is the default. However, you can also choose to upload a unique still image or use the frame the playhead is currently parked on.

7. If you click the Delete Local File After Upload option, the version of the video on your computer will be removed immediately from your drive after it uploads.

8. Click Export. A dialog will open showing the encode time.

   After the video encodes, it will immediately begin uploading it to your YouTube account. The time this takes is completely dependent on your upload bandwidth.

9. Once the dialog box closes, use a web browser to navigate to your You-Tube channel and find the video immediately available for playback. In the background, YouTube will continue to transcode different versions, making other versions available over time (this process can take a few minutes or a few hours, depending on the length of your content).

Encoding for HTML5 Video

As described in Chapter 2, until the availability of the HTML5 video element, all the video that played within a web browser has been played through third-party browser plug-ins. First there was RealPlayer, then Windows Media Player and QuickTime, and most recently Flash. But with the HTML5 specifications, there is a new standard defined to embed and play video within a web page, without the need for these plug-ins, using a <video> element. There is a catch, however. There is not a single video format that works in all HTML5 browsers. **Table 6.4** outlines by platform what each major popular browser supports.

Table 6.4 *HTML5 codec support by browser*

Codec/Container	Google Chrome	Windows Edge	Firefox	Apple Safari	iOS	Android
Theora+Vorbis+Ogg	Y	N	Y	N	N	Y
AVC+AAC+MP4	Y	Y	Y	Y	Y	Y
VP9+WebM	Y	Y	Y	N	N	Y

For a professional HTML5 video implementation, we recommend encoding your video into the following formats for maximum compatibility across HTML5 browsers:

- H.264 in an MP4 container. Note that if you are looking for maximum compatibility, use Baseline or Main. For highest quality, use High. If possible, deliver multiple copies for the widest compatibility.

- VP9/WebM in a WebM container.

- Theora/Vorbis in an Ogg container.

HTML5 Video Markup Example

HTML5 gives you two ways to embed and play video within a web page. Both of them involve the <video> element. If you have only one video file, you can simply link to it in a src attribute. This is exactly like the image tag that we all know and love: the <img src="..."> tag.

Here's an example:

```
<video src="myvideo.ogv"></video>
```

As with the <img> tag, you should always include width and height attributes in your <video> tags. The width and height attributes should be the same as the dimensions you specified during the encoding process. If one dimension of the video is a little smaller than the width or height, the browser will center the video inside the box defined by the <video> tag, rather than stretching or squishing the video.

Here's an example:

```
<video src="myvideo.webm" width="640" height="480"></video>
```

By default, the <video> element will not display the video player controls. You can create your own controls with HTML, CSS, and JavaScript. The <video> element supports the following methods: play/pause, currentTime, volume, muted.

For example:

```
<video src="myvideo.webm" width="640" height="480" controls></video>
```

HTML5 video also supports preload and autoplay. The preload attribute tells the browser that you want it to start downloading the video as soon the page loads. If you want to minimize bandwidth on your pages and ensure that a video is not downloaded unless the user actually watches it, you can set preload to none.

Here's an example:

```
<video src="myvideo.webm" width="640" height="480" preload></video> or
→ <video src="myvideo2.webm" width="640" height="480" preload="none">
→ </video>
```

The autoplay attribute will not only start downloading the video when the page loads but also start playing the video (without the user clicking the play button).

Here's an example:

```
<video src="myvideo2.webm" width="640" height="480" autoplay></video>
```

HTML5 Video Markup Example (Multiple Videos)

Since each browser supports a different video format (see the earlier recommendations), it is important to create a video element that supports the multiple video formats you have prepared for each browser. Each <video> element can contain multiple <source> elements, and a browser will go down the list of video sources in the order they are listed and play the first one it is able to play. However, this slows down how quickly the video can be rendered for the end user and creates a bad experience. Therefore, it is important to tell the browser which type of video is which by using the <source> element—each browser will play only the video it supports.

NOTE We recommend you always list the .mp4 H.264 file in your list first for compatibility with older versions of iOS (older than 4).

Here's an example:

```
<video width="640" height="480" controls>
<source src="myvideo.mp4" type='video/mp4; codecs="avc1.42E01E,
→ mp4a.40.2"'>
<source src="myvideo.webm" type='video/webm; codecs="vp8, vorbis"'>
<source src="myvideo.ogv" type='video/ogg; codecs="theora, vorbis"'>
→ </video>
```

The type attribute contains three pieces of information: MIME type, video codec, and audio codec. The earlier myvideo.mp4 example contains a MIME type of video/mp4, a video codec of avc1.42E01E, and an audio codec of mp4a.40.2.

Note that the type values have to be included in quotation marks, so you need to add another type of quotation mark to surround the entire value.

Here's an example:

```
type='video/ogg; codecs="theora, vorbis"'
```

Transcoding Job with Zencoder

Now let's set up a job to encode several HTML5-friendly videos all at once. For this, we'll use a cloud-based transcoder, rather than a desktop. Many popular sites offer encoding capabilities. For this example we're using Zencoder (*http://zencoder.com*) owned by Brightcove. While each encoding job will cost money, the costs have gotten so inexpensive for this type of service versus purchasing a stand-alone application that it is worth investigating for your workflow.

To get started, we've set up an account on the site and have selected a subscription. Because we won't be transcoding much material, choose the pay-as-you-go option, which has no monthly charge and costs only $0.05 per minute of encoded video. If you planned to do larger volumes of work per month, there are options that provide lower costs per minute.

When working with an online service like Zencoder, the assumption is that you are interacting with it programmatically, meaning you set up the jobs to execute automatically via an API. However, it's also possible to manually upload files to test specific templates, which is what we will do now. Once you've set up an output template to your liking, you would use the extensive documentation and support on the Zencoder website to set up a more automated solution.

1. In a web browser, launch the URL *https://app.zencoder.com/jobs*.

2. In the lower-right corner of the Jobs panel in the Encoding window, click the New Job button (**Figure 6.7**).

Figure 6.7 *Zencoder's homepage provides links to jobs, plus the ability to start new ones.*

3. In the Request Settings panel, select HTML5 from the Job Template menu options (**Figure 6.8**).

Figure 6.8 *Zencoder's default transcoding templates*

4. Click Choose File in the Upload A File option and browse to select the file you want to transcode (**Figure 6.9**).

Figure 6.9 *Once a file has been uploaded, note the progress bar under the name. Once it has fully turned blue, the file is uploaded and ready for processing.*

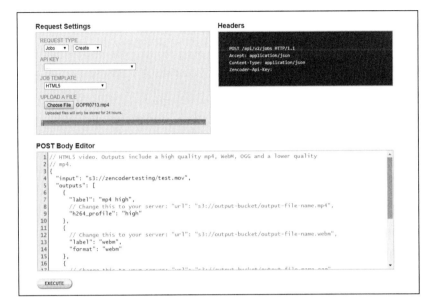

5. After selecting a clip, you will see a status bar showing its upload progress. Wait for the file to complete and do not reload or close the page while you wait. Note that this can take several minutes or even hours if the file you chose is large or your upload rate is low.

6. Scroll down and click the Execute button. As soon as the job is submitted, a new button will load called View Job. Click this to open a new page and view your job's progress.

7. On the Encoding Job page, you will see details for the file you submitted and each of the videos it is generating. In this case, we are creating a 1080p H.264 high-profile movie, a 1080p VP9 WebM movie, a 1080p Theora OGG movie, and a 360p H.264 baseline-profile movie. You can see basic statistics about each movie, and if you click the box to the right of any of the outputs, you can see detailed information about both the output file and the job itself.

8. Once the job is complete, you will see a green bar alongside each completed output (**Figure 6.10**).

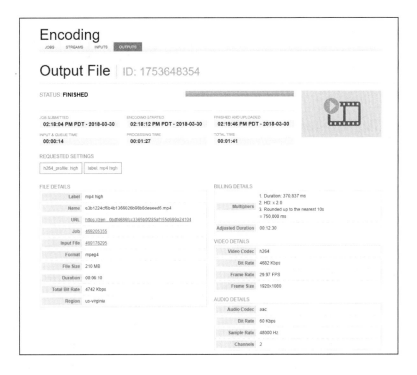

Figure 6.10 *Once a job is complete, you can click any of the encoded files to see details about that job, plus a link to download the finished video.*

9. On the detail page for each output there is a URL. Clicking the URL will play the output in your browser for review. From here you can download each asset, rename it if you choose, and then use the markup code provided earlier to embed these videos in a web page.

NOTE For those who are curious about costs of cloud-based services, the test video we ran for this example was 1 minute and 46 seconds long and cost $0.65 to encode.

Encoding an ABR File for Video-on-Demand Delivery

As we did with the HTML5 example, we will use a cloud-based service for transcoding an ABR file. This especially makes sense for adaptive bitrate content because multiple files are generated in the process, and rather than moving these around, you will want to combine hosting and delivery options with the transcode job.

For this example, we are using Azure Media Services, but as always, many other providers have similar workflows for delivering ABR content. We are using the Azure portal to set up our job; however, Microsoft also provides instructions on how to do this programmatically via .NET, Java, and REST APIs on its website (*https://docs.microsoft.com/en-us/azure/media-services/*).

This tutorial requires an Azure account that has had Media Services added to it. You can find instructions for starting an Azure account at *https://azure. microsoft.com/en-us/free/.* You can find instructions for adding Media Services to your new account at *https://docs.microsoft.com/en-us/azure/media-services/ media-services-portal-create-account.*

Since you may be new to Azure and the Media Services portal, we will break the steps down into multiple stages to make them easier to follow. Through the following walk-through, you will perform these tasks:

1. Start a streaming endpoint.

2. Upload a video file.

3. Encode a source file into a set of adaptive bitrate MP4 files.

4. Publish the asset and get streaming URLs.

5. Play the content.

Start a Streaming Endpoint

One of the most common scenarios when working with Azure Media Services is delivering video via adaptive bitrate streaming. Media Services does this through something called *dynamic packaging*. With dynamic packaging, you can deliver your adaptive bitrate MP4-encoded content in any of the streaming formats that are supported by the platform (including HLS, Smooth Streaming, and DASH).

TIP Some services can take a while to provision and be ready for use. You can check their status in a notifications section at the top of the portal page.

When you first create your Media Services account, a default streaming endpoint is added to your account in the Stopped state. To start streaming your content and to take advantage of dynamic packaging and dynamic encryption, the streaming endpoint from which you want to stream content has to be in the Running state.

To start the streaming endpoint, follow these steps:

1. Sign in to the Azure portal.

2. Choose Media Service > Streaming endpoints (**Figure 6.11**).

Figure 6.11 *Azure Media Services streaming endpoint*

3. Select the default streaming endpoint that appears to the right. The Default Streaming Endpoint Details window opens.

4. Click the Start icon (**Figure 6.12**).

5. Click the Save button.

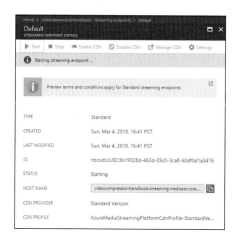

Figure 6.12 *This panel allows users to start, stop, and manage their streaming endpoints.*

Upload Files

Next, you will upload source video, encode it into multiple bitrates, and then publish the result. The first step is to upload your content.

Check the following tables to confirm the video formats and codecs you are working with are supported as inputs for the Azure Media Services encoder. **Table 6.5** (on the next page) highlights all the supported input containers, and **Table 6.6** covers all the supported input codecs in Azure. **Table 6.7** (on page 156) covers the supported audio codecs.

1. In the Azure portal (*http://portal.azure.com*), select your Azure Media Services account.

2. Choose Media Services > Assets. Then click the Upload button (**Figure 6.13**).

Figure 6.13 *Upload videos to Azure to start the transcoding process.*

Figure 6.14 *This panel will track the status of your uploading assets. It is not necessary to keep the tab open while uploading occurs.*

3. The Upload A Video Asset panel opens (**Figure 6.14**).

4. Click the folder to the right of the File Upload option and browse to the video you want to upload. Select the video and then click OK.

The upload begins. You can see the progress under the filename. When the upload is finished, the new asset is listed in the Assets pane.

Table 6.5 *Supported Azure Media Services input containers (file formats)*

File formats (file extensions)	Supported
FLV (with H.264 and AAC codecs) (.flv)	Yes
MXF (.mxf)	Yes
GSF (.gxf)	Yes
MPEG2-PS, MPEG2-TS, 3GP (.ts, .ps, .3gp, .3gpp, .mpg)	Yes
Windows Media Video (WMV)/ASF (.wmv, .asf)	Yes
AVI (uncompressed 8 bit/10 bit) (.avi)	Yes
MP4 (.mp4, .m4a, .m4v)/ISMV (.isma, .ismv)	Yes
Matroska/WebM (.mkv)	Yes
WAVE/WAV (.wav)	Yes
QuickTime (.mov)	Yes

Table 6.6 *Supported Azure Media Services input video codecs*

Input video codecs	Supported
AVC 8-bit/10-bit, up to 4:2:2, including AVCIntra	8 bit 4:2:0 and 4:2:2
Avid DNxHD (in MXF)	Yes
DVCPro/DVCProHD (in MXF)	Yes
Digital video (DV) (in AVI files)	Yes
JPEG 2000	Yes
MPEG-2 (up to 422 Profile and High Level; including variants such as XDCAM, XDCAM HD, XDCAM IMX, CableLabs, and D10)	Up to 422 Profile
MPEG-1	Yes
VC-1/WMV9	Yes
Canopus HQ/HQX	No
MPEG-4 Part 2	Yes
Theora	Yes
YUV420 uncompressed, or mezzanine	Yes
Apple ProRes 422	Yes
Apple ProRes 422 LT	Yes
Apple ProRes 422 HQ	Yes
Apple ProRes 422 Proxy	Yes
Apple ProRes 422 4444	Yes
Apple ProRes 422 4444 XQ	Yes

Table 6.7 *Supported input audio codecs*

Input audio codecs	Supported
AAC (AAC-LC, AAC-HE, and AAC-HEv2; up to 5.1)	Yes
MPEG Layer 2	Yes
MP3 (MPEG-1 Audio Layer 3)	Yes
Windows Media Audio	Yes
WAV/PCM	Yes
FLAC	Yes
Opus	Yes
Vorbis	Yes
AMR (adaptive multi-rate)	Yes
AES (SMPTE 331M and 302M, AES3-2003)	No
Dolby E	No
Dolby Digital (AC3)	No
Dolby Digital Plus (E-AC3)	No

Encode Assets in the Portal

To encode your content by using Media Encoder Standard in the Azure portal, follow these steps:

1. In the Azure portal, select your Azure Media Services account.

2. Choose Media Services > Assets. Select the asset that you want to encode. The details of the file appear in the Asset window (**Figure 6.15**).

Figure 6.15 *This panel will allow the user to encode or manage the uploaded assets.*

3. Click the Encode button.

4. In the Encode An Asset pane, select Media Encoder Standard for the media encoder name and Content Adaptive Multiple Bitrate MP4 for the encoding preset (**Figure 6.16**). To help you manage your resources, you can edit the name of the output asset and the name of the job.

Figure 6.16 *The Azure Media Services Encode An Asset panel*

5. Click Create.

Monitor Encoding Job Progress

To monitor the progress of the encoding job, at the top of the page, select Settings and then select Jobs. The progress bar will appear as your file is processed (**Figure 6.17**).

Figure 6.17 *The Azure Media Services encode monitoring panel*

Publish Content

To use the portal to publish an asset, follow these steps:

1. In the Azure portal, select your Azure Media Services account.

2. Choose Media Services > Assets. Select the asset that you want to publish.

3. Click the Publish button (**Figure 6.18**).

Figure 6.18 *Once the asset is encoded, the user must then publish the content to make it available to the public.*

4. Select Streaming as the locator type (**Figure 6.19**).

5. Click Add.

Figure 6.19 *Azure Media Services publishing to the endpoint*

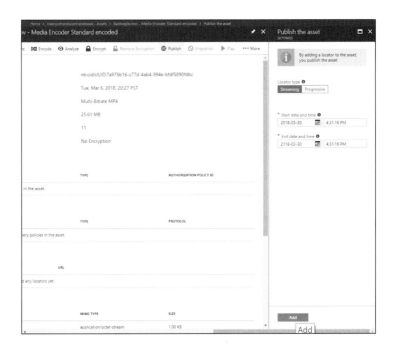

TIP When publishing your content, you can set specific dates the video is available. Use the calendar feature to choose specific start and end periods for your content. By default the content is available immediately and will end 100 years in the future.

The URL is added to the list of published URLs.

Play Content from the Azure Portal

You can test your video on a content player in the Azure portal (**Figure 6.20**).

Figure 6.20 *Published video playing in the test player*

Select the video and then click the Play button.

You should consider the following when testing your video:

- To begin streaming, start running the default streaming endpoint.
- Make sure the video has been published.
- The Azure portal's media player plays from the default streaming endpoint. If you want to play from a nondefault streaming endpoint, select and copy the URL and then paste it into another player. For example, you can test your video on Azure Media Player or any player that supports ABR content (for example, JW Player and Bitmovin).

If you return to the asset page and click the Published URLs section, a tab will open to the right showing versions of URLs that will deliver the assets as Smooth Streaming, DASH, and both HLSv3 and HLSv4. You can copy and paste these links wherever you want to deliver your newly encoded content.

Conclusion

Video on the Web has come a long way from the early days. Emerging standards such as adaptive bitrate and native HTML5 video have been widely adopted across the online ecosystem. OVPs often simplify video delivery while providing monetization and analytics tools. But while on-demand video makes up the majority of the material available to consumers, live video is actually quite a bit more popular and often generates many more simultaneous views. In the next chapter, you'll learn the differences and what you need to keep in mind for live delivery over the Internet.

Interview with a Compressionist

Name: Doug Daulton

Location: Spokane, Washington

Title/role: Filmmaker and Technical Director

Company: Verge Pictures

URL: *http://verge.pictures*

How did you get started in video compression or video streaming?

Originally, I come from the web design world. We dabbled in Flash and Sorensen Squeeze, but nothing big. When I got serious about making films, I did an internship with Pixel Corps in San Francisco. That was my first real exposure to compression and streaming.

Because I came from technical project management, I took to it quickly and was soon hired to help build out their streaming infrastructure, which was an early-stage business line at the time. Now, it is a core business for them, and they are widely considered the best at what they do.

What role does compression/streaming play in your daily work?

Now working primarily as an independent filmmaker, compression mostly comes into play when I am generating dailies or reference footage for our production team or corporate clients. Because our production teams are distributed around the globe, I am always looking for the best combination of image quality and file size I can get.

Streaming is an interesting beast for me. I've worked on several web docu-series where we capture interview footage over one or more of the various streaming services, mostly Skype. So far, because the deliverable is intended for YouTube, this has worked out pretty well.

In both cases, my time in the trenches doing high-profile corporate streams with Pixel Corps has been invaluable.

What surprises you most about video compression today?

I am constantly amazed that the industry has not come together around a common, open source, scalable codec. I fully understand the business rationale for not doing so, but I think it is short sighted and slows the pace of innovation in the space.

Google has done a lot of heavy lifting with VP9. I wish everyone, from camera manufacturers to distributors, would lock themselves in a room for a year, contribute the best features of each codec, and build one world-class codec that scales from kids goofing around on their phones to DCPs for major studio releases in IMAX.

It might be a pipe dream, but, like Elon Musk giving away the patent for the Tesla charging station, I think it would enable a lot of innovation currently locked in cross-format conversions.

For example, a common codec would accelerate the adoption of cloud-based rendering by allowing vendors to optimize media transfer and render stacks. For low-budget productions, it might even enable a distributed render farm along the lines of the Folding@Home project for disease research.

How has video compression changed in the time you've been working with it?

There are faster and more efficient transcodes and smaller footprint files and streams. Wishes for a "unicorn codec" aside, in my ten years in the space, it has been amazing to see how far we've come. What used to take a production truck can now be done, for certain use cases, with a phone and a couple of key pieces of gear, all of which fit in a backpack.

What's the one thing you wished you had known about video compression when you were starting out?

I wish I had known how fast the deliverable environment would change. When I started, 1080p capture, 720 renders, and SD streams were cutting edge. Now, the minimum is 4K capture, 2K renders, and 1080p streams. With consumer AR/VR/MR right around the corner, the current standards will likely seem quaint within five years.

Had I understood how quickly the landscape would change, I would have been a bit less rigid early on.

What's the next big thing we should be watching in the world of video compression?

The obvious answer is compression for AR/VR/MR. Headsets like the Oculus Rift are just the tip of the iceberg. As the screen moves closer to or, eventually, in the human eye, the need for image fidelity will greatly increase. Couple that with delivery in real time, and the need for better, faster compression algorithms is self-evident.

Like most, I am fascinated by AR/VR/MR and am currently working on a project involving it. But, what I am most excited for is how advances in that space will reduce the real costs (e.g., dollars, time, accessibility) for producers of "traditional" 16:9, fixed-frame media. The compression advances that enable virtual reality will eventually reduce, if not eliminate, the need to travel to capture inexpensive, high-quality real-time interviews with subjects from across the globe. As a producer with young kids and a desire to be closer to my family, I find that really exciting. In theory, it allows me to have it all.

Compression for Live Delivery

7

The previous chapter covered a lot of ground about online video but focused on video-on-demand (VOD) content. While this may make up the majority of your work as a compressionist, video delivered in real time online is growing exponentially. Viewers spend much more time watching live streaming video than on-demand video content, with the length of time varying by device. According to data gathered by Livestream, people spend an average of 2.8 minutes watching on-demand videos on mobile devices but spend 5 minutes on live streams per session. On tablets (which are called out separately from phones in this survey), on-demand video gets about 4 minutes of viewing time, while live streams earn more than 7 minutes. Top viewership goes to desktop users, with live streams earning an impressive 34.5 minutes of viewing time, while on-demand videos receive only 2.6 minutes.

This chapter breaks down some key differences between live streaming and VOD. We'll cover the basic equipment you'll need and give you some other considerations for setting up for live streaming. Finally, you'll work with some recipes for creating live streams on Facebook and YouTube using encoders.

Basic Live Streaming Equipment

While it's possible today to stream directly from your phone to sites like Twitter, Facebook, or YouTube, we aren't covering that particular process here. Those platforms have made it really simple and straightforward, and you really don't need any help getting started. We do, however, want to highlight the basic equipment you'll need for a live stream of your own.

Camera

As with all video, first you'll want to consider how you'll capture it. You might have some sort of USB webcam, but the quality of the image it captures is probably fairly poor. For a high-quality production, at the minimum you'll want to use a digital SLR or prosumer-level video camera (**Figure 7.1**). Something with a decent lens that can produce at least 1080p over HDMI is a good way to go.

Figure 7.1 *The Canon XF100 is a good example of a camera that's less than $2,000 that will make for a good live-streaming source.*

Capture Device

If you are going with a USB camera, then you can skip this part. However, if your camera uses HDMI or some other connection for video output, then you'll need a capture device. There are a wide range of hardware-encoding devices that can do this. Some are external devices that plug in between your camera and computer, and others are available as cards that can be installed in desktop computers. The El Gato line of capture devices is popular for streaming high-quality 60 fps live streams. Some hardware encoders even allow you to bypass the need for a computer completely.

Encoder

Next, you'll need to encode the signal. Unlike a file-based transcoder, the live encoder will need to be powerful enough to handle live video in real time. This could be a dedicated hardware-based solution (and potentially portable), or it could be a software-based encoder running on a computer. Hardware solutions will cost anywhere from a few hundred dollars to several thousands of dollars depending on the features you are looking for. Software encoders vary in price, from free and open-source options like Open Broadcaster Software (OBS), which we will cover in more detail later in this chapter, to pro-level packages like Telestream's Wirecast Pro.

Video Streaming Host

Finally, you'll need a video-streaming host or an online platform that has the bandwidth and streaming server configuration to take your video input and stream it to viewers, whether that's just a few, thousands, or more. This could be a service you pay for at an over-the-top online video platform (OVP), such as Ooyala or Brightcove, or it could be a free service at a social media site such as YouTube or Facebook.

Cloud-Based Transcoding

Cloud-based transcoding plays a big role in live streaming. Realistically, if you are looking to reach a large audience, you'll need to support multiple formats and resolutions. It's impractical and expensive to do this on location and then upload to a server for delivery. Instead, you want to stream one high-bitrate video to the cloud (as high a bitrate as your connectivity allows you to deliver in real time) and then use services in the cloud to transcode the stream to the final deliverable (**Figure 7.2** on the next page). If you are using a social media service, such as YouTube or Facebook, they are already doing this work for you; you just have to deliver the single stream. Think of the high-bitrate stream as analogous to the mezzanine files we discussed earlier for VOD workflows.

Figure 7.2 *A cloud-based transcoding workflow for your live stream moves the encoding of the video deliverable from the ground to the cloud.*

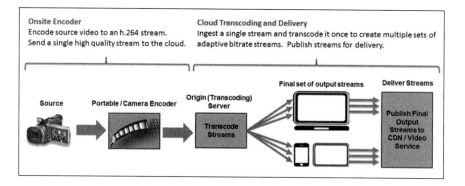

Live Streaming Considerations

In addition to the hardware and software you'll be using, we want to pause for a moment to highlight some of the other areas you will need to consider as you approach your live-stream production.

Push vs. Pull

By and large, the terminology laid out for on-demand encoding also applies to live streaming. "Push vs. pull" is one such phrase shared by both methods of video delivery.

In a pull scenario, a request is made by a client computer to receive a stream from an encoder or streaming server. This works in much the same way as any web page on the Internet works where the information isn't sent until requested. In a push scenario, the connection is instigated by the encoder to a streaming server (or service), which often requires a username and password or API key. The streaming server then redistributes the stream to the users. Push and pull methods get used for different scenarios. Pull scenarios most often occur within the network where multiple servers may pull a feed from a primary source. Ingesting live streams into the network, however, is most likely a push scenario.

Live vs. Live Linear

Live streaming video adds another couple of terms to your vernacular, but these aren't really technical. If you are working in this space, you will run across them and want to know the difference. People use *live streaming* as the term most typically associated with a live event video. Think large-scale events such as the Super Bowl, the Oscars, or even the local news. All of these are special events taking place in real time that are also being delivered in real time. *Live linear*, on the other hand, is prerecorded content that is streamed in real time in the same way a live event is delivered (instead of as a VOD asset). All of the primetime TV shows you watch (except for live events) are live linear broadcasts in which prerecorded shows are delivered in real time.

While the workflows are more or less similar for the two, the source differs. Live events may be delivered from virtually anywhere in the world via a camera and encoder and a data connection to deliver your stream to the world. Live linear will most likely start from a broadcast source, such as the feed from a television station or a server playing programs on a set schedule.

Content Delivery Networks

A content delivery network or content distribution network (CDN) is a geographically distributed network of proxy servers and their data centers. Their purpose is to distribute content to end users to provide high availability (multiple redundancies) and high performance. CDNs serve a large portion of the Internet content today, including web objects (text, graphics, and scripts), downloadable objects (media files, software, documents), applications (e-commerce, portals), live streaming media, on-demand streaming media, and social networks.

CDNs are a layer in the Internet ecosystem. Content owners pay CDN operators to deliver their content to their end users. In turn, a CDN pays ISPs, carriers, and network operators for hosting its servers in its data centers.

If you are streaming your content into an existing platform, such as YouTube or Facebook, then you're just reusing their CDNs to distribute your content. If, however, you're setting up your streams to deliver to large audiences on your own site, then understanding CDN costs and requirements will become critical to your live streaming workflow.

Challenges to Live Streaming

There is no shortage of challenges facing those of you who are delivering live streams at scale. Here are just a few of the challenges live streaming faces over traditional VOD encoding.

Bandwidth Limitations

Connectivity issues almost always plague live streaming setups. Trouble-shooting network connections and understanding which data rates can realistically be delivered over your specific connection are critical skills for compressionists involved in live streaming. Many streaming producers try to avoid Wi-Fi or wireless technologies as much as possible because the additional overhead can make delivering in real time problematic. If you are streaming from a remote location, underlying network issues may be exacerbated by relying on a wireless connection to the Internet.

Latency

The very nature of live-streaming technology is that there is some delay, known as *latency*, from the time the image is captured until it is delivered to the end user. The goal is for this latency to be as low as possible. In most situations, latency levels under 10 or so seconds are acceptable. In some scenarios, such as gamers streaming their gameplay while chatting with viewers, they want the latency to be around 3 seconds or less.

Costs

All that equipment we discussed in the previous section can quickly add up, cost-wise. Even a relatively inexpensive live streaming kit will likely cost between $3,000 and $10,000 and can quickly run into the hundreds of thousands of dollars, depending on what you're streaming and from where.

Social Media and Live Streaming

Live streaming isn't simply a replacement for cable TV programming. Twitch, Twitter, Facebook, and other social media sites have been rolling out live-streaming features and promoting them heavily. The same demand for live content by consumers is driving demand for live content on social platforms; and in the case of e-sports and gaming, live streaming has created an entirely new culture.

Popular Live Streaming Platforms

Here is a quick rundown of the current most popular live streaming social media platforms.

Periscope

Periscope (*https://www.periscope.com*) is a Twitter-owned and operated platform that is tightly integrated with Twitter. Periscope has more than 10 million users, more than 2 million of whom log in daily. Two hundred million hours of video have been broadcast to date, with roughly 350,000 hours per day. The service lets users live stream from their mobile devices and push out those streams on Twitter.

Facebook Live

The fact that Facebook offers a live-streaming feature is really not surprising at all, and using it is straightforward. Users can "go live" directly from a computer or mobile device using the Facebook app (*https://live.fb.com*), but it also supports the ability to stream a feed from a professional streaming setup as described earlier. The section "Recipes for Live Streaming Video" offers a step-by-step guide for using OBS to stream video from your computer to Facebook.

YouTube Live

The home of online video, YouTube has continued its quest to bring video of all kinds to its more than 1 billion users. With YouTube Live (*https://www.youtube.com/live_dashboard_splash*), the company can utilize its expansive creator and advertising network to generate even more hosted and monetized content. As with its on-demand video services, YouTube makes it easy to deliver live-streaming video in multiple ways. The section "Recipes for Live Streaming Video" includes details on live streaming to YouTube using XSplit.

Twitch

Twitch (*https://twitch.tv*) is the live-streaming platform owned by Amazon, and it's been around since 2011. It's the biggest and oldest service of its kind online, boasting approximately 10 million daily active users. While the platform was initially focused purely on gaming (and this continues to be its primary content), Twitch Creative was added in 2015. Twitch Creative allows artists (broadly interpreted as anyone from a writer to an illustrator to a chef) to live stream their work to viewers.

Mixer

Mixer (*https://mixer.com*) is the youngest platform covered here and was launched in early 2016 as Beam.tv before being acquired by Microsoft later that year. Similar to Twitch, you'll find live and previously broadcast gaming-focused content on Mixer. Mixer stands apart from the rest of the platforms by offering a much more interactive experience for viewers. For example, viewers can actually influence the gameplay by giving weapons or tools to the player that immediately become available for use. Because it's run by Microsoft, it's also a service easily available to Xbox and Windows 10 users.

The Most Unlikely of Stars in the Most Unlikely of Places

In March 2018, Twitch broke its record for most-viewed stream by a single player when pro-gamer Tyler "Ninja" Blevins assembled an unlikely supergroup to play the extremely popular game Fortnite by Epic Games. Ninja was joined by NFL rookie JuJu Smith-Schuster, rapper Travis Scott, and pop superstar Drake. At its peak, the stream was trending on Twitter and hit 628,000 concurrent viewers, smashing the previous record of 388,000 viewers for a single-player stream. While these viewer figures don't exactly match primetime television numbers, well over half a million people were logged on to watch a professional gamer and his famous friends playing video games live. This was an event that wasn't marketed or otherwise planned in any way, yet the next day it was covered by all the major broadcasters and nearly a month later is still referred to in the press.

Recipes for Live Streaming Video

Now that we've talked through some of the live-streaming considerations, let's dive in and try some simple live-streaming examples. For these guides, we will focus on streaming from a Mac or PC to a social media service such as Facebook or YouTube because these are easy first tests for delivering a live stream to an audience.

Streaming to Facebook Live via OBS

Open Broadcaster Software is a free and open source software suite for recording and live streaming. It acts as a mixer, allowing users to combine multiple sources and then either record that locally or deliver it to one of a number of supported streaming sites, such as Twitch, YouTube, or Facebook.

Creating the Stream on Facebook

Before we stream to Facebook, we first have to create the stream on the platform.

1. Go to *https://www.facebook.com/live/create*. Sign in to your Facebook account.

2. Click the Create Live Stream tab. The Connect screen opens (**Figure 7.3**).

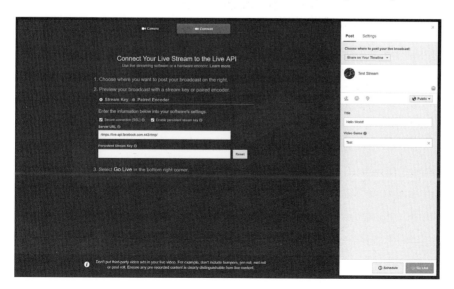

Figure 7.3 *On the Facebook Create Live Stream Connect page, you can also choose to have the video go live immediately or schedule it for a future date.*

3. Choose where you want your live broadcast to be posted, such as your Timeline, in a Group, or on an Event page.

4. Choose Stream Key under step 2.

5. Select Enable Persistent Stream Key if you want your stream key to be permanent. If this isn't selected, you won't be able to use this stream key again after the stream ends.

6. Copy and paste the server URL and stream key or persistent stream key into the settings of OBS (see "Setting Up OBS").

7. Next, write a description and title, and add any tags you feel are appropriate (such as a topic), which Facebook can use to help users discover your stream.

8. Leave this web page open, as we will come back to it after setting up OBS.

NOTE The server URL may differ from user to user. The correct one will automatically populate this field for you. Also, remember that the stream key is unique for every user—anyone with your key will be able to stream to your Facebook page!

A Few Things to Keep in Mind During Your Facebook Live Stream

During your live stream, people will be able to react and comment. You can write replies to comments or respond to them in your streaming broadcast. If you're live streaming to your timeline, you'll be able to choose the audience. When you end your live stream, the video will stay where you shared it as a video post.

Also, don't share your stream key or persistent stream key. Anyone who has access to your stream key information can stream video to your post. You won't be able to use a stream key again after your live stream ends. A persistent stream key, which is created by selecting Enable Persistent Stream Key when creating a live stream, is permanent and can be used again after a live stream ends. Keep in mind that you can broadcast only one live video at a time with your persistent stream key.

Finally, you can embed your live stream on a website outside of Facebook. Once you have gone live, your browser page will have a preview showing your live stream. Near the bottom-right corner of this screen is an HTML code that you can copy and paste onto your website.

Setting Up OBS

Now let's set up OBS to stream to your Facebook page.

1.   Launch OBS Studio.

2.   At the bottom right of the opening screen, click the Settings button and then select Stream from the Settings panel.

3.   Select Streaming Services for Stream Type (**Figure 7.4**).

4.   Select Facebook Live in the Service drop-down menu.

5.   Select Default for Server.

6.   Paste your stream key into the Stream Key field.

Figure 7.4 *OBS Stream Settings panel*

7.   On the Output tab, set Video Bitrate to 2500 (this is Kbit/s, so you're set-ting it to 2.5 Mbit/s).

8.   On the Video tab, make sure Output Resolution is set to 1280 × 720 (the maximum that Facebook Live supports). See the sidebar "Facebook Live Streaming Guidelines" for details on Facebook video specifications.

9.   Click OK to return to the main screen.

10. Set up your canvas for streaming by adding all the different inputs your project requires. OBS supports the ability to have multiple inputs. For the purposes of this example, we've added our desktop and a cropped inset of our webcam.

NOTE To learn more about setting up your canvas, see the sidebar "The Ultimate Guide to OBS Studio."

Facebook Live Streaming Guidelines

Here is a quick rundown of the currently supported specifications from Facebook (keep in mind these may change over time):

- The recommended max bitrate is 4000 Kbit/s (4 Mbit/s).
- The maximum resolution is 720p (1280 × 720), at 30 frames per second.
- An I-frame (keyframe) must be sent at least every 2 seconds throughout the stream.
- Titles must have fewer than 255 characters or the stream will fail.
- You can have H264-encoded video and AAC-encoded audio only.

11. Click Start Stream. A small green square icon lights up in the lower-left corner along with stats about your stream (**Figure 7.5**).

Figure 7.5 *You can see the stats about your stream on this screen.*

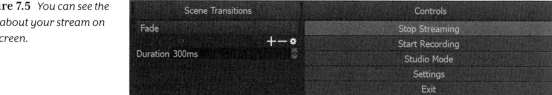

The Ultimate Guide to OBS Studio

The guidance here will get you started, but we can't possibly cover everything about OBS in this book. Fortunately, we don't have to. Producer/Editor Adam Taylor (*www.eposvox.com*) created and maintains the OBS Studio Master Class, both as a Google Docs file and as a YouTube Video. The 40-page guide delves into every feature OBS offers, and his 6+ hour video on YouTube walks users through every possible action they'd need for streaming on OBS.

Google Doc: *https://tinyurl.com/obsultimateguide*

YouTube: *https://tinyurl.com/obsvideo*

12. If you go back to the Facebook Live Stream page, you will now see a preview of your stream (**Figure 7.6**). Notice the Go Live button is now also available. You can choose to go live immediately or schedule it to go live at a future time.

Figure 7.6 *Go live immediately or click the Schedule button to select a date and time for your stream.*

Streaming to YouTube Live Using XSplit

XSplit is a live streaming and video-mixing application developed and maintained by SplitmediaLabs. There are two products under XSplit: XSplit Broadcaster and XSplit Gamecaster.

XSplit Broadcaster acts as a video mixer, switching between various media configurations (known as *scenes*) while dynamically mixing them with other sources such as video cameras, screen regions, game capture, and others. These sources are used to create a broadcast production for both live streams and local recording for on-demand distribution on the Web.

NOTE Similar to OBS, XSplit users need to set up their input sources (called scenes) prior to streaming. For details, visit *https://www.xsplit.com/broadcaster/manual*.

XSplit Gamecaster, on the other hand, is a more turnkey application. It's designed for casual gamers who immediately want to start live streaming or recording their gameplay with minimal setup and configuration.

Similar to OBS, XSplit provides a convenient way to link several platforms directly to your application for streaming. Here we walk you through linking your app to YouTube and then live streaming to it.

1. Launch XSplit Broadcaster.

2. Choose Outputs > Set Up A New Output > YouTube Live (**Figure 7.7**).

Figure 7.7 *XSplit output options*

3. In the dialog that appears, click Authorize.

4. Sign in with your Google account. If you have turned on two-factor authentication, Google may ask you for a second confirmation.

5. After successfully signing in, XSplit will ask for permission to access certain things on your YouTube account (**Figure 7.8**). Click Authorize.

Figure 7.8 *XSplit YouTube Properties panel. Click Authorize to pair your YouTube account to XSplit.*

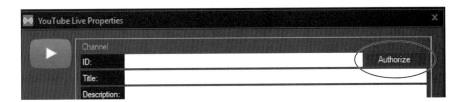

6. To ensure streaming to YouTube Live is enabled on your channel, go to YouTube.com, click your user icon, and click Creator Studio (**Figure 7.9**).

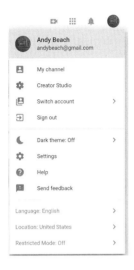

Figure 7.9 *Access YouTube Creator Studio from settings found under your user icon.*

7. Click Channel Settings and make sure Live Streaming is enabled.

8. Choose Status And Features from the Channel drop-down menu (**Figure 7.10**). In the Embed Live Streams box, you'll notice either a green or red line at the bottom. If a green line appears, you are set and ready to stream. If, however, there is a red line, click Learn More to resolve any issues.

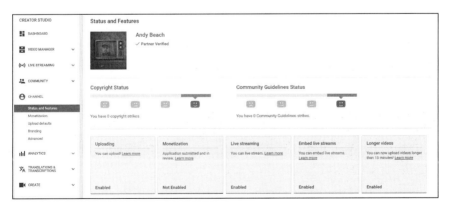

Figure 7.10 *The YouTube Creator Studio Status And Features page*

Restrictions on YouTube Live Streaming

Your live-streaming ability may be automatically disabled for any of the following reasons:

- Your channel received a Community Guidelines strike.
- Your live stream or archived live stream is blocked globally.
- Your live stream or archived live stream receives a copyright takedown.
- Your live stream matches another copyrighted live broadcast.

Live-stream restrictions last for 90 days or until the associated issues are resolved. You can check your channel's access to live streaming under Status And Features at any time.

9.   Return to XSplit and choose Output > YouTube. Enter the details for your stream in the dialog that appears and then select Start Broadcast (**Figure 7.11**). After a few moments, a pop-up menu confirms you are streaming to YouTube.

Figure 7.11 *XSplit Broadcaster's Start Broadcast button*

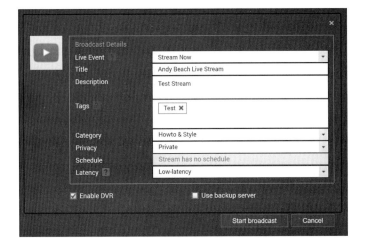

Mirroring a Stream to Multiple Sites

One last suggestion if you are streaming on a regular basis: You may want to consider making your content live on multiple platforms simultaneously to make it more discoverable and to increase your audience size. If you tried to deliver a stream to each and every one, you'd quickly outstrip your bandwidth's ability to deliver. There are, however, solutions out there that allow you to deliver one stream that then gets redirected to multiple services. One such service is Restream.IO (*www.restream.io*). Create an account there and then connect the services you want to deliver to. Then on your own system, set up OBS, XSplit, or whatever encoder you are using to stream an RTMP stream directly to your Restream account (this will require pointing at the correct server and adding your API key). With this done, now every time you go live, your content will be delivered to all the platforms you've set up. One thing to note is such services will add some noticeable lag to the streams because they are being redirected multiple times as part of the delivery.

Conclusion

If you are interested in streaming online, these guidelines should help get you started. However, you may still need physical media as part of your workflow. Encoding for physical media has changed dramatically from the heyday of disc delivery over ten years ago, so it's important to know what applies today and the best ways to prepare your content.

Compression for Optical Discs

8

For some compressionists, optical media, whether via standard-definition DVD or Blu-ray Disc, will be the sole, or certainly primary, delivery medium for their compressed content. Although optical media formats are in decline and seem to be giving way to more dynamic media streaming technologies, they still play a critical role in delivering certain types of content, mainly educational pieces to schools or independent films to certain film festivals.

To understand the optical disc landscape, you have to take a quick trip back in time to the turn of the century. Affordable DVD players were released in 2000 and, after a couple of Christmas seasons, eventually dethroned the almighty VHS tape as the crowned king of home video. DVD became the best choice for delivery of standard-def content because of its ubiquitous nature. A few years later, it became clear that high-definition video also needed a consumer delivery medium. In 2002, technology companies assembled themselves into two camps backing two different disc formats: HD DVD and Blu-ray Disc.

Before commercial Blu-ray or HD DVD recorders became available, "hybrid" disc technology appeared, which allowed producers to record high-definition video footage onto regular DVD discs. You got only about 20 to 30 minutes of video per disc (double that for dual-layer DVDs), but that sufficed for many applications. Of course, you still needed either a Blu-ray or HD DVD player to play the results.

Between 2006 and 2008 there was an all-out format war. For those old enough to remember the original home video format war of the early 1980s, it was VHS vs. Betamax all over again. In February 2008, the main leader of the HD DVD group, Toshiba, announced it was abandoning the platform just after Warner Bros. announced it would be releasing its movies exclusively on Blu-ray.

So today, we have two disc formats popular enough to release content on: good ol' standard-def DVD and the high-definition Blu-ray.

What's a DVD?

At a high level, DVDs are incredibly simple. All DVDs have two components: content consisting of things such as video, slideshows, and audio; and the menus used by the viewers to navigate and access that content.

In the first days of DVD creation, you created/edited your content in one application and "authored" your actual DVD in another. Since then, programs have become more integrated. Still, DVD authoring is straightforward in concept: you create your menus and then link to your content.

What gets a little more complicated are the specific requirements necessary to ensure that your DVD plays on your target player. Although most authoring programs shield you from many of these technical details (because in theory all players should be standardized against one specification/standard), it helps to understand these requirements before starting production.

Producing SD DVDs

The first thing you'll want to know when producing DVDs is what your target player is going to be. There are lots of different models of players at different price points with different features. Blu-ray players can also play SD DVDs but will usually upconvert your SD content to HD on playback (which sometimes doesn't look all that great) on today's HDTVs.

Because there are lots of different models of players, you have to produce your disc for the lowest common denominator. So, if you're producing a disc to play on an end user's $19.95 Walmart DVD player, you'll have to use a certain kind of media and a limited set of compression technologies.

DVD Disc Types

In the early days of DVD recordable media, there was another format war between –R/RW (pronounced "dash R" or "dash RW") and +R/RW (pronounced "plus R" or "plus RW") and their respective recorders. The R stands for recordable and can be used only once, while the RW stands for rewritable and can be erased and rewritten.

What's the Difference?

When shopping for recordable media, you'll find yourself staring at a lot of – and + symbols. But what do those symbols actually mean? The only difference between the formats is the way they determine the location of the laser beam on the disc.

DVD-R discs use tiny marks along the grooves in the discs, called *land prepits*, to determine the laser position. DVD+R discs do not have land prepits but instead measure the *wobble frequency* as the laser moves toward the outside of the disc.

That small difference between the disc formats used to make a much bigger difference before hybrid ± drives were introduced. If you have a ± drive, you can use either format. DVD-R is still the more popular choice, but you should be fine since both are widely supported.

Though both –R and +R will play on standard DVD players, DVD-R recorders required DVD-R media, and DVD+R recorders required DVD+R media. Since different vendors supported different standards (HP backed +R, while Apple went with –R), producers with different computers often needed to stock multiple standards of recordable media. Add rewritable and dual-layer media to the mix, which are also standard-specific, and your shelves could easily be filled with stacks and stacks of different discs.

Fortunately, after a few years of that nonsense, affordable "dual RW" recorders appeared that could record to media of both types. If you have a dual RW recorder, you can use both media standards; otherwise, you'll need either +R or –R recordable media.

Note that both +R and –R are available in both single and dual layer, with the capacities shown in **Table 8.1** (on the next page). If you're producing a single-layer disc of either type, you have a capacity of 4.7 GB, which adds up to about 74 minutes of audio/video at a combined 8 Mbit/s, which is the highest recommended rate.

Table 8.1 *Standard disc types and their characteristics*

Standard options	DVD±R/RW	DVD±R/RW dual-layer
Number of layers	1	2
Capacity	4.7 GB	8.5 GB
Video at 8 Mbit/s (in minutes)	74	135

Compatibility Risks of Recordable Media

Virtually all Hollywood DVDs are produced using a different process than DVD recordable, often called *replication*. Playback compatibility for these replicated discs on the wide variety of DVD players is near 100 percent since the raison d'être for these players is to play Hollywood DVDs, and their manufacturers test accordingly.

Unfortunately, recordable media didn't become widely available until long after DVD players started selling, so lots of players were on the market before most recordable media brands became available for compatibility testing. As a result, many of the earliest DVD players can't play recordable discs. Playback incompatibilities can be absolute or can relate to recorder, media brand, or even recording parameters.

If you're producing for your own use, you can use a combination of media and recorder that plays on your player—no big deal. When producing for wider distribution, however, the risk of playback incompatibilities becomes much more significant.

You can minimize (but not eliminate) compatibility risk by doing the following:

- Use name-brand premium media. We use Ridata and Verbatim exclusively. Once you find a media brand that works for you, don't switch.
- Use recordable (R), rather than rewritable (RW), media.
- Record at a combined audio/video data rate of less than 8 Mbit/s, or even 7 Mbit/s if serving a broad base of customers who may have older or cheaper players, which will choke and sputter on recordable media with video encoded at high data rates.

These same principles apply to high-definition recorders and recordable media. That is, early Blu-ray players couldn't be tested for compatibility with recordable media because it didn't exist when they shipped, which obviously increases the risk of compatibility issues. Fortunately, you're producing for a much smaller target audience, so you can and should test compatibility early in the process. Expect incompatibilities, test to minimize the risk, and warn your customers and clients that issues may occur.

Dual-layer discs in both formats can hold up to 8.5 GB, sufficient for about 135 minutes of audio and video at 8 Mbit/s. Note that dual-layer discs have two layers on a single side, so you don't have to turn the disc over to either record or play the disc. There are some dual-sided media around (mostly from Ritek) that you have to turn over to record and play, though we haven't seen this type of disc used much.

One final caveat before moving on: not all recordable discs will play on all DVD players. See the sidebar "Compatibility Risks of Recordable Media" for more details.

SD Codecs

Now that you have the media side down, let's address the codec side of this DVD you're producing for your end user's $19.95 Walmart DVD player. On a DVD, the only video codec you can use is MPEG-2, and all assets containing visual images will be compressed to MPEG-2.

For example, if you use your DVD-authoring program to create a slideshow, the authoring program will encode the slideshow into MPEG-2 video during the authoring process. If you create motion menus for your DVD, these will also be encoded into MPEG-2.

You probably won't need to actually *do* anything to choose MPEG-2. As you can see in **Figure 8.1**, in the Project Properties dialog from Vegas DVD Architect, you really don't have a video codec option, just an audio codec option.

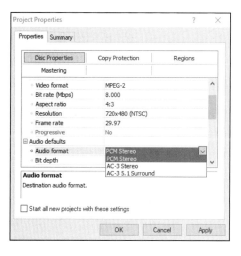

Figure 8.1 *The Project Properties dialog from Vegas DVD Architect. All SD DVDs use the MPEG-2 video codec and either Dolby Digital, PCM, or MPEG (not shown) audio compression.*

NOTE There are two versions of the Dolby Digital encoder: Standard and Professional. Dolby Digital Professional offers better-quality encoding, but not all applications will offer both, so if audio quality is extremely important, you may want to investigate which version you are using.

You have a bit more flexibility on the audio side, where you can choose Dolby Digital or PCM compression and sometimes MPEG-1 Layer II audio compression. All DVD players sold in U.S. markets *must* support the first two formats, while support for MPEG audio compression is *optional* (although most players do support it).

Most prosumer and professional authoring programs offer Dolby Digital, and when it's available, it's the best option. You can recognize a Dolby Digital file by its .ac3 file extension. Some consumer programs offer only MPEG and PCM, and typically we'll choose MPEG in that instance. If you choose PCM, it has a data rate of about 1.5 Mbit/s. To meet your 8 Mbit/s total target, this means you'll have to drop your video data rate to 6.5 Mbit/s.

In contrast, both MPEG and Dolby Digital have configurable data rates that usually go as high as 400 Kbit/s or so, though most producers stick to 192 Kbit/s or less. At this rate, you have 7.8 Mbit/s to devote to video, which is about 20 percent higher than the 6.5 Mbit/s you'll have with uncompressed audio. For this reason, it almost always makes sense to use some form of compressed audio, with Dolby being the best choice when available.

What the Heck Is a VOB?

As you may already know, if you produce an MPEG-2 file on your computer, it typically has an .mpg, .mp2, .mpv, or .m2v extension. Yet if you scan the contents of a DVD in Windows Explorer or Finder, you won't find any files with that extension. Rather, as shown in **Figure 8.2**, you'll see that all the large files have .vob extensions.

Figure 8.2 *During the compiling stage, the authoring program combines menus and content into VOB files that DVD players know how to read.*

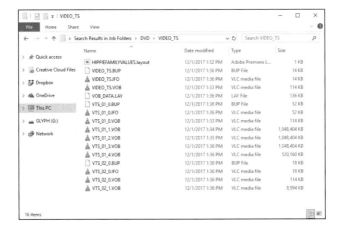

Technically, a video object (VOB) file is a "container format" for the disc's menus and content. If you copy a .vob file to your hard drive and change the extension to .mpg, your default MPEG player will probably play the video, though you'll likely lose any interactivity.

More important, you should know that you can extract the original MPEG-2 files from a DVD using many consumer authoring and editing programs such as Adobe Premiere Elements or Pinnacle Studio, assuming the DVD isn't copy-protected. This is often useful when you need to access videos that you've previously produced to DVD but have since deleted the source files from your production station.

In addition, if you do see a bunch of MPEG-2 files on the DVD, it probably won't play on a desktop DVD player. Instead, you'll need the VOB files in the proper Video_TS folder for the DVD to play. That's why you need to go through the authoring stage to produce a DVD that will work on a TV-attached player.

> **NOTE** We mentioned transport streams as they relate to MPEG-2 in Chapter 2, but that is not the only way this codec gets bundled and used. Two more common stream formats exist known as program streams (PS) and elementary streams (ES). Program streams, also referred to as MPEG-2 PS, are the standard format for storing MPEG-2 video multiplexed (muxed) with other streams (such as audio or subtitles). Elementary streams, on the other hand, are the individual audio and video files that haven't been muxed together. Each channel of the audio would be an individual file, so a 5.1 surround sound export would include six individual files.

What's a Blu-ray Disc?

As Blu-ray Disc (BD) is the HD successor to DVD, what will content producers and compressionists need to know to be prepared to deliver in the Blu-ray format? The first thing you'll need to do it is to get familiar with the basic specs, such as overall disc capacities (which directly affect bit budgeting), video resolution, and frame-rate support. Most important, you'll need to wrap your head around codec support, which is a little more complicated with DVD because there is more than just one option. **Table 8.2** provides the lowdown on Blu-ray Disc.

Table 8.2 *Desktop producer's view of Blu-ray Disc features*

Features	Blu-ray details
Capacity: Single/double layers	25/5/0 GB
Video formats	AVC/VC1/MPEG-2
Video resolution (maximum)	1920 × 1080 24p or 50/60i HDTV
Maximum video bit rate	40 Mbit/s
Audio formats	Dolby Digital/DTS/PCM
Interactivity	Blu-ray Disc Java (BD-J)
Recorders availability in the United States	Since January 2007

We didn't list all supported audio codecs, but Dolby Digital should clearly be the codec of choice for most desktop producers. The Blu-ray format enables interactivity beyond that offered by SD DVDs, although no prosumer program that we're aware of supports these features. Rather, they simply extend current SD DVD features to the higher-capacity discs (and higher-quality video codecs).

Rumors of HD DVD's Demise *Not* Exaggerated

Once upon a time there were two physically distinct and mutually incompatible high-definition disc formats: HD DVD and Blu-ray Disc. These formats battled to succeed DVD as the standard for HD content delivery on optical disc. On the manufacturing and patent side, HD DVD was essentially a Toshiba format, while Blu-ray Disc was backed by Sony, Pioneer, Panasonic, and roughly 150 other companies. That said, HD DVD did carry the endorsement of the DVD Forum, which had been the leading industry advocacy group for DVD (including many DVD patent holders), and the support of some major movie studios, which many felt would be a key factor in determining which format would win out. Other advantages of HD DVD included its manufacturing similarities to DVD, which meant that the replication plants that crank out DVD movies could adapt their existing lines to HD DVD production with less effort and cost than it would take to migrate to Blu-ray Disc.

Blu-ray Disc, meanwhile, offered greater capacity per layer on each disc (25 GB versus 15 GB for HD DVD) and arguably more opportunities for adding interactivity and web connectivity on the authoring side, although most of those haven't been explored yet. And it had a lot more companies behind it. But as far as consumers were concerned, the formats were functionally the same: both could deliver full 1080p HD movies on disc, with some nice additional improvements over DVD such as pop-up menus. But what was frustrating was that the presence of two formats meant a kind of stalemate that was keeping manufacturing and sales volumes low, player and disc prices high, and most consumers wary of choosing one or another format lest they get burned as Betamax users did in the late 1970s when VHS doomed their format of choice to instant obsolescence. And that went double for content producers who needed the consumer market to stabilize before they could confidently start developing for one format or another with assurance that their customers could play the discs they produced.

The stalemate broke in January 2008 at the annual Consumer Electronics Show (CES) in Las Vegas when Warner Bros. announced that it would exclusively back the Blu-ray format and deliver its high-def movies only on Blu-ray Disc. With several other key players having already jumped ship, Warner's defection tipped the scales decidedly in Blu-ray's favor. The HD DVD camp's immediate response was to cancel the HD DVD party they'd planned for the first night of the show and initiate a fire sale on all the HD DVD players in inventory. In rapid succession, similar announcements followed from Netflix, Best Buy, Walmart, and others, and by mid-February, rumors were circulating that Toshiba would be announcing the death of HD DVD very soon. That announcement came on February 19, and HD DVD was history.

Though there are levels of complexity in Blu-ray authoring, from the viewpoint of a desktop disc author, there's very little difference between producing SD DVDs and high-definition Blu-ray Discs. That is, your menu and interactivity options are nearly identical to those offered on a DVD. Although you may want to choose a different video codec and a larger disc capacity when recording to your Blu-ray recorder, there's no real learning curve for SD producers moving to desktop high-definition production.

With all of this in mind, let's take a quick, high-level look at some of the issues related to producing Blu-rays; then we'll dig in and actually produce an SD DVD and a Blu-ray Disc.

Producing Blu-ray Discs

To produce Blu-ray Discs, you have to understand the different types of Blu-ray Discs produced by the different authoring programs and how their differences might affect playback compatibility. In addition, some programs, such as Adobe Encore, can format and write full-length Blu-ray Discs to Blu-ray recorders. In contrast, some consumer authoring programs can produce Blu-ray-compatible discs on DVD media, allowing producers to produce discs with about 20 to 25 minutes of HD video *without* a Blu-ray recorder.

> **NOTE** You can find instructions for installing Adobe Encore in the sidebar "Installing Adobe Encore," which appears in the section "Recipe for Producing Blu-ray Discs."

Blu-ray Overview

There are three types of Blu-ray Discs. The richest set of authoring functionality is available with the HDMV (Movie Mode) specification, which includes pop-up menus, interactive graphics, and other content. To access this level of functionality, you'll need a professional authoring program such as Scenarist BD, which is priced several times higher than prosumer programs such as Adobe Encore.

For the most part, only Hollywood producers use HDMV to author and then replicate their discs for mass-market consumption. Again, from a compatibility perspective, this type of disc is safest in terms of both media and format since replicated media is the most reliable and all consumer Blu-ray Disc players have been tested for compatibility with replicated HDMV discs.

Thoughts on DVD and Blu-ray Software

The HD DVD/Blu-ray format war took several years, which meant other technology had time to advance quite a bit while the two camps battled it out. Content producers started to look beyond optical discs as the primary means of distribution and found a somewhat perfect delivery medium in the Internet. Starting with downloads from services such as iTunes and moving later to streaming platforms such as Netflix and Hulu, file-based delivery online started to change the home video scene. Once HD DVD went away, Blu-ray didn't quite reach the popularity that DVD enjoyed because consumers were starting to get used to content delivered on-demand instead of on-disc. As such, Blu-ray authoring programs were also not as popular. Many of the software companies that sold Blu-ray creation tools have either stopped supporting them or have sold off their applications. Both Apple and Adobe have essentially abandoned DVD Studio Pro and Encore, which were two of the most popular disc-making tools on the market. So, while the demand for Blu-rays and DVDs may still exist from corners of the market such as education and film festivals, the tools for compressionists to make discs are going away rapidly.

Next is the Blu-ray Disc Movie (BDMV) specification, which offers the same level of authoring functionality as current DVDs but can include Blu-ray content and can write to Blu-ray media. This is the level of functionality provided by Adobe Encore, which essentially extends its DVD authoring capabilities to Blu-ray.

The least functional specification is Blu-ray Disc Audio/Visual (BDAV), which is offered by consumer-level programs such as CyberLink's PowerProducer. BDAV discs don't have menus, and viewers choose videos via a file manager available in all Blu-ray players. This can make playback comparatively primitive compared to BDMV options, at least until the video starts playing, at which point the quality of the high-definition video should be identical.

Recording Blu-ray Discs

There are essentially three ways to create a disc that will play in Blu-ray players.

- Record a BDMV-formatted project to a full-capacity disc on a Blu-ray recorder. This is *probably* what most readers want to do, and it's what we'll demonstrate with Adobe Encore in this chapter.

- Record a BDAV-formatted disc to a full-capacity Blu-ray Disc on a BD recorder, which is the level of Blu-ray support afforded by most consumer video-production programs, including CyberLink PowerPro-ducer, which is shown in **Figure 8.3**.

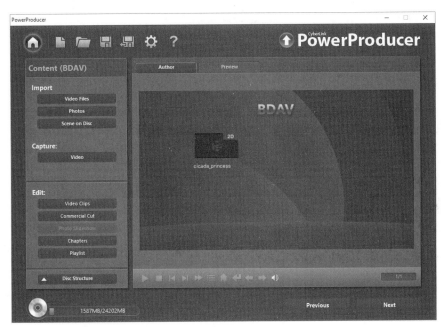

Figure 8.3 *Producing a BDAV disc in CyberLink's PowerProducer. This is a full-capacity single-layer Blu-ray Disc.*

- Record a BDMV-formatted disc to an SD DVD. Though recorded on SD media, this disc will play back only on Blu-ray players. We're recording to a dual-layer disc that will provide up to 63 minutes of Blu-ray video at the default 17,000 Kbit/s. This "hybrid" approach has the advantage of enabling HD production on normal DVD drives.

With this technical information as background, let's look at the different workflows you'll deploy to actually produce your DVDs.

That Whole Bit Budget Thing

For those of you jumping in at this section, *bit budgeting* refers to assigning audio and video bitrates to your source footage to make sure the compressed footage fits on your selected media. If you're working with an integrated editing/authoring solution, you probably have to bit budget only when you're ready to produce your disc. With most programs, you'll have some kind of meter showing disc capacity as your guide.

On the other hand, when working with separate programs such as Adobe Premiere Pro and Adobe Encore, you'll want to perform your bit budgeting before rendering from your editor to avoid double compression. Fortunately, bit budgeting is pretty simple. Each disc has a known capacity, and you have a certain number of minutes of content, so divide the latter into the former to figure out the data rate you need to fit the content on disc.

Complicating this equation is that capacity is measured in giga*bytes*, while data rate is measured in mega or kilo*bits*; in addition, you probably care more about *minutes* of content on the disc, rather than *seconds*. To simplify things, we've illustrated the math in **Table 8.3** and **Table 8.4**.

Specifically, Table 8.3 answers the initial question you should always ask when producing a DVD: "Do I have to care?" That is, if you encode at the maximum data rate supported by the device, do you have sufficient disc capacity for the video in your project?

Table 8.3 *Bit budgeting for DVDs at maximum capacity*

Measurement	Blu-ray	Standard DVD
Capacity (in bytes)	25,000,000,000	4,700,000,000
In bits (times 8)	200,000,000,000	37,600,000,000
Per sec max	40,256,000	8,000,000
Seconds	4,968	4,700
Minutes (divide by 60)	83 (79)	78 (74)

For Blu-ray devices, if you encode at the maximum bit rate, which probably isn't necessary, you still have 83 minutes of capacity, though we always round the calculated number down by 5 percent to be safe, which brings us to the number in parentheses, 79. For DVD, where it's recommend you stay below 8 Mbit/s combined audio and video data rate, the number is 74 minutes. If you have less content than any of these numbers, you're safe.

If you're exceeding that number, you must compute the bit budget for each second of compressed video, which is illustrated for a project with 100 minutes in Table 8.4. Briefly, you use the same capacity divided by the seconds of video in your production. Again, the computed rate for 100 minutes is shown first, and then 95 percent of that is in parentheses.

Table 8.4 *Bit budgeting for projects with 100 minutes*

Measurement	Blu-ray	Standard DVD
Capacity (in bytes)	25,000,000,000	4,700,000,000
In bits (times 8)	200,000,000,000	37,600,000,000
Minutes of content	100	100
Seconds of content (times 60)	6,000	6,000
Per second data rate	33.33 (31.67) Mbit/s	6.27 (5.95) Mbit/s

Remember to include the capacity needs of motion menus, slideshows, and first-play videos in your computation of total minutes of video. If you have unusually lengthy audio menus, you should subtract the total bit rate for that audio from the available capacity before dividing the balance by the number of minutes of video.

Once you have the total data rate, you're in charge of divvying up that bit rate between audio and video. We typically use 192 Kbit/s for stereo audio and allocate the rest to video. If you're producing in six-channel, 5.1 surround sound, you might go as high as 448 Kbit/s.

As they say in the construction business, when you calculate bit budget, "Measure twice, cut once." Encoding video can take quite a long time. You don't want to spend hours and hours encoding just to find out that your content won't fit on the disc.

Note that there are several online sites with bitrate calculators, including *www.videohelp.com/calc.htm*, which even lets you download the calculator for desktop use when not online.

Whew! That's enough background. Let's produce some discs. We'll start with creating a Blu-ray Disc with Adobe Encore and then briefly cover a way to create a simple DVD using Apple's Compressor.

Recipe for Producing Blu-ray Discs

While Adobe Encore is officially unsupported, your Creative Cloud still gives you access to it. See "Installing Adobe Encore" for more information. With Encore you get BDMV authoring, which is basically the same feature set you get with SD DVDs, and you can burn single-layer Blu-ray Discs that can hold 25 GB of data.

Installing Adobe Encore

Adobe announced that its disc-authoring application Encore would not be updated past version CS6, effectively marking the end of its life. But the software still works, and if you have a Creative Cloud license, you can install it with a little bit of work.

1. Open the Creative Cloud menu and click the Apps tab.

2. Find the listing for Premiere Pro CC and click the triangle button to the right of the Open/Update/Install button (**Figure 8.4**).

3. Choose Other Versions and click the install button next to CS6 (**Figure 8.5**).

Adobe Premiere CS6 will begin to install, and with it comes Adobe Media Encoder and Encore.

Figure 8.4 *Choose Other Versions to reveal the installer for older versions.*

Figure 8.5 *Click the install button for CS6 to install Premiere Pro CS6, which will also install Adobe Media Encoder and Adobe Encore.*

Encore is fairly compatible with most Blu-ray burners available. We've had good luck with drives from LaCie and LG but have run into problems with the Pioneer BDR-101. Preference is given to external USB drives because it simplifies working on multiple systems.

We've successfully used both Ridata and Verbatim media with the LaCie unit but can't vouch for any other brands. Find one that works for you, and stick with it.

From a bit budget perspective, let's keep it simple. Let's say that you have 80 minutes of video, which, according to Table 8.3, you can encode at the maximum data rate of 40 Mbit/s and still fit the video on disc.

Working in Premiere Pro

You can and should insert chapter markers in Premiere Pro since this gives you frame-accurate placement and the ability to view the audio waveforms, which makes it simple to find periods of quiet and/or applause that mark many chapter points.

To set a chapter marker, follow these steps:

1. Move Premiere Pro's Current Time Indicator to the target frame, right-click, and choose Set Chapter Marker (**Figure 8.6**).

Figure 8.6 *Right-click the Current Time Indicator to access the context menu.*

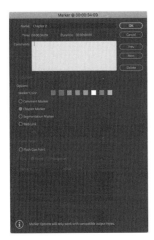

Figure 8.7 *Inserting a chapter marker in Premiere Pro*

2. In the dialog that appears, type the desired chapter name in the Chapter Marker Name field, and click OK (**Figure 8.7**). Encore can use this field to name buttons that you link to when creating your menus, so we always name our chapter markers precisely, including the capitalization we want for that button in our menu.

Producing an H.264 Blu-ray-Compatible File in the Adobe Media Encoder

To create an H.264 Blu-ray-compatible file from Premiere Pro using Adobe Media Encoder, follow these steps:

1. Choose File > Export > Adobe Media Encoder. In the Export Settings window (**Figure 8.8**), choose the following:

   Format: Choose H.264 Blu-ray.

   Preset: Choose a preset that matches your source footage and quality goals. In this example, we'll use HD 1080p 23.976.

   Export Video/Export Audio: Choose which content types to include in the final stream. We'll select both.

   Source Range: Choose either Entire Sequence or Work Area.

Figure 8.8 *Initial export settings in the Adobe Media Encoder*

2.   Customize your video settings for H.264 video by selecting the Video tab
(**Figure 8.9**) and choosing the following:

Figure 8.9 *Encore's H.264
Blu-ray configuration
options*

Video Dimensions [pixels]: This should follow your choice of preset.
If incorrect, change to match your source footage.

Frame Rate (fps): This should follow your choice of preset. If incorrect,
change to match your source.

Field Order: This should be Progressive if the preset is a 1080p preset.
If the chosen preset is interlaced, then it should be Upper.

Aspect Ratio/Profile/Level: If configurable (as shown), accept the
default values.

TV Standard: Choose the appropriate standard. The standard for the
United States is NTSC.

Bitrate Encoding: VBR, 1 Pass, and 2 Pass encoding are available. Choose
the desired method.

Target and Maximum Bitrate [Mbit/s]: We could fit our 80 minutes of
video at Blu-ray's maximum bit rate of 40 Mbit/s, but this increases the
risk of playback problems. Stick with the presets here unless the footage
is very challenging.

3. Configure your audio settings. Select the Audio tab (**Figure 8.10**), and choose PCM for the Audio Format. (We'll encode to Dolby Digital in the next section in Encore.) Leave all other encoding options at their defaults.

Figure 8.10 *Choose PCM as the format in the Audio Format Settings.*

4. Select your output destination and name the file. Click the green Play button in the upper-right corner to begin the encode process.

Creating a Blu-ray Disc in Encore

Now that you have your assets encoded, it's time to start work in Encore. Here are the steps:

1. Launch Encore, and choose New Project in the Encore splash screen (or choose File > New Project in Encore). On the Basic tab of the New Project window (**Figure 8.11**), choose the following:

Figure 8.11 *If working with 1080p content, your project settings should match these.*

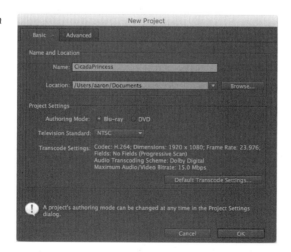

Authoring Mode: Choose Blu-ray.

Television Standard: This should be NTSC if your project is 29.97 or 23.976 frames per second.

2. Click the Default Transcode Settings button (**Figure 8.12**), and choose the following:

Automatic Transcoding: Choose the desired maximum.

Audio Transcoding: Choose Dolby Digital.

Then click OK to close the dialog, and start the new project.

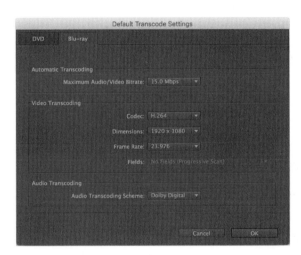

Figure 8.12 *Setting advanced encoding options as the Default Transcode Settings.*

3. Import the encoded content from the previous step.

Now you have your project set up and assets imported. The main concerns at this point are to make sure you don't re-encode the video or audio unnecessarily. You can resolve both issues on the Project tab (**Figure 8.13**).

Figure 8.13 *The status of the content on the Project tab*

For example, you can see that the H.264 file CicadaPrincess_071614_ v1.m4v has Don't Transcode in both the Blu-ray Transcode Status and Blu-ray Transcode Settings columns. This means that Encore finds the asset Blu-ray Disc compliant and won't re-encode when recording the disc; it will simply copy the content to the disc. If you see Untranscoded for video files that you've attempted to encode into Blu-ray format, Encore will automatically transcode the video while building the disc, which can make the build process take much longer.

4. Before you panic, check to make sure you're looking at the right column and are looking at the Blu-ray Transcode Status column, not DVD Transcode Status, which precedes Blu-ray status in the window (you can adjust which columns display by right-clicking the label area, choosing Columns, and then choosing the desired column). If you're looking at the Blu-ray Transcode columns and the video columns say Untranscoded, you have to review your encode settings in Media Encoder.

5. Select both the video and audio and then click the Page icon at the bottom of the project window. Select Timeline. A new timeline with your encoded content in it will appear.

6. Connect any menus and configure the timeline's end action by clicking the timeline in the Project panel and then adjusting settings in the Properties panel (**Figure 8.14**).

Figure 8.14 *The Properties panel allows you to specify an end action such as play another timeline, play that timeline again (loop), or simply to stop the player.*

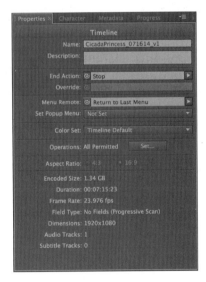

7. When you're ready to produce your disc, choose File > Build > Disc.

8. Choose Blu-ray as the Format option and Blu-ray Disc as the Output option and then click Build (**Figure 8.15**). If you have problems, first try creating a Blu-ray image, save that to your hard drive, and then use it as your source for the next attempted burn. If you can create the image but can't successfully record it to Blu-ray Disc, try a third-party recording program, or try copying the image to a different computer and recording to disc there.

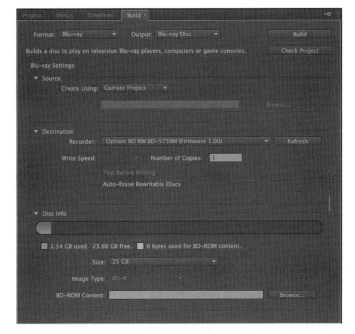

Figure 8.15 *Building your Blu-ray Disc*

Recipe for Producing SD DVDs

If you need to make a full-fledged DVD with multiple menus and custom buttons, you'll need to find a copy of an application like Apple's DVD Studio Pro (which Apple no longer supports) or Vegas DVD Architect or install Adobe Encore (see the previous "Installing Adobe Encore" sidebar for instructions). But if all you need is to make a simple auto-play disc as a work-in-progress screener or as a backup for a film festival, you can use Apple Compressor to encode and create the disc or disc image for you. Just follow these steps:

1. Import the movie to be encoded into Compressor.

2. In the settings panel on the left of the interface (you may have to click the Show/Hide Settings & Locations button in the top-left corner of the window), drag the Create DVD settings group onto the item in the batch window (**Figure 8.16**).

Figure 8.16 *Adding the Create DVD settings group to the batch list item*

3. Select the output location of your encoded files by right-clicking the default location and choosing Location from the contextual menu.

4. Select the batch item and the job inspector on the right, scroll down until you find the Action section, and choose Create DVD as the post-encode action. Adjust the settings as desired (**Figure 8.17**).

Figure 8.17 *The Action panel is where the options to create a DVD or disc image live in Compressor.*

5. If you want to simply build a disc image to burn later, select Hard Drive under Output Device, and then choose File under Build Type. If you want to burn a disc right away and have a DVD burner connected, you can choose that device. We usually recommend creating a disc image

first and then using the Finder or a program like Roxio's Toast to burn the final disc. This allows you to go through the creation process once and then burn as many copies as you need without rebuilding the disc each time.

6. Click Start Batch to begin encoding. An .m2v file and an .ac3 file will be saved to the output location, and if you selected Hard Drive in the Action settings, an .img file or DVD folder will be there as well. If you selected your DVD drive under Output Device, you'll be prompted to insert a blank disc.

Using HD Source Material for DVD

Apple's Compressor has come a long way since the initial release. In older versions, there were issues with creating nice-looking DVD downconversions. Compressor 4 appears to have fixed some of the problems with using 1920 × 1080 source material with the MPEG2 DVD encoder. However, if you aren't happy with the image quality you get from the automatic/default settings, you can sometimes get a higher-quality encode by splitting the resize into a separate operation from the encode.

All content on a DVD is encoded at 720 × 480, with pixel aspect ratios of 0.9 for 4 × 3 content and 1.33 for 16 × 9 content. If you want to take control of the resize, you can use a program like Adobe After Effects to resize your program from 1920 × 1080 to 720 × 480 with a pixel aspect ratio of 0.9 and render to a codec like ProRes. This will create an anamorphic intermediate file that will appear squeezed (everyone and everything will look too tall). When you bring this anamorphic intermediary into Compressor, you can dive into the DVD video settings and switch the Anamorphic setting from Automatic to On, which will apply the correct pixel aspect ratio to your squeezed footage, and turn it back into wide-screen video when played in a DVD player. You'll know you've done it right because in your final DVD player, the window will be rectangular in shape rather than square, and your content will appear normal.

Separating the resize operation from the encode is a great way to isolate visual artifacts to a specific part of the process. This allows you to adjust settings related to the portion of the compression process directly responsible for creating unwanted artifacts in your efforts to avoid them.

Apple's Compressor is a good way to get a down-and-dirty DVD out the door with minimal effort and hassle. While it doesn't give you much control over menu styles or the ability to create a disc with multiple tracks, it works for those times when you just need to get a piece of content onto a disc quickly.

While the need to create DVDs has greatly diminished in recent years, you still might need to create one every now and again. Having a DVD creation tool in your toolkit is still recommended, even if you don't use it often.

Conclusion

Delivering video content on physical media is almost a thing of the past. There are several areas where Blu-ray and even DVD discs are still very much a required delivery format. But the software tools are becoming extinct, and it won't be long before creating discs will be almost a completely niche process.

But then again, you may very well not care about DVD and Blu-ray distribution, and you wouldn't be alone. Many people are skipping physical media altogether and going straight to the Web with their content. Compared to DVD encoding, creating and encoding video for the Web is a lot less standard—nearly anything is possible. While that may seem liberating, it actually makes optimizing the video more difficult because you have almost too many options.

Interview with a Compressionist

Name: Aaron Owen

Location: San Francisco, California

Title/role: Cofounder

Company: Cinematiq

URL: *https://www.cinematiq.com*

How did you get started in video compression or video streaming?

While in high school, I worked on a cable-access TV show, and the producer sent the editors to a class where we thought we'd be learning Final Cut Pro. Instead of learning about how the nonlinear editor worked, the instructor spent most of the time explaining the ins and outs of compression.

He introduced us to a piece of software called Media Cleaner and reinforced that pretty much everything in digital video involves compression in one way or another. The class came with a book called *QuickTime for the Web*, which I read cover to cover.

What role does compression/streaming play in your daily work?

Much of what we do at Cinematiq involves preparing our clients' content for delivery. We create DCPs for digital cinema, Blu-ray and DVD discs (yes, there's still a market for DVDs apparently), and files for web delivery. Each of these formats requires specific compression requirements, and we pride ourselves on developing workflows to deliver our clients' work at the highest quality possible.

What does your encoding workflow look like?

We use Adobe Media Encoder and Apple Compressor for quite a bit of what we do. They are solid tools that have really come a long way over the years. We also use a JPEG 2000 encoder from Fraunhofer called easyDCP and a garden variety of other software tools for handling files that are hard to work with.

For hardware, we use a mix of custom-built Windows PCs and Macs all sharing the same files from a NAS system.

What surprises you most about video compression today?

I'm surprised I still have to deal with legacy issues like fractional frame rates such as 29.97. I thought for sure that the future would simplify video, and in some ways it has. In other ways, the ecosystem is more complex than it's ever been. Back in the day, there used to be only two or three video standards like NTSC and PAL. Now there's not really anything that's "standard." There are about four common delivery frame sizes and something like nine common frame rates, which means there are *lots* more ways to skin the proverbial cat these days.

How has video compression changed in the time you've been working with it?

An editor I used to work with once said, "There were no good ol' days. Everything is better now," which I find to be true for the most part. That said, I've often found that the faster we make computers, the faster we figure out ways to slow them down. We are now processing images at sizes that are *so* much larger than what we used to. I just worked on a project where we delivered image sequences at 14k × 14k in 16 bit. That just seems nuts compared to what we were doing 20 years ago in trying to make video look good at 640 × 480. Internet speeds have gotten so much faster, which means there's a lot less pressure to make the files as small as possible and more of a focus on delivering a quality image.

There's also been a shift from content producers and owners compressing and delivering their own content to meet a specification to platforms like Netflix and YouTube doing most of the heavy lifting on the encoding with heavily optimized proprietary encoders. So, yeah, everything is better than it used to be.

What's the one thing you wished you had known about video compression when you were starting out?

If I had to pick one thing, it's probably that different encoders use a different base unit for bitrate. Some use kilobytes per second, some use megabits per second, while others use megabytes per second. But I'm not sure that there's just one thing I wished I knew. When I was just starting out, a 30-second commercial took around 10 minutes to encode to Sorenson Video 3 with our in-house settings. In those days, I wished for faster computers so that I could run more test encodes to see with my own eyes exactly how each parameter affected the final output. Like I mentioned earlier, there was a lot of pressure to deliver really good-quality results at the smallest file size possible so that clients with limited Internet speeds wouldn't have to wait forever to download works in progress. I wanted the ability to run lots of tests quickly because the encoders weren't as good as they are today.

What's the next big thing we should be watching in the world of video compression?

In the world of video compression, the only constant is that things are always changing. HDR, VR, and augmented reality are going to have a huge impact on the future technology that will be developed for compressionists. I think we're approaching the upper limits of spatial resolution and that the next big advances will be in how to best increase temporal resolution without negatively impacting aesthetics. Rethinking temporal resolution has the ability to completely upend the entire pipeline from acquisition onset all the way to delivery. It's an exciting time to be involved with video for sure.

Compression for Digital Cinema and Broadcast

9

One method of video delivery that used to be relegated to the realm of "big-iron" post houses and studios that could afford the expensive equipment is cinema and broadcast delivery. The recent convergence of video and IT technology, however, has made it possible for software solutions to replace the industry's reliance on dedicated hardware systems. In practice, this means both the cinema and broadcast worlds have transitioned to digital systems that are file based.

A Brief History of Package Formats

Let's take a step back to look at how we got to this point. In 2002, the major Hollywood studios and distributors decided that there were significant cost advantages in transitioning the motion-picture industry away from a photochemical and celluloid system to a digital one. At the time, there were quite a few competing systems beginning to be installed at theaters around the world, and studios realized that it was to their advantage to create a single standard that could be adopted worldwide. The studios and distributors formed an alliance called the Digital Cinema Initiative (DCI). The idea was to create a single digital cinema standard based on open technologies. Afraid that a single technology provider could gain a monopoly as some had done in the past, DCI chose to restrict itself to only using technologies in this new standard that were unencumbered with intellectual property and licensing issues.

Many of the engineers involved with DCI had been involved with the creation of other digital standards including DVD, HD DVD, and Blu-ray, so it's no surprise that the approach taken bears quite a few similarities to that which had come before. Audio and video were to be encoded and stored separately, and subtitle and captions were to be rendered at the time of display (projection) without the need to "burn in" the words to the picture. These design choices meant that movies could be delivered in many different versions without needing to completely re-encode the video each time, saving these large content studios millions of dollars per title.

What emerged from the DCI alliance was a new format called the Digital Cinema Package (DCP). The chosen video codec was JPEG 2000, which is a high-quality wavelet-based codec with support for multiple resolution levels. This means a DCP created at 4K would be able to be played on a 2K projector without any special equipment or re-encoding. Audio would be encoded as 48 kHz, 24-bit PCM audio with support for up to 16 channels. Subtitles and captions could be rendered either as PNG files with alpha channels or as text in an XML document and placed over the picture by the projector. These separate media assets would be glued together by XML files that would contain the specific instructions about how to correctly play the title in the theater. On July 20, 2005, version 1.0 of the specification was completed, and the DCP format was born. However, this initial spec was intended to be a temporary solution while the Society of Motion Picture and Television Engineers (SMPTE) ratified a more full-featured specification as a suite of international standards.

After the initial DCP specification was launched, many in the film industry wanted to apply the lessons learned from the development of the DCP spec to releasing a mezzanine mastering format that could help keep versioning under control for various distribution channels such as broadcast, Blu-ray and DVD, and VOD platforms such as Netflix and Hulu. Content owners were finding it harder to keep up with the sheer volume of file-based deliverables they needed to create, manage, and archive. Using the evolved DCP specification as a starting point, engineers at SMPTE created the Interoperable Master Format (IMF).

These package formats are increasingly important to anyone seeking any sort of digital distribution release, be it online or in theaters. You'll learn about IMF in greater detail at the end of this chapter. For now, let's take a look at this question: what exactly is a DCP?

Dissecting a DCP

The Digital Cinema Package can take one of two forms: the older InterOp (IOP) format and the newer SMPTE format (**Figure 9.1**, **Figure 9.2**, and **Figure 9.3**).

NOTE Support of the SMPTE DCP format is still being rolled out globally. For now, the older InterOp format is much safer and less likely to fail.

Name	^	Size	Kind
▼ CoinOperated_SHR_S-239_EN_51_2K_20170310_CMQ_IOP_OV		--	Folder
7898e0d5-7477-41d0-a0a4-1aa578f7c59e_j2c.mxf		6.92 GB	Media Exchange Format
a5e912c5-caff-42be-8cdb-72686535e8ba_pcm.mxf		272.5 MB	Media Exchange Format
ASSETMAP		2 KB	TextEdit Document
CPL_138eabd4-1527-4c01-8913-892c8edaa71d.xml		11 KB	XML
PKL_8fc9f684-7861-4e07-91af-6418a966370e.xml		11 KB	XML
VOLINDEX		337 bytes	TextEdit Document

Figure 9.1 *This is what a simple InterOp DCP looks like on your computer.*

Name	^	Size	Kind
▼ Schattenlicht_SHR_F-178_GSW-en_51_2K_20171212_CMQ_SMPTE_OV		--	Folder
78098905-cc1f-495e-9a0f-a80878f9b868_pcm.mxf		354.5 MB	Media Exchange Format
ASSETMAP.xml		2 KB	XML
ba5ef593-f7bb-4951-baed-b2157aefcf3c_j2c.mxf		2.55 GB	Media Exchange Format
CPL_8260c333-c990-444b-a65d-3286070859a8.xml		11 KB	XML
PKL_4c1e6ac2-ea71-4a3b-92a1-f87e98dd6a04.xml		11 KB	XML
VOLINDEX.xml		194 bytes	XML

Figure 9.2 *This is what a simple SMPTE DCP looks like on your computer.*

Name	^	Size	Kind
▼ SUM-OF-HISTORIES_FTR-2_S-239_NL-XX_51_2K_20171002_CMQ_IOP_OV		--	Folder
2af7372b-2b2a-4efe-bd2b-7d3364f8d843_pcm.mxf		1.04 GB	Media Exchange Format
39e80a6a-9df8-4864-a5a3-8545838983a2_j2c.mxf		29.41 GB	Media Exchange Format
68c778c3-c1ab-4888-947b-fe0c6a0ff322_pcm.mxf		1.04 GB	Media Exchange Format
98f00c3d-d9fd-472c-937a-95a50ffa02d9_j2c.mxf		28 GB	Media Exchange Format
69419e6c-093c-478b-a380-b4949f49b99b_pcm.mxf		1.04 GB	Media Exchange Format
ASSETMAP		3 KB	TextEdit Document
c8089043-9f93-4dfc-94a1-1bd64bcd9d63_pcm.mxf		404.1 MB	Media Exchange Format
CPL_ea128d23-f9b3-43fd-b27b-bcda22785ca2.xml		14 KB	XML
ddaf7c73-6971-43c0-ad7c-4f173c70910d_pcm.mxf		1.04 GB	Media Exchange Format
ed7c96f8-cccb-44e9-9a5f-3c485a0d13f0_j2c.mxf		29.06 GB	Media Exchange Format
f6c4a555-9387-4302-adaf-effab719f197_j2c.mxf		6.77 GB	Media Exchange Format
f3329499-ad4c-437a-9fbd-d2a8d57105f7_j2c.mxf		30.59 GB	Media Exchange Format
PKL_98f0e7c6-c8c3-4b27-838f-a1d6f9562bd7.xml		13 KB	XML
VOLINDEX		337...ytes	TextEdit Document

Figure 9.3 *This is an example of an InterOp DCP with multiple reels.*

Essentially, a DCP is the digital equivalent of a 35 mm film print. Traditionally, movies are finished in reels. In the days of 35 mm film, each projection reel was 2000 ft, which translates to about 22 min. A feature-length movie usually had about five or six reels. One of the goals of the transition to digital was to make it as easy as possible to transition to digital using established postproduction workflows, so this concept of reels was built into the DCP format from the beginning. We'll come back to this in a moment.

What Comprises a DCP?

At the highest level, a DCP is a collection of various files that when combined into the same folder allows the playback server in the theater to play your movie. Each one of these files has an important role, and without all of them, the package wouldn't be valid, and the server won't recognize or play it.

The simplest DCP is composed of at least six files.

- **ASSETMAP file:** The ASSETMAP is an XML file that lists all of the assets, along with their universally unique identifiers (UUIDs) and paths to the specified files on the delivery drive. The purpose of the ASSETMAP is to associate the UUID with the file path so that the ingest system can find the files it needs.

- **VOLINDEX file:** This is an old and mostly deprecated file that allows DCPs to span multiple physical disks. This file assigns a volume number to each disk. Because disks today are much larger than they were at the beginning of the standard, almost all DCPs can fit onto a single disk. As such, VOLINDEX isn't really relevant but is still required.

- **Composition playlist (CPL):** The CPL file is the heart of a DCP. This XML document contains all the instructions about how to play the composition. In the CPL there's information about the reel list, asset list, edit rate (frame rate), duration, unique IDs associated with each media asset, screen aspect ratio, content title, issuer, and creator. It also contains the digital signature, which ensures the content is authentic and hasn't been altered in any way between creation and projection (**Figure 9.4**).

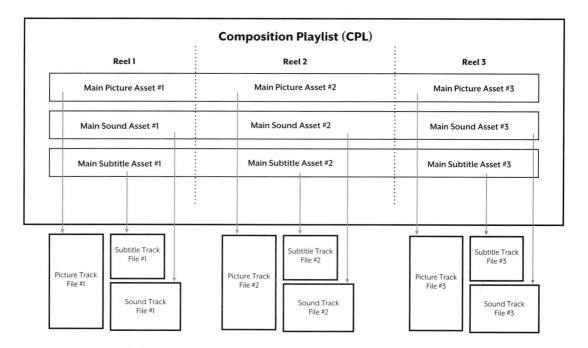

Figure 9.4 *A diagram of a multireel composition playlist and how the CPL combines and sequences the various media essence files into tracks for playback*

- **Packing list (PKL):** The PKL is another file that tells the ingest system what assets are contained in the package and lists what role they play in the package.

- **One main picture essence per reel:** A DCP is composed of one or more *reels.* This emulates how celluloid film was broken up into shorter pieces to make transport and handling easier. Each reel must contain a *main picture* essence, which is an MXF file with containing frames encoded using the JPEG 2000 codec.

- **One main sound essence per reel:** In addition to the main picture, each reel must contain a *main sound* essence, which is a separate MXF file containing multiple channels of audio encoded at 48 KHz, 24-bit, PCM audio.

When all of these elements are in place inside the same folder structure, the finished DCP is ready for playback (**Figure 9.5** on the next page).

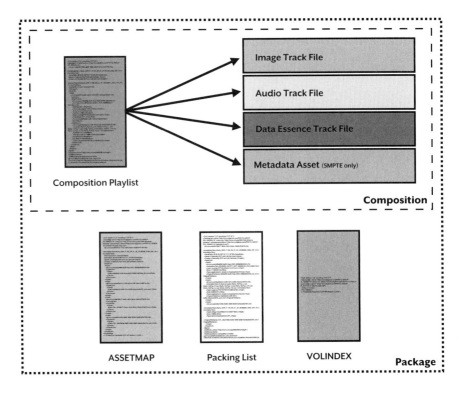

Figure 9.5 *A diagram of the finished sample DCP*

Digital Cinema Naming Convention

The simple example listed in Figure 9.1 doesn't contain subtitles because the film appears to be in English, supports surround sound, and uses the scope container. How can you tell? By reading the name of the folder, which adheres to the Digital Cinema Naming Convention. This naming convention was put into place by the Inter-Society Digital Cinema Forum (ISDCF), an industry group tasked with documenting best practices, recommending changes for the IOP and SMPTE specifications, and facilitating industry discussion of any technical issues that might arise (**Figure 9.6**).

The Digital Cinema Naming Convention standardized the abbreviation of certain important metadata elements such as content type, resolution, date of release, studio, rating, creation facility, version number, and so on. The goal of the naming convention was to ensure that projectionists received files named consistently regardless of what facility or studio the movie came from. The idea was that this would reduce the number of projection errors associated with the automation of the projectionist job once the transition to digital was complete.

If you think this naming convention seems confusing and error prone, you're not alone. It was developed as a bit of a workaround in the InterOp days when this important metadata couldn't be embedded into the package. It's important to note that the newer SMPTE format contains specific places where this metadata can be placed and therefore read automatically by the projection system. Any piece of information that can be put into the naming convention should be placed into these special fields if you're creating an SMPTE package.

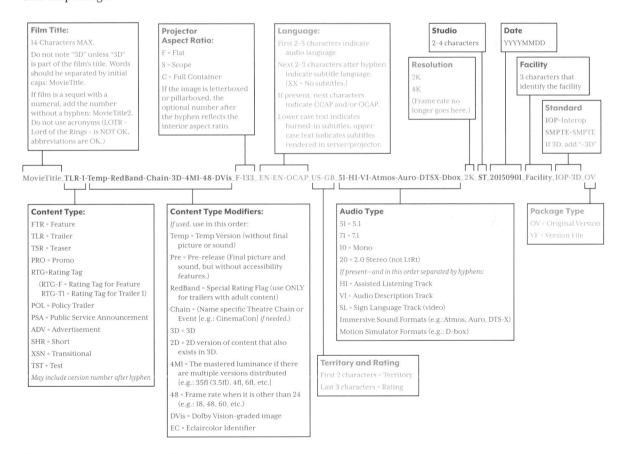

Figure 9.6 *The Inter-Society Digital Cinema Forum provides the digital cinema naming convention for the industry. You can find the up-to-date version at http://isdcf.com/dcnc/.*

More About CPLs

As mentioned earlier, the heart of the DCP is the CPL. This XML file is human-readable and can be opened in a text editor. Even though all the media is contained in separate files, this is the file that is accessed and played by the server in the theater. Without it, the server would just have a lot of different MXF media files but no idea about what order to play them in; how to synchronize audio, video, and subtitles/captions; and what frame rate to play everything at. Basically, it would be a mess.

The CPL glues all of these disparate files together into something coherent. The same media essence files can be reused by multiple DCPs that may be on the same drive if they are referenced by multiple CPLs. For example, if a movie is being shipped with multiple language versions, there would be a CPL that specifies the use of an English language audio track in one DCP, and a separate CPL could reference the same video files and specify the use of an alternate language such as Spanish. In this way, the DCP format was designed to minimize the amount of re-encoding of the video assets, thus saving time and disk space.

Encryption

A DCP can be either *unencrypted*, which means that anyone with the right equipment would be able to play it, or *encrypted*, meaning the recipient needs a key to *decrypt*, or unlock, it. This key is called the *key delivery message* (KDM), and it allows the DCP to be unlocked and played back. These KDMs are XML files that are usually emailed to the theater and then put onto USB sticks for ingest into the playback system. Each KDM grants the theater to play a specific DCP on a specific server for a specific window of time. If the theater wants to move the movie from one screen to another, a new KDM must be issued.

In the independent film world, festivals that request DCPs usually request them to be sent unencrypted if they aren't coming from a major distributor. The KDM was Hollywood's answer to the fear of piracy and unauthorized screenings. The system was put into place by the studios, and it is there to serve their business model. If you are making a DCP or need to work with them in some regard, your life will be much simpler if you don't have to deal with encryption or KDMs. However, because anyone with the proper hardware or software can read your DCP whenever they want, the risks of sending out unencrypted DCPs need to be weighed against the convenience.

Version Files

Let's say you have a film that is going to cinemas in the United States and then later it might go to theaters in Mexico. You could create separate DCPs for each region like you might with QuickTime files. But with DCP that's not necessary. Instead, you create the original version (OV) for the United States, which is an unsubtitled version of the movie with an English audio track. For Mexico, you create a *supplemental* DCP or version file (VF), which is a separate package that *references* material contained in the OV along with the new Mexico-specific material.

Let's say you want to create two versions for Mexico: one with English audio and no subtitles and another that is subtitled in Spanish. By using supplemental packages, all that would need to be contained in the VF would be the new subtitle elements that aren't present in the OV. This vastly decreases the amount of re-encoding that needs to happen to create different versions of a film, as well as total file sizes since elements can be reused between versions.

So, for the version with English audio and Spanish subtitles, the video and audio track would come from the OV, while the new subtitle track would come from the VF. It's important to also realize that the CPL would also come from the VF because the CPL is the recipe for how to put all of the elements together (**Figure 9.7**).

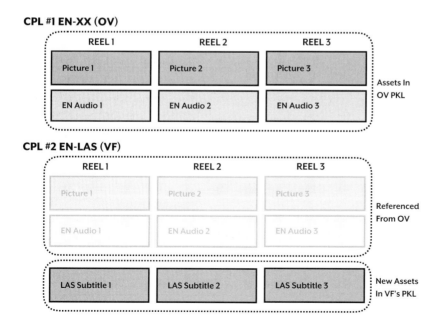

Figure 9.7 *Supplemental DCPs or VFs contain new Spanish subtitle material and references to the master picture and English audio from the OV package in order to create a new Spanish subtitled version.*

So, now you know that supplemental VF packages can be used to modify the original package with new or region-specific content. But how does this actually happen inside the playback server? Inside the ASSETMAP for each package, each element is assigned a UUID. This UUID will always be unique to the particular asset, no matter who or where it was created. Because each element in every DCP ever made has a UUID, elements can be cross-referenced in a CPL without actually being part of that package. This is much better than the alternative, which would be to reference files by file paths (which can be unreliable). Note that in order for a VF to work, both the OV and the VF must be loaded in the correct order: the OV first and then the VF.

Creating a DCP

Creating a DCP isn't quite as simple as exporting a QuickTime or MP4 file, but it's not as difficult as it used to be because of the advancement of the software tools used to create them.

Workflow for Creating a DCP

From a high-level view, creating a DCP follows similar steps as making a Blu-ray or DVD.

1. Encode the audio and video assets (separately).

2. Create subtitle and caption assets if required.

3. "Author" or wrap the assets into the standardized package.

4. Copy the package onto properly formatted delivery hardware.

Seems fairly straightforward, right? Let's unpack each step.

Encoding Picture Assets

One of the great things about a DCP is that it is a standard, and as a standard, there are certain prescriptions that must be followed. There are rules governing almost every aspect of the video-encoding process. Frame size, frame rate, aspect ratio, color space, and gamma are all defined by the standard. That means there's not much wiggle room in the encoding process, but it also means that you, as the compressionist, have fewer decisions to make along the way. The first and most time-consuming step in creating a DCP is encoding the picture assets into JPEG 2000 frames, which are then stored inside an MXF file.

Let's take a look at the standard for each component of our picture track.

Aspect Ratio and Container Size

There are two main aspect ratios in use in cinemas today: 1.85:1, or *Flat*, and 2.39:1, or *Scope*. Each of these aspect ratios can come in one of two container sizes: 2K or 4K. There is also a default container, *Full Container*, which is not typically used for delivery. **Table 9.1** shows the most common container sizes for DCP. There are two main resolution types and two main aspect ratios. All DCPs must fit into one of these four containers regardless of active picture area or aspect ratio.

Table 9.1 *DCI-compliant frame sizes*

Container	2K	4K
Flat (1.85)	1998 × 1080	3996 × 2160
Scope (2.39)	2048 × 858	4096 × 1716
Full Container (1.9)	2048 × 1080	4096 × 2160

Resolution Confusion

In cinema, the terms 2K and 4K used to mean a specific resolution. 2K meant 2048 × 1556 pixels, and 4K meant a frame size of 4096 × 3112 pixels. This was mostly used in the VFX industry because they were the first to work with digital files scanned from film. Then the entire world went digital, and different people adopted the terminology using it to mean a variety of things. These days, 2K has come to mean a frame size of roughly 2000 pixels wide, and 4K refers to a frame size of roughly 4000 pixels wide. There's a lot of marketing hype (mostly by camera manufacturers) surrounding 4K and beyond. If you are old enough to remember the megapixel wars of the mid-1990s among digital still camera manufacturers, it's similar.

You might be noticing that the Full Container width is the same as the Scope width, and the height is the same as the Flat height. This is because the Full Container frame size defines the *maximum* frame size that a DCP is allowed to be encoded at for each resolution category.

The technical specification says that for a DCP to be considered DCI compliant, one side of the frame size must match the Full Container size. The standard resolutions for the Flat and Scope containers do indeed follow these rules. However, this does not mean you should create a DCP using a nonstandard container size even if you adhere to this rule. Some projection systems expect these standard frame sizes and may give you problems if they receive something different, even if it's technically correct. For these compatibility reasons, you'll want to choose the Flat or Scope container for your DCP, even if your active image aspect ratio is different. For example, if your aspect ratio is 4:3 (1.33), you could place your active image into the Flat 1.85 container and use black pillar-boxing to fill out the rest of the container.

A common situation where the active picture area can differ from the image container occurs when making DCPs from 16 × 9 content (1.78:1) (**Figure 9.8**). The most common frame size in this aspect ratio is 1920 × 1080. This resolution technically adheres to the one-side rule (the 1080 height matches the Full Container height, which makes it legal), but in practice it's usually better to encode the content using the Flat container at 1998 × 1080 with a slight pillar box.

Figure 9.8 *This image shows an active picture area of 16 × 9 inside a Flat container (1.85:1).*

Frame Rate

Now that we've established the spatial resolution (frame size), let's look at the temporal resolution (frame rate). Digital Cinema only uses integer frame rates, which means that 24 fps really means 24 and not a fractional rate like 23.976. Likewise, 30 fps really means 30, not 29.97 as it does in the television/video world. The most common digital cinema frame and edit rate is 24 fps. Support for other common frame rates such as 25, 30, 50, and 60 is more limited and only in relatively new equipment. IOP supports only 24 (and 48 for 3D films), so if you're creating a DCP at any other frame rate, you must use the SMPTE format.

This means that if you're working with content that was shot, edited, and finished at a video rate, you'll need to convert the frame rate. This doesn't really affect the picture so much, as long as you're simply converting from a fractional rate to the corresponding integer rate. The number of frames in the movie isn't going to change. It's only the amount of time each frame will be onscreen that will change. This will affect the audio sync, so when you prepare your audio, you'll need to take this into consideration. Otherwise, the sound will drift out of sync over time.

Color Space and Gamma

This is where things get a little technical and you have to pay close attention. Digital Cinema uses a much different color space and gamma setting than what's used in the video world.

While video is typically encoded in either a Y'CbCr or RGB color space, DCP uses a color space called X'Y'Z' color space (described in CIE Publication 15:2004, *Colorimetry, 3rd Edition*). This is typically abbreviated as XYZ. Similarly, video typically uses a gamma value between 2.2 and 2.4, while DCP uses a gamma of 2.6. One way to arrive at this color space is to perform the final color grade in this space. This is the best way to achieve the highest-quality DCP. But for many projects, a theatrical DCP is a secondary output format. In these cases, a more economical workflow is to grade in a video color space and then perform the color conversion during the DCP encode process.

To perform this color conversion, you'll use a lookup table (LUT), which takes the color value from source space and translates it to the corresponding value in the destination space. Mainstream DCP creation and encoding toolsets have options built in for handling this common color and gamma conversion. It is worth noting, however, that to perform an accurate color conversion, the exact parameters of the source material need to be known. Otherwise, unintended issues such as washed-out blacks can occur.

Codec

Here's one place where there aren't many options. In fact, you have only one. The DCP spec requires the use of the JPEG 2000 codec (sometimes abbreviated as JPEG2K, which has no relationship to 2K frame sizes), and many encoders only allow the operator to adjust bitrate. JPEG2K is an intraframe codec, which means each frame is encoded completely independent of each other. For most DCPs, the highest bitrate allowed is 250 Mbit/s, so your encoding software may limit your bitrate if it is specifically designed for digital cinema.

It should be noted that not all JPEG2K encoders are built for digital cinema. There's a special digital cinema flag that is necessary, and even if your encoding software can output JPEG 2000 files, it's possible that this special flag may be missing. This means your picture content won't be compatible and may not play. To avoid this, make sure to encode with software specifically designed to encode JPEG2K for digital cinema.

Preparing the Audio

Preparing audio for packaging in a DCP can be both straightforward and slightly tricky, depending on the exact circumstances of the project. The DCI specification allows up to 16 mono channels of 48 kHz, 24-bit PCM audio (but there must be an even number of channels). In practice, all this means is that you'll want a single channel of mono audio per speaker channel. **Table 9.2** shows the ISDCF-standardized audio channel assignments as outlined in Document 4 published on the ISDCF website. For more information, see *http://isdcf.com/papers/ISDCF-Doc4-Audio-channel-recommendations.pdf.*

Table 9.2 *The standard audio channel configurations*

Channel in package	Configuration			Notes
	5.1	7.1 SDDS	7.1 DS	
1	L	L	L	Left
2	R	R	R	Right
3	C	C	C	Center
4	LFE	LFE	LFE	Screen low-frequency effects
5	Ls	Ls	Lss	Left surround (or left-side surround)
6	Rs	Rs	Rss	Right surround (or right-side surround)
7	HI	HI	HI	Hearing impaired (with emphasis on dialogue)
8	VI-N	VI-N	VI-N	Visually impaired narrative (audio description)
9	—	Lc	—	Left center
10	—	Rc	—	Right center
11	—	—	Lrs	Left rear surround
12	—	—	Rrs	Right rear surround
13	Motion Data			Synchronous signal (currently used by D-Box)
14	Sync Signal			Used for external sync (e.g., FSK Synch). Only used for SMPTE-DCP, not INTEROP-DCP
15	Sign Language Video			See Note 9
16	—			Not used at this time

We've talked a bit about frame rate conversions as they apply to video. If you've converted the frame rate from a fractional rate to an integer rate, you have a bit of work to do to synchronize the audio to match the converted frame rate. If your source rate is 23.976 and your destination frame rate is true 24, you'll need to perform what's known as *audio pull-up*. The slightly faster video rate means that the video will finish before the audio if left alone. To properly sync the audio to the video, you have to change the sample rate to have the playback system play the audio slightly faster to match the new video frame rate.

Once the audio pull-up is complete, you'll have changed the duration of the audio, and it will now sync with the 24 fps track.

Creating Subtitles and Captions

What's the difference between subtitles and captions? In a DCP, the difference is partly content, partly labeling, and partly metadata flags that alert the playback system what the intent of the content owner (you) is.

Content

The main difference between subtitles and captions is the content. With subtitles, the main goal is to translate the audio from one language to another. Subtitles are most common for English films going to international film festivals or markets. Captions, on the other hand, are meant to give additional audio information to someone who is deaf or hard of hearing. This may mean that in addition to the dialogue, there may be onscreen text describing sound effects or music.

Labeling

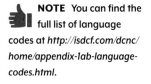 **NOTE** You can find the full list of language codes at *http://isdcf.com/dcnc/home/appendix-1ab-language-codes.html.*

If the text track is meant to be a subtitle, then the Digital Cinema Naming Convention requires a two-character language code following the audio's two-character language code, separated by a dash (**Figure 9.9**). If the text track is a caption file, then the naming convention requires that you specify whether the captions are *open captions* (OCAP) or *closed captions* (CCAP). Open captions are meant to be displayed onscreen and visible to everyone in the theater just as a subtitle track would be. Closed captions are meant to be streamed to a special device to display the text so that only those who have access to the equipment can see the captions.

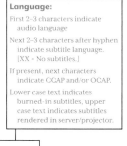

Language:

First 2–3 characters indicate audio language

Next 2–3 characters after hyphen indicate subtitle language. [XX = No subtitles.]

If present, next characters indicate CCAP and/or OCAP.

Lower case text indicates burned-in subtitles, upper case text indicates subtitles rendered in server/projector.

MovieTitle_TLR-1-Temp-RedBand-Chain-3D-4Ml-48-DVis_F-133_EN-EN-OCAP_US-GB_51-HI-VI-Atmos-Auro-DTSX-Dbox_2K_ST_20150901_Facility_IOP-3D_OV

Figure 9.9 *The Language section of the Digital Cinema Naming Convention has special instructions for how to label audio language and subtitles.*

Metadata

There are various DCP creation software packages, and most support adding subtitles and captions to your DCP. Depending on the type of track you want to add, there will be a way to add metadata to define that track as either a subtitle (or open caption) or a closed caption. This will tell the composition playlist what kind of track you're adding, which then tells the playback system what do to.

Methods

There are a couple of methods for subtitling a film for a foreign language or providing captioning for the hard of hearing and the deaf. The first is to *burn in* the text data to the picture so that it is always displayed. The second is to let the projector render the text and key it on top of the clean picture.

Burning your subtitles into the picture is the most foolproof way to ensure that your subtitles are seen as intended. Many film festivals have requirements that subtitles must be burned in. Most of the time this is because they've had a foreign-language film play without subtitles to an audience who can't understand the audio. This might sound like the simplest way to deliver your DCP, and many times it is. But there are some drawbacks as well. If you plan on releasing your title to multiple language markets, you'll have to create a new DCP for each language. This can quickly become very costly in terms of either encoding time or money.

The alternative to burning in subtitles is to create a DCP without subtitle text and have the projector render the words over the picture (**Figure 9.10** on the next page). This allows for greater flexibility, and you can change the text content without needing to re-encode the picture or audio tracks. Additional supplemental DCPs can be created for each new language version. This greatly reduces the size of your delivery and is the way the major Hollywood studios release their films internationally.

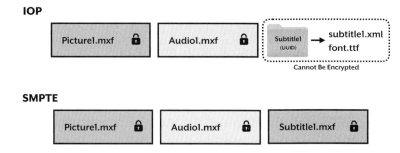

Figure 9.10 *Subtitles are handled in slightly different ways between the IOP and SMPTE formats. With IOP, subtitles are contained in a folder named for the subtitle.xml's UUID. This folder contains the timed text in an XML file, along with any ancillary files such as fonts or PNGs. With SMPTE, the subtitles (and ancillary files) are wrapped into an MXF, which can be encrypted just like the video and audio.*

Wrapping Assets into a Package

Once you have encoded all of your audio, video, and timed text assets, it's time to wrap it all up into the final DCP. This step is taken care of by your DCP creation software, and the results are files that resemble Figures 9.1 through 9.3.

Delivering the Package

DCPs are typically ingested into a theater management system (TMS), a library management system (LMS), or the playback server itself. Larger cineplexes will use either a TMS or an LMS, while smaller single- or double-screen theaters will ingest directly onto the playback server. The drive on which you send your DCP needs to be recognized by these computer systems for the system's software to ingest your DCP and validate it. Playback systems don't typically play the content from your delivery drive. Rather, they copy the DCP files onto their own super-fast internal storage RAIDs.

In an attempt to standardize the industry onto the same delivery hardware, DCI originally chose the CRU Dataport DX115 drive sled. This decision was based on the fact that the design was originally intended for a military setting and was known for being exceptionally rugged and could be plugged and unplugged hundreds or thousands of times before failing. The main reason to use the CRU drive was to increase the speed of ingest as the CRU is connected over an internal SATA connection. This means copying data from these drives is much faster than over a USB 2 connection.

Many festivals and theaters still require the use of the CRU drive as the delivery drive of choice (especially for feature-length content). However, large USB 3 thumb drives are now being used as support for USB 3 becomes more prevalent on the ingest systems found in theaters.

Anyone familiar with computers knows that filesystem compatibility across different operating systems and manufacturers is usually problematic. Playback servers usually run on a variant of Linux, and the TMS/LMS systems usually run Windows. Formatting the drive so it can be read across all systems worldwide is quite important. ISDCF has set forth its guidelines in Document 3, which state the delivery device is to be formatted according to the following guidelines:

1.2 Partitioning

Storage devices shall contain a standard "MBR" partition table. This is meant to specifically exclude "GPT", "BSD", and other partition table types. The MBR partition table shall contain one and only one partition record. The single partition record shall be the first Primary partition record.

1.3 Formatting

The partition on the storage device shall be formatted as EXT3 or EXT2, with the inode size set to 128 bytes. NOTE: These are not standard settings for the default Linux formatting command, as the defaults have evolved since this configuration was agreed upon. Following is a suggested command to format a distribution device from a Linux prompt. Various GUI-based formatting programs may require you to explicitly specify these settings.

The suggested Linux commands for both partitioning and formatting are:

```
$ parted -s /dev/sdX mklabel msdos
$ parted -s -a optimal /dev/sdX mkpart primary 0% 100%
$ mkfs -t ext3 -I 128 -m 0 /dev/sdX1
```

> **NOTE** You can download the full set of DCP delivery recommendations from *http://isdcf.com/papers/ISDCF-Doc3-Delivery-Recs.pdf*.

Even though there's a universal standard that's been defined by the definitive authority, there have been reports in certain territories (Australia, for one) of theaters not having the appropriate software on their TMS/LMS to allow their Windows computers to read Linux-formatted drives. Because exact compatibility depends on a variety of factors, unless specifically asked to provide something else, it's best to follow the ISDCF recommendations. Deluxe Technicolor, one of the largest companies responsible for sending out drives all over the world on behalf of Hollywood Studios, uses the ISDCF-recommended best practice for all its delivery drives worldwide. If you won't know ahead of time where your DCP will be playing, it's best to adhere to the ISDCF guidelines. It's also not recommended to deliver IOP and SMPTE DCPs on the same drive.

Recipes for Creating a DCP

Just like there are many different tools to create QuickTime files, there are many tools that can be used to create a DCP. Depending on your toolset, the workflow may vary.

Example DCP: Recipe 1

NOTE See the sidebar "Additional Tools for DCP Creation" later in this chapter for other tools you can use instead of those used in the examples.

In this example, we'll go through a complete sample workflow using off-the-shelf, professional software, including Adobe After Effects CC, Avid Pro Tools, easyDCP Standalone JPEG 2000 Transcoder, and easyDCP Creator.

In this example, we'll use a 1920 × 1080, 23.976 fps, ProRes QuickTime file without subtitles.

Step 1: Create Intermediate Image Sequence and Audio Sync QuickTime with Adobe After Effects CC

The first step in this particular workflow is to create an intermediate image sequence from the Digital Source Master (DSM) QuickTime file. In this example, you'll use After Effects to render out an image sequence of 16-bit TIFF files (to be encoded at a later point) and a reference 24 fps QuickTime to sync your audio.

To render out an intermediate image sequence, follow these steps in After Effects:

1. Open After Effects and create a new project. Adjust the project's color settings to 16 bit by opening the Project Settings window (Command+Option+Shift+K or Ctrl+Alt+Shift+K), clicking the Color Settings tab, and setting Depth to 16 bits per channel (**Figure 9.11**). Click OK.

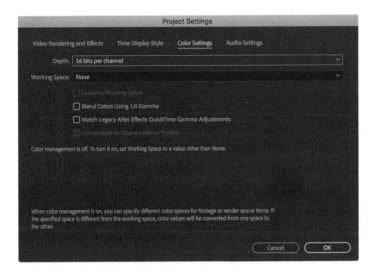

Figure 9.11 *Changing After Effects to a 16-bit project*

2. Import the DSM into the project and interpret the footage. Right-click the clip and choose Interpret Footage > Main. Click the Conform To Frame Rate button and enter **24** as the frames per second (**Figure 9.12**). Confirm that the footage is Rec. 709 by clicking the Color Management tab and checking the Embedded Profile (**Figure 9.13**).

Figure 9.12 *Conforming the clip's frame rate from 23.976 to the required true 24 fps*

Figure 9.13 *Double-check the embedded profile is Rec. 709 on the Color Management tab.*

3. Create a new composition from the conformed clip by dragging it onto the new comp button at the bottom of the project window.

4. Change the composition frame size from 1920 × 1080 to 1998 × 1080 by opening the Composition Settings panel (Command+K or Ctrl+K) and entering the new frame width. Click OK. The result should be a

pillar-boxed image with vertical black bars on the sides of the original image. The image should not be stretched to fill the screen.

5. Add the composition to the render queue (Command+Option+M or Ctrl+Alt+M) and open the Output Modules settings by clicking the blue text that probably says "Lossless." Configure the output module to render a TIFF sequence, making sure to select Trillions Of Colors as the Video Output Depth setting to ensure 16-bit output (**Figure 9.14**). Click the Format Options button to confirm that the option for LZW Compression is not checked (**Figure 9.15**).

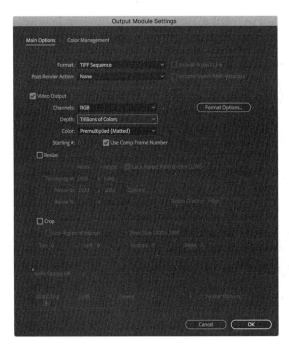

Figure 9.14 *Output Module Settings for the intermediate image sequence*

Figure 9.15 *Both boxes should be unchecked.*

6. Name the output by clicking the blue text next to the Output To label. Make sure that there are enough pound (#) signs in the name to account for the total number of frames in the movie. For example, if your Quick-Time file has 100,000 frames in it, you'll need at least six pound signs.

7. Since you're converting the frame rate from 23.976 to 24 fps, you'll also need to render out a picture reference file that you'll use in step 2 ("Step 2: Create Final Audio Tracks with Avid ProTools" on page 234) when prepping the audio. This file also can come in handy to create subtitles or caption files. Duplicate the output module by pressing Command+D (Mac) or Ctrl+D (Windows), and change it to render out a 666 × 360, H.264 QuickTime movie at 24 fps (**Figure 9.16**).

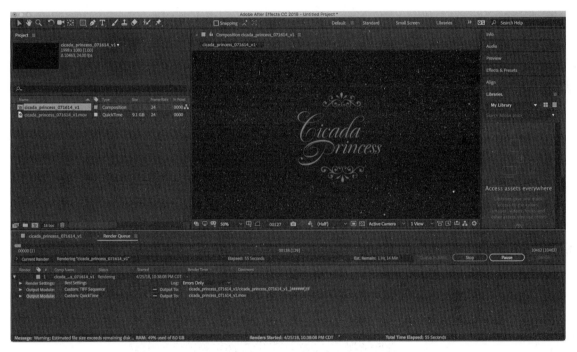

8. Click Render. Once finished, you should have a folder with a separate TIFF file for each frame in the movie (**Figure 9.17**).

Figure 9.16 *After Effects rendering out an intermediate image sequence and audio sync QuickTime file*

Figure 9.17 *The final sequence is a numbered image sequence with each file representing a separate frame.*

Step 2: Create Final Audio Tracks with Avid ProTools

For this step, you'll use Avid ProTools to prep the final audio that will be wrapped into the DCP. You'll convert the frame rate from 23.976 fps to 24 fps to match the audio sync QuickTime file. To perform this conversion, follow these steps:

1. Create a new ProTools session and select BWF as the file type, 24-bit as the bit depth, and 48 kHz as the sample rate (**Figure 9.18**).

Figure 9.18 *ProTools session settings to begin the project*

2. Import the audio sync QuickTime file rendered from After Effects in step 1 by choosing File > Import > Video. If asked, choose New Track and Session Start for the destination.

3. Import the audio mix as a WAV file by choosing File > Import > Audio. In the top part of the Import Audio dialog, browse to the WAV file for the audio mix (**Figure 9.19**). In the bottom half of the dialog, select the audio file in the Clips In Current File window. Click the Convert button. Select the Apply SRC box, and choose 48048 for the new sample rate. Applying the sample rate conversion is what performs the audio pull-up to match the video frame rate. Click Done.

Audio Pull-Up Math

To sync the 23.976 audio to the new 24 fps picture, you need to conform the sample rate of the audio so that it plays back 0.1 percent faster (in other words, 24/23.976 = 1.001001 or a 0.1 percent difference).

The audio sample rate is currently at 48 kHz, which can also be written as 48000 Hz. If you multiply your original sample rate by 0.001, you find that 0.1 percent of 48 kHz is 48. If you add this to your original sample rate, you get 48,048 Hz.

Thus, if you tell ProTools that your source file's sample rate is 48048 and import it into a 48 kHz project, it will play back 0.1 percent faster and sync with the 24 fps picture track.

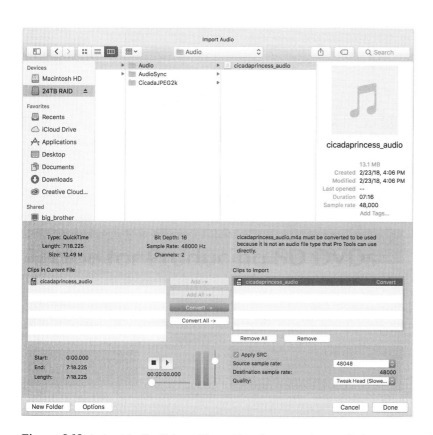

Figure 9.19 *Import Audio dialog with sample rate conversion applied*

4. Choose a destination to save your converted files to. Click OK.

5. Create a new track by dropping the sample rate converted audio below the video track. The duration should match identically (If not, trim the audio to match the length of the video). Verify that the track's output routing is routed to the correct output track.

6. Play the audio to check for lip sync problems against the audio sync QuickTime file. If correct and your duration already matched the video duration exactly, you can use the ProTools generated files as is. (You can find these in the destination you chose in step 4.) You should have a mono file for each channel.

7. If you had to trim your duration to match, you'll have to "bounce" (export) your audio to separate MONO Broadcast Wave (.wav) files, one per track (in multiples of 2). Choose File > Bounce > Disk. Select the Offline box to utilize faster than real-time exporting (**Figure 9.20**).

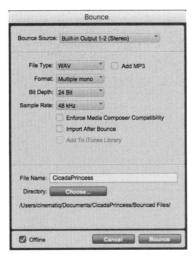

Figure 9.20 *Bounce dialog*

Step 3: Encode Intermediate TIFF Files to JPEG 2000

In this step, you'll use easyDCP Standalone JPEG 2000 Transcoder to create the final J2C image sequence that is going to be wrapped into the MXF video essence file with easyDCP Creator. Since the source was finished in the Rec. 709 color space, you'll need to convert to the XYZ color space (which will also change the gamma from 2.2 to 2.6). This is where you need to be precise with your color settings; otherwise, your color won't appear in the theater as you'd expect.

1. In easyDCP JPEG 2000 Standalone Transcoder, select the first TIFF file for the First Input File Name (**Figure 9.21**).

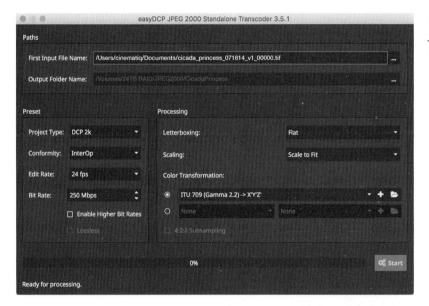

2. Select your output folder name.

3. Match the settings shown in Figure 9.21. Click Start.

4. When the encoding finishes, you'll have a folder that should be the same as your intermediate TIFF's folder, except all the frames are now .j2c files. When you open the file in Photoshop, you'll see that the color has been transformed and doesn't look "correct." This is the result of the conversion to XYZ and is completely normal.

Step 4: Check Source Files, Map Audio Tracks, and Generate Name

Now that you have your encoded picture track, with final audio files, you'll need to make sure there are no issues with the source files. EasyDCP Creator makes this simple with a built-in source file checker.

1. Launch easyDCP Creator and create a 2k InterOp 24 fps project.

2. Import the .j2c files from earlier by clicking the green +Picture button.

3. Right-click the video clip and choose Check Source Files. Select all the file checks and click Start. The source files are checked (**Figure 9.22**). If the files don't pass the check, you'll see the results of any corrupt frames to re-encode.

Figure 9.22 *Setting up source file check in easyDCP Creator*

4. After the source files check is complete, click the +Sound button. Select the correct preset for the number of audio channels you have. In this case, it's stereo. Click the three dots (…) on the left channel, and select the converted audio file from earlier. Do the same for each channel, making sure the correct file is mapped to the correct channel following the ISDCF channel layout mentioned in Table 9.2 (**Figure 9.23**). Finish the import by clicking Add Sound Track.

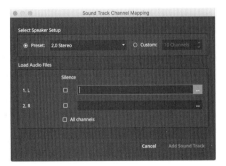

Figure 9.23 *Importing and mapping audio tracks in easyDCP Creator. If you route the wrong source channel to the wrong output channel, it will sound bad in the theater at best and potentially blow out the theater's speakers at worst.*

5. Drag the video clip and the audio clip into the box labeled New Reel.

6. In a field just below the label Package Content, you'll see a name field. This is where you can enter the content title text. Click the three dots (…) button at the right, and the Digital Cinema Naming Convention dialog opens. Refer to Figure 9.6 for the specific guidelines for entering this information and generating the name (**Figure 9.24**). Once done, click OK.

Figure 9.24 *The easyDCP Digital Cinema Naming Convention dialog makes it easy to create the DCP name according to industry guidelines.*

7. Select the entire name and copy and paste it into the PKL parameters and Composition Annotation text, which are the two other fields that require the same information. This is what generally shows up on the ingest system. Refer to **Figure 9.25**.

Figure 9.25 *Once you have a suitable name that adheres to the DCNC, you'll need to copy and paste it into these two other metadata fields.*

Step 5: Wrap Essence Files and Generate Package

This is the moment you've been working toward! easyDCP is aptly named because now that you've prepared and checked everything ahead of time, you can click a single button to have a bunch of things happen at once.

1. Click the Generate button. If you have any errors, a warning dialog appears alerting you to what isn't quite right. If everything is OK, the Generate Package Wizard opens.

2. Choose where you want your DCP to be generated, ensuring that there's enough space on your drive to build the package (**Figure 9.26**). The name of the folder should also be the same as the title of the DCP. Click Next.

Figure 9.26 *Choose an output folder where easyDCP will create your DCP.*

3. Ensure that Max Bitrate is set to 250 Mbps and click Next.

4. Double-check the summary to ensure everything is as you expect, and click Next (**Figure 9.27**). If you have Force Re-encoding Of JPEG 2000 Codestreams set to Yes, the picture will be re-encoded. To avoid this, open the easyDCP preferences and uncheck the Force Re-encode box.

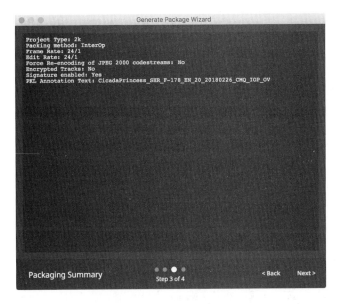

Figure 9.27 *Double-check the settings summary before the rendering the final DCP.*

5. You package will begin rendering to the location specified for audio tracks first. Once finished, a summary page appears (**Figure 9.28**).

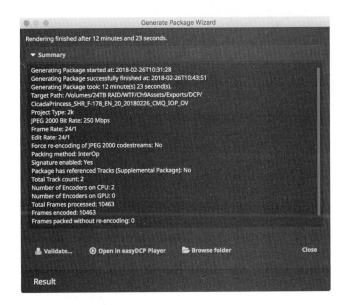

Figure 9.28 *Once your package is finished rendering, all the files necessary to play your DCP will be in the folder you specified.*

Step 6: Play Your DCP

This is where the rubber hits the road and where more than a few folks run into snags. DCPs are meant to play in theaters on expensive and sophisticated playback servers with fast storage and hardware-accelerated decoders.

If you have easyDCP Player, you can simply click the Open In easyDCP Player button to use the software player to play the DCP to check for accuracy and completeness. Aside from easyDCP, there are a number of other software players on the market including NeoDCP, Telestream Switch, and Dolby CineAsset Player.

If you're creating DCPs using 5.1 surround sound, you'll need a 5.1 surround-sound system and need to make sure that the software player supports multichannel outputs.

In short, there's a lot to be aware of and potentially a number of expensive tools you'll need to have if you want to view or validate your DCP on your computer.

Thoughts on Quality Control

Because creating a DCP is a complicated procedure and there are many steps where conversions take place, you'll want to make sure you've done everything correctly before putting your content in front of an audience. Simply playing back the DCP using a software player on the same system used to create the DCP is not a thorough QC. The only way to really see what your audience will see is to take your DCP to a theater and watch it played from a theatrical playback server through a DCI-compliant projector in the XYZ colorspace. If your film has 5.1 surround sound, then you'll really want to make sure the film sounds like you remember it from your mix session.

More often than not, QC screenings reveal issues with your audio mix that you didn't hear in the mixing studio. Audio postproduction facilities with 5.1 rooms are usually much smaller than even the smallest of theaters. Surround mixes sound can sound quite a bit different when you're physically 5 ft to 10 ft away from the speaker in the mix room than when you're 30 ft to 50 ft away in the theater. Small unwanted sounds that might have been missed in the mix are often amplified in the larger room when played at full volume. In smaller rooms, mixes that feel "surround" when audio is coming from the rear speakers can feel much more frontal when you get into the theater. There are several different software players that can give you a good idea of what you'll see on the screen, but the only real way to be sure is to go into a theater.

Step 7: Create Delivery Drive

The ISDCF guidelines can be quite tricky to adhere to unless you have a strong background in Linux systems administration. Even then, the default settings on a couple of the commands will give you results that aren't compliant and may not be read by certain cinema servers. DCP Transfer (**Figure 9.29**) is a tool that makes it super simple to format either a CRU or USB flash drive with a couple of clicks.

NOTE It's worth noting that DCP Transfer was created by author Aaron Owen's company Cinematiq after a lot of frustration making delivery drives using the Linux command line.

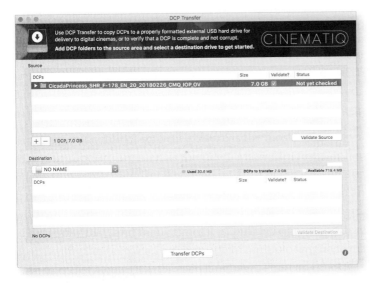

Figure 9.29 *DCP Transfer formats DCP delivery drives according to the ISDCF guidelines and performs package validation.*

1. In DCP Transfer, import your DCPs into the source area by dragging the DCP folder into the source window or by clicking the + button and locating the folder on your computer.

2. Select the drive you want to use as your destination drive. Click Transfer DCPs.

3. The options panel appears. You can validate the source and destination automatically as part of the transfer. Once you are satisfied with your options, click Start Copy (**Figure 9.30** on the next page).

Figure 9.30 *If your drive is not formatted correctly for delivery, you'll see a red X next to the drive selector in the interface and will be forced to reformat (which will erase everything on the drive).*

4. DCP Transfer begins the transfer operation. Once finished, the Transfer Successful screen appears with a summary of the operation (**Figure 9.31**).

Figure 9.31 *The ext2-formatted drive is now ready for delivery to a digital cinema.*

Example DCP: Recipe 2

While the first example used several different programs and many steps to prepare audio and video separately from each other, this example uses only two programs: Adobe Premiere Pro CC and easyDCP Publisher. easyDCP Publisher is a pay-as-you-go software that means it is free to use to create and view DCPs within the software. You pay a fee when you "publish" the DCP, which means the DCP becomes unlocked and can be sent to the theater.

Step 1: Prepare 24 fps QuickTime Files

You can use Adobe Premiere to conform your source movie to 24 fps from its native 23.976 fps.

1. Import the source file into Premiere Pro, right-click the clip, and choose Modify > Interpret Footage (**Figure 9.32**).

Figure 9.32 *Choose Interpret Footage from the Modify section of the contextual menu.*

2. Select Assume This Frame Rate and type in **24** (**Figure 9.33**). Click OK. If your audio is included in the source movie, Premiere will keep the audio in sync. If your audio is external to your video file, you'll need to use an application like SOX or ProTools to perform the sample rate conversion.

Figure 9.33 *Conform the clip to 24 fps.*

3. Create a new timeline by dragging your modified clip onto the New Item button at the bottom of the Project window.

4.   Choose File > Export > Media. In the Video tab within the export dialog, select a mezzanine format such as ProRes or a high-bandwidth H.264 file (**Figure 9.34**). Click Export.

Figure 9.34 *Exporting the timeline from Premiere Pro to a ProRes HQ file. Enable 16-bpc (bits per channel) encoding to avoid banding and other artifacts associated with 8-bit imaging.*

Step 2. Wrap DCP with easyDCP Publisher

1. Open easyDCP Publisher. Once you've logged in to your easyDCP account, click the New button at the top of the window to create a new project (**Figure 9.35**). You're going to create a 2K, monoscopic, 24 fps SMPTE DCP in this example.

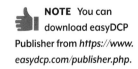 **NOTE** You can download easyDCP Publisher from *https://www. easydcp.com/publisher.php.*

Figure 9.35 *Creating a new 2K, 24 fps SMPTE DCP project in easyDCP Publisher*

2. Click the green Picture button in the top left to import the movie file from the previous step. If you have audio tracks in your movie file, those will automatically be brought in as a separate audio clip (**Figure 9.36**).

Figure 9.36 *easyDCP Publisher's UI after importing a 24 fps movie file*

3. At the bottom-right corner of the video clip, there are two icons, one for color and one for aspect ratio. Click the Color Processing icon and set it to RGB (ITU-R BT.709) (**Figure 9.37**). This interprets your clip according to video/legal levels and applies a gamma value of 2.2.

Figure 9.37 *Setting the Source Color Space for the video track.*

4. You didn't change the frame size in Premiere Pro, so you'll need to adjust the aspect ratio to conform to one of the DCI container sizes. Since the source is 1920 × 1080, choose Flat and Scale To Fit, which will result in adding a slight pillarbox (**Figure 9.38**).

Figure 9.38 *Setting the aspect ratio to Flat*

NOTE You can find the DCP language codes at *http://isdcf.com/papers/ISDCF-Doc7-DigitalCinemaLanguage Codes.pdf.*

5. Drag the video and audio clips into the area labeled Reel 1. Hover the mouse over the reel, and in the top-right corner of the reel area, you'll see the Edit Composition Parameters button. Select the appropriate Content Kind setting, and enter the two-character Issuer Language code (**Figure 9.39**).

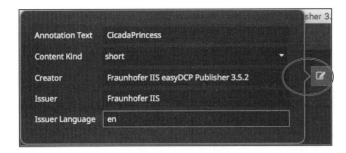

Figure 9.39 *Entering composition metadata*

6. At the bottom right of the window, click the red Preview button (see Figure 9.36). The content title text is replaced by the appropriate Digital Cinema Naming Convention name. This name is also automatically entered into the composition and PKL's Annotation Text field behind the scenes.

7. In the Preview Wizard, click Next twice, and you'll see the DCP begin to render (**Figure 9.40**). Audio will be packaged into the MXF essence first. Then the movie file will be transcoded into JPEG 2000 and those frames will be wrapped into the picture essence MXF.

Figure 9.40 *Transcoding and wrapping the DCP in one step*

Once the picture and audio essences are complete, the rest of the package elements are generated. Upon completion, a summary is shown (**Figure 9.41**).

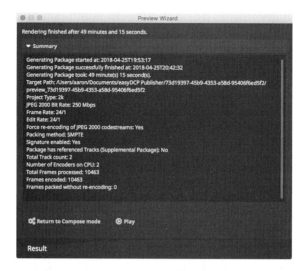

Figure 9.41 *Package generation summary*

8. Click the Play button to launch the previewer (**Figure 9.42**). This player will allow you to play your DCP and see the finished package before purchase and export.

Figure 9.42 *DCP playback in easyDCP Publisher's preview window*

9. To finalize your DCP and export it for distribution, click the Publish button at the bottom-right corner. The Publish window appears. This will walk you through the process of paying for your DCP (**Figure 9.43**).

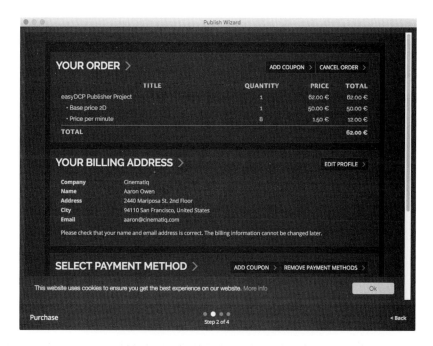

Figure 9.43 *Pricing is based on a base fee plus a per-minute fee.*

10. Once your order is complete, you'll be asked to fill out the final name. Then your DCP will be unlocked and copied to an unencrypted package available for distribution (**Figure 9.44**).

Figure 9.44 *Unlocking your final DCP*

When unlocking is complete, you'll have the option to browse/open the folder or inspect the published DCP (**Figure 9.45**). Your final DCP is complete.

Figure 9.45 *When the DCP is published, you can copy your package to an external drive or review it in a pre-view mode.*

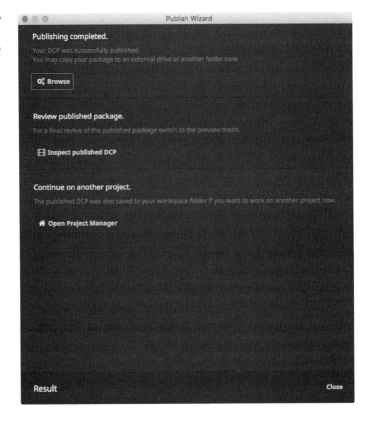

Step 3: Create Delivery Drive

Step 3 is the same as step 7 in the previous recipe, "Example DCP: Recipe 1." Refer to the instructions in that section, "Step 7: Create Delivery Drive."

Closing Thoughts on DCP

Creating a DCP can take quite a bit of time. If you are attempting to create a DCP for the first time, make sure you have enough time to make mistakes along the way before your delivery deadline. The example recipes are by no means the only way to accomplish the entire process, and there are a lot of different tools that you can use along the way.

Additional Tools for DCP Creation

In our example recipes, we used Adobe After Effects and Premiere, ProTools, easyDCP JPEG 2000 Transcoder, easyDCP Publisher, and easyDCP Creator. While these tools represent a fairly easy-to-use professional toolset, it can also be quite expensive to license all of these software applications. It's worth noting several other tools that may be less expensive than the ones used in the examples.

easyDCP Resolve Plug-in
This is a lower-cost option than buying the full version of easyDCP Creator. This option adds the ability to export a DCP package from within Black Magic Design's Resolve. It works quite well and is fairly straightforward to use.

Blackmagic Resolve Studio
In version 15 of Resolve Studio, Blackmagic added the ability to export a DCP without the need of a plug-in. This native feature is quite minimal and is limited to unencrypted packages only.

DCP-O-Matic and Open DCP
These open source tools are definitely appealing because they are free to download and use. However, there are lots of ways you can mess up the process, and just like with all DCP creation tools, you really need to understand the DCP requirements and process to create a completely compliant package.

SOX
This tool is a command-line audio conversion tool useful for performing the audio pull-up to convert 23.976 audio into 24 fps without using ProTools. You can install SOX on a Mac using the Homebrew package manager. The command to use to pull up the audio from 23.976 to 24 fps is as follows:

```
sox [inputFile] [outputFile] tempo 1.001
```

See the "Audio Pull-Up Math" sidebar for more details.

WraptorDCP Adobe Media Encoder Plug-in
Bundled with Adobe Premiere and Media Encoder is a tool called WraptorDCP. It works in the same way that the easyDCP Resolve plug-in works. However, in our experience, DCPs created with Wraptor aren't always compatible with cinema playback servers. It's really tempting to use because it's free and built-in, but because of these compatibility issues, we highly recommend against using the Wraptor plug-in that's bundled with Adobe's tools.

Understanding the Interoperable Master Format

For the past 30 years (and arguably longer), cinema and television have been on a convergent path. This convergence is possibly best seen when comparing DCP and IMF. Just as the Digital Cinema Package was created in response to the major Hollywood Studios' challenges in digital distribution, IMF was built to solve a similar but entirely different set of challenges for content owners. The main problem that IMF was created to solve was in delivering multiple versions of the same show for different distribution channels.

For example, HBO is the producer of the hit show *Game of Thrones*. After an episode is completed, a master (or more accurately, multiple masters) is sent out for playback on its cable channel, streaming on both desktop and mobile platforms, Blu-ray and DVD, 4x3 versions for airlines, and versions for use in various international markets. When you add it all up with different subtitles and audio languages, there could be hundreds of versions of the same episode. All this digital delivery leads to an asset management nightmare for larger content producers. In response, around 2012 SMPTE started work on publishing the IMF standard.

What IMF Is Not

IMF is meant to be a mezzanine (intermediate) format. This simply means that, unlike DCP, it isn't meant to be a format that is played back for the end user. It's meant to deliver all the necessary assets to a distribution platform that would then be prepared specifically for that channel. Over time we may see additions to IMF/IMP to make it more suitable for archival use.

A great example of this is if you needed to deliver the same show to iTunes, Netflix, and Hulu. Before IMF, a content owner would need to receive the delivery specs from all three channels, which would all probably be different. The idea with IMF is to allow producers to ship the same IMF to each outlet and let the various content ingest teams transcode the show specifically for their platform. In reality, though, each outlet still has very specific requirements leading to the creation of channel-specific packages.

IMF's Heritage

Because the creators of IMF used DCP as their template, it looks quite a bit like DCP in the overall structure, with a couple of additional concepts specifically aimed at digital delivery use cases outside of cinema. Because these extra-use cases have much more variance than the digital cinema world, it's not quite as strict when it comes to codecs, resolutions, and frame rates. SMPTE (the standards body responsible for IMF) has decided to take a little bit more of a modular approach to take these different use cases into account.

The IMF standard is based on a core framework that shares quite a bit of DNA with DCP, and then specific applications have been developed for specific workflows. IMF calls each of these specific workflows *applications*. The best way to think about an application is that it's a specific combination of codecs, frame sizes, and frame rates meant to serve a specific market.

IMF Applications

Like DCP, the original IMF spec only included JPEG 2000 as the acceptable codec. But later, it was revised to include almost every video codec imaginable. Currently, there are five main applications called Application #2, #2E, #3, #4, and #5. Gotta love it when engineers get to name things, right? Aside from the terrible names, each application is slightly different.

Application #2: Specifies the use of the JPEG 2000 codec. There is also an *extension* of this application (**Application #2E**) that adds support for UHD and HDR among other things (**Table 9.3**). Application #2E is currently the most popular application. There is also a different flavor of #2E that uses Apple ProRes instead of JPEG 2000.

Table 9.3 *Comparing Applications #2 and #2E*

Application	HD	UHD/4K	4:2:2	4:4:4	Rec.709	Rec.2020	HDR	JPEG 2000
Application #2	X	—	X	X	X	—	—	X
Application #2E	X	X	X	X	X	X	X	X

Application #3: Specifies the use of the MPEG-4 video codec using the professional studio profiles with frame sizes up to 4K.

Application #4: Sometimes referred to as Cinema Mezzanine, this application also specifies JPEG 2000 as its codec but includes a wider range of legacy/historical frame rates.

Application #5: Using the ACES color system, this application was developed with long-term archival in mind.

Packages that are created under each application are meant to be compatible, as long as the recipient is using tools that support that particular application. The great part about this modular approach is that if there are enough companies that have a specific workflow that needs to be accomplished with specific parameters not covered by a current IMF application, IMF can be adapted to the latest technology without having to reinvent the wheel from scratch. You as a user probably won't be involved with creating these applications, but it is important to know they exist and that there are various flavors of IMF.

Anatomy of an IMF and IMP

Just like DCP, IMF can be broken down into two parts: elements that belong to the composition and elements that comprise the package that is sometimes referred to as an Interoperable Master Package (IMP) (**Figure 9.46** on the next page).

In the composition are the following components:

- **Composition playlist (CPL) (XML):** This is an XML file that ties all of the track files together. You can think of this as the recipe to put your show together correctly. In essence, it is a more complicated version of an edit decision list (EDL). There can be more than one CPL per IMP because there may be multiple versions of a show contained in the IMP. For example, if there are multiple language versions, multiple CPLs would refer to the same video element but different audio files.

- **Image track files (MXF):** This is where your picture elements live. There can be multiple image MXFs in an IMP.

- **Audio track files (MXF):** Audio in an IMF is 24-bit uncompressed and can contain any number of tracks or soundfields (e.g., Dolby Atmos). There can be multiple audio MXFs in an IMP.

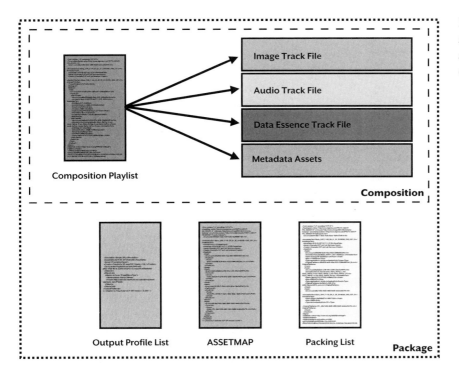

Figure 9.46 *The overall structure of an IMP looks similar to a DCP but adds an extra element in the OPL file.*

- **Data essence track files (XML):** This is where your subtitle and captioning information goes. Just like video and audio, you are allowed to have multiple data tracks.

- **Metadata track files (XML):** IMF supports so-called dynamic metadata, which is a fancy way of saying metadata that changes over time. IMF supports some pretty cool advanced workflows by allowing the creator to specify color correction, pan and scan, data related to stereoscopic (3D) applications, and descriptive metadata.

Rounding out the final package are the familiar elements from DCP.

- **ASSETMAP:** As with DCP, this file provides a way to link each asset's UUID to actual locations in a file system on the delivery drive/media. There is only one ASSETMAP per IMP.

- **Packing list (PKL):** The same as with DCP, this file defines all the assets belonging to an IMP. It refers to each asset using a UUID and provides a hash value for each asset. The hash value is created upon package creation and can be recalculated at any time to verify the integrity of a particular asset. If the value does not match, then the content has been changed or corrupted in transit. There is only one PKL per IMP.

And then there's a new file specific to IMF.

- **Output profile list (OPL):** This is where part of the power of IMF comes to life. An IMF creator can create multiple output profiles that are part of the same IMP, allowing the recipient to transcode correctly according to the instruction set specified in the OPL. A single IMP can have multiple OPLs and can be as simple as instructions to "play CPL" or can be complex with various output, preprocessing, colorspace/conversion, and transcoding parameters. It should be noted that while the specification for the OPL has been published, support across the industry is extremely limited, and interoperability is still being tested. This part of the IMF standard is still under active development, and it may be some time before broad adoption takes place.

Supplemental IMPs

Just like you saw with DCPs, IMF supports supplemental packages to modify content for specific uses, with a couple of really neat additions. Remember when we said that you can also think about the CPL as a slightly more complex version of an edit decision list? This is where that shows up.

Let's say you have an original version of a TV show with the main title and credits in English. In this scenario, both of these are over the picture so that the only way to swap out the text would be to edit a new version of the shot from cut point to cut point (**Figure 9.47**).

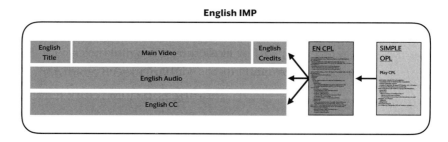

Figure 9.47   *This IMP contains the main picture, English audio, and English closed captions. In this example, the main picture track is encoded as one MXF (a single essence) that also contains the English opening title and end credits.*

If you wanted to create a French version of the show complete with French audio and closed captions, you would only need to encode the opening title and end credits video segments and include the new audio and closed captions. With a supplemental IMP, it's possible to package up only the new material needed in the new CPL, which references both the original content and the new content (**Figure 9.48**).

This works just like it did with DCP, except you can replace segments of video from a specific in point to a specific out point.

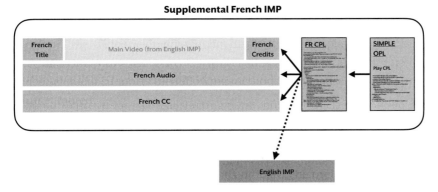

Supplemental French IMP

Figure 9.48 *The supplemental IMP contains only the new elements needed for this version, as well as a CPL that pulls the correct elements together from various packages needed for a specific version of the show.*

Because you're able to deliver an OV IMP and supplemental IMPs for region or alternate versions of content, there is a reduced need to export/render "long play" files of multiple versions of the whole show for simple changes (provided all outlets will accept the same package). You can simply update the OV with a supplemental package. That could end up saving hundreds of hours and thousands of dollars over the life of a show.

QC and IMP

Quality control is always a huge part of any compressionist's job, and with IMF/IMP, the story is no different. But part of the issue specific to IMPs is how to check to make sure that all the assets are present and that the resulting final encodes/transcodes that are made from the IMF/IMP are correct. Several companies are starting to develop automated QC systems. As with all automated QC systems (such as those found in the digital cinema world), results may vary. Keep an eye on these developments as IMF continues to mature.

Conclusion

DCP and IMF are both "package" formats. Both package flavors are similar to each other but are designed for very different use cases. DCP is meant to be played back in theaters, while IMF is meant to be an intermediate "mezzanine" format suitable for transcoding for specific digital delivery platforms. IMF builds on the lessons learned from DCP and minimizes the amount of separate versions content creators need to manage when preparing programs for distribution.

Compression for Virtual Reality and 360 Video

10

Of all the video delivery methods we have discussed so far, this one is by far the most unique and emerging. There is a lot of buzz around virtual reality (VR) and 360 video, but what are they really? Most importantly, how do we adapt our existing workflows to support delivering content for them? What is AR? How does FOV play into it all? Let's find out.

VR Concepts

To understand how we approach compression for VR and 360 video, let's begin by discussing all the various forms of reality that have littered this space with acronyms.

What Is Virtual Reality?

The ultimate goal of *virtual reality* (VR) is immersion—the feeling you are in another place without being physically there. The video-gaming industry spearheaded modern VR technology so that players could immerse themselves in the digital world and spend a lot of their time there, closer to the story and the action. In VR, the player controls the game directly using their head and hands and receives the visual and auditory information back through a VR headset rather than a static screen. The VR headset provides a larger *field of view* (FOV) than most monitors, which means players feel like they have more direct control and feedback of their digital world interaction. VR is best used for storytelling and conveying experiences. You can take a tour through a remote location or nonexistent location. You can engage in a training experience that would otherwise be expensive or difficult to do, such as operating heavy equipment. Or, you can simply enjoy fantasy experiences or new forms of art. The value of virtual reality is a more intuitive way to interact with the digital world and a deeper immersion in the digital experience.

What Is Augmented Reality?

Let's now take a look at *augmented reality* (AR). If you have played Pokemon Go, then you are already at least a little familiar with the concept of AR. Unlike VR where you are bringing the user into a digital world, augmented reality is used to bring digital information into the real world. Facebook and Snapchat selfie filters are also prime examples of augmenting real life with digital information. The ultimate goal of AR is to provide digital information to the user in the context of the real world, delivered as they need it. Applications of AR include highlighting traffic signs and providing GPS information while driving, visualizing furniture and other products in your room before buying (**Figure 10.1**), and translating signs in other languages in real time while traveling.

Figure 10.1 *Ikea's iOS app, built on Apple's ARKit, allows users to preview what furniture would look like in their homes before they buy it.*

What Is Mixed Reality and Extended Reality?

Unlike AR and VR, *mixed reality* (MR) and ex*tended reality* (XR) are more abstract concepts. They describe combinations of the other technologies. The general understanding is that MR is "in between" AR and VR and that XR is an over-encompassing term that includes AR, VR, and MR (**Figure 10.2**). Microsoft HoloLens is a good example of mixed reality. HoloLens takes the full interactivity of VR and adds it to real life by projecting hologram images in front of the user's eyes in a headset. This combination of real life and virtual interactivity is interesting for educational and industrial applications in addition to gaming and entertainment. For instance, imagine doctors having a heads-up display of patient vitals while making a diagnosis or a mechanic accessing a repair manual while working on a car.

If this all sounds confusing, well, it is. Keep in mind this whole area is new and the nomenclature is still being built up to support it. Expect things to change rapidly in this space.

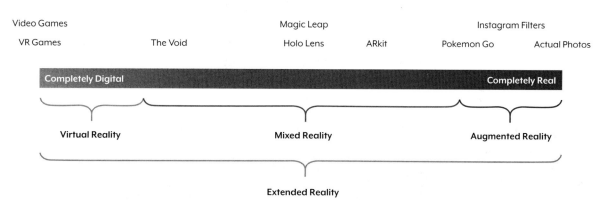

Figure 10.2 *The various two-letter acronyms can get confusing when talking about the world of virtual reality. This graphic attempts to show more clearly where the concepts appear on a spectrum from a completely digital to full reality world.*

VR Hardware

There isn't a single type of VR headset. At the time of this writing, there are three basic types of VR headsets, with the lines being continually redrawn as manufacturers add new technologies to the mix. For now, assume that the headsets are either a basic handheld mobile phone, a premium smartphone headset, or a computer/console-tethered full-immersion experience.

Degrees of Freedom (DOF)

As you review types of hardware available for VR, you will see the acronym DOF, which stands for "degrees of freedom" and is part of the mechanics of VR you need to understand.

DOF refers to the movement of a rigid body inside space. It could be explained as the basic ways in which an object can move. There are only six DOF in total, and there are two different types, translations and rotations.

Translation movement is where a body is free to move in three degrees of freedom: forward/back, up/down, left/right.

Additionally, a body can have *rotation movement* in three degrees of freedom, known as the pitch, yaw, and roll.

Any possible movement of a rigid body, no matter how complex it is, can be expressed as some combination of the basic six DOF. For instance, when you hit a tennis ball with a racket, the complex movement of the racket can be expressed as a combination of translations and rotations.

Basic Handheld Kits

Thanks to the sophistication of today's mobile phones, they can act as a first foray into VR with some cheap additions. In 2014, Google launched a product called Cardboard, a foldable cardboard headset that a user can drop a phone into and then wear like a visor to experience VR. This works because of the accelerometers and gyroscopes in modern smartphones that allow them to work in this environment. Multiple versions have since been released, and Google has even certified other companies to complete sturdier versions, but ultimately, this entry-level solution costs users around $15 (plus a smartphone, of course).

Premium Smartphone VR

Next is the premium smartphone category. Technically, you could lump this category in with the first because it is ultimately a device you secure a smartphone into and then wear visor-style for a VR experience. However, we are differentiating this class of headsets because they do have some advantages over cardboard. Generally, these products are plastic and can securely hold your phone in place. They have straps and padding to make them much more comfortable as well. Some include Bluetooth-based game controllers, allowing for much more interactivity than their cardboard cousins. Premium headsets generally run between $100 to $200 and are often tied to a specific smartphone. For example, Samsung's Gear VR is designed to work specifically with Samsung's Galaxy line of phones (**Figure 10.3**).

Figure 10.3 *Samsung's Gear VR is a relatively inexpensive way to experience VR when you combine it with one of the Samsung Galaxy smartphones.*

Tethered Headsets

The last category is what we would consider a "true" VR experience, the tethered headset. While this category is the most immersive experience you can have, it's also the most expensive. These devices offer a far more robust experience, with different input devices and higher-fidelity graphics.

The most famous entry in this list is the Oculus Rift. Oculus first launched its Kickstarter campaign in August 2012, which at the time generated worldwide buzz for the company. Oculus was acquired in 2014 by Facebook for $2 billion. The final version of the headset didn't release until 2016 (though prerelease developer units were available before that). Facebook has continued to innovate in this space and is still releasing new hardware under this brand (see the sidebar "Oculus Go").

As you may have guessed from the category title, all these headsets must be connected to a computer with a relatively good graphics card to work. The user's headset is tethered via a series of cables to the computer, which limits the range of motion a user can experience. Prices of the headsets in this category have been dropping a little bit, but they still cost between $400 and $700, depending on additional hardware, such as game controllers and sensors for tracking the user's movement in space. Keep in mind this cost is on top of a computer that is powerful enough to run a VR headset, which will likely cost another $500 at a minimum.

In the fall of 2017, Microsoft announced a line of VR headsets on which it partnered with manufacturers. These MR headsets are designed to specifically work with Windows 10 laptops and PCs and have slightly lower price points, coming in at around $300.

One last area worth mentioning here is the VR experience for gaming consoles. We are putting this in the tethered category, as like the other headsets we've mentioned, it must be tethered to the device (in this case the game console) to properly work. As of today, only one game console has released a VR headset. The PlayStation VR launched in the fall of 2016 and is designed to connect to a PlayStation 4 gaming console. This allows users to play VR games and use the headset in "cinematic mode," which renders a larger projector screen in space for the user to watch videos on.

Oculus Go

In the fall of 2017, Facebook announced it was working on a stand-alone version of its VR headset, the Oculus Rift, that would not need to be tethered to operate. At its developer's conference in May 2018, Facebook released the Oculus Go model to the world for $199. Little is known about this hardware yet, as only reviewers have been able to get their hands on it. However, it could be an entire new category of VR headset, living somewhere between the premium mobile headsets and the computer-tethered ones. Assuming the quality of the headset lives up to expectations, even more people will begin experimenting with VR, as a $200 price point is much more obtainable to end users than the current $300 to $600 price tag plus a computer.

360 Video Overview

360-degree videos, also known as *immersive videos* or *spherical videos,* are video recordings where a view in every direction is recorded at the same time (**Figure 10.4**). Unlike normal videos that capture whatever is within the camera's field of view, these videos capture the entire 360-degree scene and are designed for viewing in VR headsets (though Windows 10 PCs will allow desktop users to natively view the videos, and Mac users can use third-party solutions such as VLC to pan around the 360 space). A common way to depict 360 videos in VR is by wrapping a video to cover half of a sphere's inner surface and placing the user at the dome's center. The viewer is able to look all around them, in any direction. While VR and 360 video are sometimes used interchangeably, the reality is that 360 video, while immersive, is still more of a viewing experience and not the interactive experience that true VR encompasses.

Figure 10.4 *360 video cameras vary greatly, from inexpensive to high end. The more expensive models include multiple cameras capturing simultaneously to create the full 360-degree field of view.*

Monoscopic vs. Stereoscopic

Most of the 360 video content on the Web is monoscopic, meaning there is no depth information between background and foreground and the same image is displayed to both eyes. Our brains can still partially make up for the lack of depth information by comparing objects to each other and guessing their size at distance, but these types of 360 videos appear essentially flat. Stereoscopic 360 videos (or 3D 360 videos), on the other hand, deliver two distinct images rendered individually to each eye, allowing the brain to perceive depth the way it does in real life. This addition of depth information can dramatically improve the experience of a 360 video.

Video Resolution vs. Perceived Resolution

One of the challenges with 360 video is resolution for playback. It is common for first-time video VR content creators to be dismayed at the apparent low resolution of their content, even when it is encoded at 4K or higher. The issue is the difference between the video file itself and the small chunk of that video file that the user actually sees. Remember, the entire sphere of video is 360 degrees, but the user is looking only at 90 to 110 degrees of the field of view at a time. A 4K video file viewed with a 90-degree field of view would result in a perceived resolution of roughly 1K. In practice, to get 4K perceived definition within a 90-degree FOV, the actual resolution of the video would be roughly 16K!

Equirectangular vs. Cube Map vs. Pyramid Projection

The shape the video is stored in greatly impacts the file size when it comes to 360 videos. The most common projection type is equirectangular. This style resembles a sphere flattened into a two-dimensional rectangle (similar to a world map versus a globe). Very quickly, however, developers realized that while this method creates a uniform experience for users, it was somewhat unnecessary. The VR viewer's attention is typically focused on distinct areas of action, and changing the warp of the projections to save bits doesn't degrade the image. By changing the style to a cube map, the 360 video is folded for projection, which would drop the required bitrate by 25 percent without reducing the quality of the image to the user. Facebook is further experimenting with a pyramid-style projection technique, which it says reduces bitrate requirements by 80 percent. The pyramid geometry technique takes flat frames, turns them into spheres, and places them inside a pyramid (**Figure 10.5**).

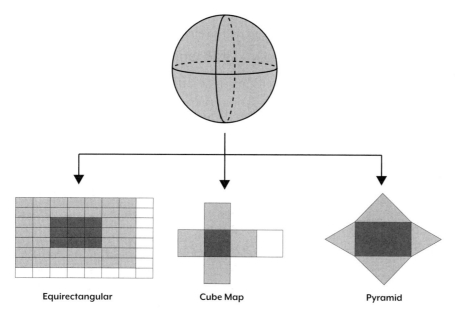

Figure 10.5 *This diagram shows how the styles of storing and projecting video differ for equirectangular, cube map, and pyramid.*

Equirectangular   Cube Map   Pyramid

Codecs

VR headsets all support the same popular delivery codecs we discussed in Chapter 2. However, because of the potentially very large files sizes you may be working with based on differences in perceived resolution, 360 video benefits greatly from modern codecs such as HEVC. Read the documentation for the headsets you are planning to support closely and make sure you are choosing codecs that offer hardware decode of the video over software decode. Hardware decoding generally has a considerable performance and power efficiency advantage over software decoding, as the latter requires a lot of CPU work, a particularly precious resource on such devices. To avoid overheating and excessive battery consumption, hardware decoding formats are preferred over software decoding formats. This may mean falling back to H.264, VP9, or other more established codecs.

Streaming vs. Downloading

An important consideration is whether the content will be streamed or available for download and what's appropriate for the experience you want to deliver. While most online consumption of video is streaming, much of the VR content available to consumers today is a download experience. Once again, this is changing rapidly, but for now, those experimenting in the space may need to plan on supporting a download of their 360 video content until more streaming options for VR headsets are made available.

Device-Specific Targeting

Because the VR/360 video space is still so new, there are few headsets available. Because there is no single VR platform but instead nearly one per device manufacturer, it is challenging for a compressionist attempting to target multiple headsets with a single video. Instead, it is common to see publishers create device-specific videos that optimize the content per device, based on its capabilities.

Ideally, as this area matures and the platforms begin to consolidate, we'll see a more standardized offering. For now, plan to support multiple resolutions of your content that are device specific to get the best playback experience.

Pixvana (www.pixvana.com) has built a software development kit (SDK) that allows content creators to create 360 video content and then deploy to any of the devices easily. Its Spin Studio software allows content creators to take their ideas from storyboard all the way to market. Companies like this will be key for VR filmmakers who want to focus on their content and not on the technology surrounding It.

Optimizing Your 360 Video

As mentioned, there is no standard regarding supported codecs and resolutions. Support is based purely on what hardware is used and how the video will perform optimally, so results are extremely varied today. But generally speaking, a good starting point for 360 video is either H.264 or HEVC video, with a resolution around 3840 × 2160 at 30 fps or greater. **Table 10.1** outlines the supported codecs, resolutions, and frame rates for some of the popular headsets across all categories.

Table 10.1 *Supported codecs and resolutions for 360 video platforms*

Platform	Codec	Resolution
Gear VR	H.265	3840 × 2160
Cardboard Android	H.264 (baseline level 4.2)	3840 × 2160
Cardboard iOS	H.264 (baseline level 3.1)	1920 × 1080
Oculus Rift	H.265/h.264	4096 × 4096

VRencoder

Since this is an emerging area, there are no software encoders with 360 video templates built in currently; however, encoders will no doubt be updated to include templates soon. That said, anyone could build their own device-optimized settings in their favorite application to do the job.

For anyone getting started, rather than taking this route, we suggest experimenting with a free encoding tool called Purple Pill, developed and released by VR Studio, (www.purplepill.io). The company has created a whole set of tools that will be useful to those interested in creating VR content; you can find them at https://purplepill.io/tools.

For compressionists interested in encoding 360 video content, VR Studio created a simple tool called VRencoder (https://purplepill.io/vrencoder/). This application is built on top of FFmpeg and has a simple user interface that allows you to select source material and then target specific devices for delivery. It then creates the multiple necessary versions of your content for each device (**Figure 10.6**).

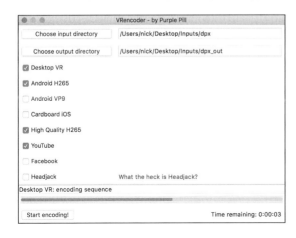

Figure 10.6 *VRencoder is a simple tool for quickly encoding your 360 video to target specific devices for playback.*

Conclusion

360 video and VR are rapidly evolving, and the hardware improvements that have occurred just in the past few months have radically changed what is possible in terms of video playback. As prices drop on the headsets, even more people will try VR for the first time, which will bring content creators to the space to experiment. Will VR replace your television? Absolutely not. There will still be a place in our lives for a shared-screen experience for viewing. However, there is a wealth of opportunities around immersive entertainment and education where VR will play a huge role, so it's worth keeping an eye on the technologies and understanding the changing requirements around delivering a video experience in this medium.

Index